ORGANIC COTTON

ORGANIC COTTON

From field to final product

edited by
DOROTHY MYERS and SUE STOLTON

INTERMEDIATE TECHNOLOGY PUBLICATIONS 1999

Intermediate Technology Publications Ltd,
103–105 Southampton Row, London WC1B 4HH, UK

© The Pesticides Trust 1999

A CIP record for this book is available from the British Library

ISBN 1 85339 464 5

Typeset by Dorwyn Ltd, Rowlands Castle, Hants
Printed in the UK by Biddles, Guildford

Contents

Finishing / Dying   57, 78+

Foreword

THIS BOOK IS rich with details of successes, difficulties and challenges. It is about organic cotton, though it also tells a wider and vitally important story — about how agriculture can become more sustainable while making significant improvements to people's lives.

In recent years, many agricultural systems across the world have begun an extraordinary transition towards sustainability. It used to be thought that being good to the environment was a luxury that only the rich could afford. That myth is no longer true. What is clear is that sustainable agriculture can mean more from less. It can mean new opportunities for better livelihoods for poorer groups. Being good to the environment actually does mean being good for the economy.

Any approach that seeks a transition towards sustainability implies thinking carefully about assets. All systems, whether farms, livelihoods, communities or national economies, rely for their success on five types of capital asset: natural capital (nature's goods and services); social capital (the cohesiveness and trust in communities); human capital (the capacities and skills of individuals); physical capital (infrastructure); and financial capital (money, savings, remittances).

Sustainable systems accumulate capital assets over time, while non-sustainable ones spend capital like income, so depleting assets for future generations. A vital challenge for all of us is to find ways to accumulate these assets. Organic cotton production exemplifies one of these approaches.

Cotton is a globally important fibre, providing returns to many small farmers in developing countries, as well as being worn at one time or another by most of the world's population. But most cotton is produced in a way that causes great dmage to the environment. High productivity comes at great environmental and health costs. A well-designed and sustainable production system can, however, make the best use of nature's free goods and services — from the predators that control pests to the legumes that fix nitrogen.

Organic cotton systems also offer opportunities for new partnerships between the private sector concerned with creating 'clean' supply chains, as well as with NGOs, farmers' groups, and government agencies. Such new relationships are in themselves important, as trust is a key foundation for the spread of sustainable systems.

The Pesticides Trust has helped to bring together many stakeholders in the organic cotton business. It began by being primarily concerned with pesticide reduction and elimination, and has helped to integrate wider concerns for sustainability. Through this book, it points to an alternative path for fibre and textile production — a sustainability path. But it will be neither simple nor straightforward. Many do not yet believe that organic systems can work. Many others believe the only way forward lies in genetically-modified cotton. There will be new threats to the emergent successes. There will be backward steps. But what is clear is that the Pesticides Trust and the authors of this book have illustrated in a clear and compelling fashion that another more sustainable future does exist for those who wish to work towards it.

JULES PRETTY,
Centre for Environment and Society,
University of Essex
December 1998

Preface

Why this book?

THE PURPOSE OF this book is to draw attention to organic cotton production and processing. Organic agriculture provides important environmental, economic and social benefits compared with conventional cotton production. It is hoped that the book will be of interest to those contemplating involvement in organic cotton at the production, processing or consumption level. It is also intended to appeal to a wider audience, both North and South, including policymakers, journalists, those involved in industry and commerce, farmers' organizations, environmentalists, agronomists and informed consumers.

Commercial organic cotton production is a new area of activity—barely 10 years old—and is still very much 'work in progress'. Research and analysis are at an early stage and little relevant written material exists. This first book on the subject draws together experience from a diversity of sources with the objective of providing a comprehensive overview. Chapters are arranged according to the stages in the 'cotton chain', from farmer to consumer, and are intended to cover topics as authoritatively as possible. Illustrative case study material is particularly important and forms a substantial proportion of the text. Most of the current organic cotton projects worldwide are discussed.

The book summarizes the problems of the dominant cotton production system and the current state of organic production, processing and use (Chapters 1 and 2) with a special focus on small-scale farming systems in developing countries. Technical aspects of production are covered in Chapter 3, and Chapter 4 looks at project support requirements. Problems at the processing level, and approaches which are more environmentally responsible, are discussed in Chapter 5. The book also examines economic and marketing aspects and developments in regulatory systems (Chapters 6, 7 and 8). Case study material is drawn from both well-established projects and experimental projects, to present an overview of developments to date (Chapters 9 to 14 and throughout). Perspectives on current problems and future developments are reviewed in Chapter 15 and resources available to those who wish to pursue the topic further are listed in the appendices.

The conventional cotton 'chain' from farmer to consumer is notoriously complex and lacking in transparency. Cotton fibre, yarn, fabrics and clothing are moved around the globe, with those involved usually having no knowledge of the origins or final destination of the goods that they are handling. The new developments in organic cotton production and processing are often more open and less complex but it is nevertheless a multi-faceted story. This is reflected in the numerous and varied contributions to the book from a wide array of sources and experiences—from agriculturalists, researchers, certifiers, industrialists and business people (see the appendices). The process of gathering, systematizing, consolidating and checking such a diverse collection of material has been a long and challenging task, but has hopefully also served the purpose of linking many of the actors in the system and building capacity to tackle problems and move ahead. To this extent, the book is both product and process.

The future

What is described in this book is only a beginning. Much, much more is still to be done if the experience developed so far is to be built upon to make an impact on the conventional cotton production and processing system. There are indications that environmentally responsible textiles are moving from the niche market into the mainstream (Chapter 8). However, there are still few answers and many questions. Existing experience needs to be carefully analysed and further research topics identified. Social aspects, including the gender implications of the changes taking place, especially at the household and community level in the South, have received little attention so far and must be investigated and acted upon (Chapter 1).

The dissemination of information and experience in suitable forms to growers, consumers, policymakers, companies and governments is vitally important, as is raising consumer awareness and developing markets both internationally and domestically. We hope *Organic Cotton* will make a contribution to that process. In a rapidly changing area of activity such a book can quickly become out of date. We therefore invite readers to contribute to the process with a view to producing future editions. Please send any relevant material to: The Cotton Project, the Pesticides Trust, Eurolink Centre, 49 Effra Road, London, SW2 1BZ, UK.

Terminology

The editors have found, in the process of compiling this book, that a multiplicity of terms are in general use. Further confusion arises from linguistic and regional differences. Decisions had to be taken early in the editing process about standardizing terminology.

'Production' is used to describe agricultural production and 'processing' is used to describe the transformation which takes place after the cotton crop is harvested. At the production, or growing, end of the cotton chain, 'conventional' cotton production describes the current dominant production system, which is dependent on synthetic chemical inputs. 'Organic agriculture' is used to describe various systems for producing food and fibre according to specific established standards and certified as such (see Chapter 6) which promote environmental, social and economic health. This does not imply that all those millions of farmers who practise 'sustainable' forms of agriculture which are free of synthetic chemical inputs are not following 'organic' principles, but for present purposes 'organic' is used only to describe systems and products which are certifiable. The farms of producers who have made the positive choice to convert their production to an organic system are referred to as 'in-conversion', which involves going through a conversion period before products can be certified as fully organic. In the USA, this period is termed 'transitional'.

There are also references in the book to 'biodynamic' agriculture, a system which developed out of the teachings of Rudolf Steiner, founder of the anthroposophical movement, in the mid-1920s. Many basic elements—including approaches to soil fertility, botanical diversity in rotations, use of farm-produced manures and cultural practices—are common to both organic and biodynamic agriculture. Biodynamic agriculture has some features which distinguish it from organic agriculture including, for example, emphasis on the use of special biodynamic preparations.

Whereas organic agricultural production systems have been described and measured and a terminology has been established, the situation is much more complex and confused in cotton processing and marketing. At the height of the 'eco-trend' (a period in the early 1990s when environmental considerations had an influence over a wide-range of consumer choices from food to clothing), a plethora of descriptions and labels appeared to describe textiles which may, or may not, have been processed in more environmentally benign ways. Terms such as 'natural', 'ecological', 'eco-friendly', 'clean', 'green' and 'hand-picked' have been widely used to market products in the North and have led to widespread customer confusion. The term 'environmentally responsible' is used throughout the book to describe processes which have taken some steps towards reducing environmental impact. The textile products from these processes are described in this context as 'eco-textiles'.

Finally, there has been considerable interest in recent years in the use of cotton varieties which are grown for their colour. Many terms have been used for this type of cotton including 'naturally coloured' and 'colour-grown'. The term 'naturally pigmented' is used in the book to distinguish these types of cotton from cotton which has been naturally coloured through environmentally responsible dyeing.

The reader is also referred to the Glossary.

DOROTHY MYERS, *The Pesticides Trust,*
and SUE STOLTON, *Equilibrium Consultants.*

Acknowledgements

THIS BOOK IS THE RESULT of the collaborative efforts of many people, all of whom are participants in some way or other in the organic cotton chain. In particular, we recognize the daily efforts of farmers, workers in processing factories, those involved in design and manufacturing and all the other steps in the cotton chain who carry out the day-to-day work of producing textiles and clothing. In realizing this project, we are indebted to a large number of people who have contributed in many different ways on the basis of their varied experience. We want to thank all of them for their contributions, and for their patience. First of all, they include the following.

Bo van Elzakker who worked on developing the book idea with the Pesticides Trust, provided ideas and information, contributed a major part of the text and, at key stages, read and commented on several draft versions of the whole book; Lynda Grose who helped assemble material from the United States and contributed text and comments; Nathan Boone who contributed text and comments on drafts; Ros David, Barbara Dinham, Nigel Dudley, Jules Pretty and Margaret Reeves who read and commented on drafts of the whole book; and Kristina Plenderleith who edited the case study material.

We would like to thank the many people who have contributed chapters or parts of chapters or provided comments on chapters. They are: Stephan Bergman, Tadeu Caldas, Richard Charity, Alexander Daniel, Ernst Ehrismann, Ahmed El-Araby, Kate Fletcher, Bernward Geier, Polly Goldman, Luis Gomero, Susanne Hagenfors, Dan Imhoff, Norberto Mahalambe, Klaus Merckens, César Morán, Fortunate Nyakanda, Bo Ottosson, Sam Page, LaRhea Pepper, Gerd Ratter, Gunnar Rundgren, Mayumi Morizane-Saito, Kevin Sweeney, Sean Swezey, Abou Thiam, Peter Ton, Ngone War Toure, Roberto Ugás, Jill Vlahos, Simplice Davo Vodouhe, James M. Vreeland Jnr, Nicole Waayer and Brent Wiseman.

In addition, many people have contributed information or comments and we would like to thank them all. They are:

Uygun Aksoy, Celik Aruoba, Rainer Bächi, Christine Bärlocher, Birgit Boor, Mike Brown, Ute auf der Brücken, Rafiq Chaudhry, Dimitris Dimitriadis, Jürgen Ehlenburg, Atila Ertem, Bakary Fofana, Harry de Vries, Peter Förster, Richard Göderz, Sally Gurley, Roxanne Halper, Oliver Hanschke, Ulrich Helberg, Iqbal Javaid, Per Jiborn, Sergio Kalierof, David Katz, Onno Kuik, Wilfried Leupolz, James Liebmann, Dagmar Parusel, Pedro Jorge B. F. Lima, Alfonso Lizárraga, Therese Malmestrom, Robert Mensah, Andreas Scharf, Ulrike Schönherr, Demba Sy, Micha Tiser, Marck van Esch, Wilhelm Giesbrecht Wiebe and Emelda Wingwiri.

The lists above are very long and aim to be comprehensive but mistakes happen and we apologize for any errors of ommission or accuracy. Contact details for many of the contributors can be found in the appendices.

The Pesticides Trust is grateful to its donors for support for the Cotton Project of which this book is a part. They are Comic Relief, Novib, the Rausing Trust, The Patagonia Foundation, Ralph Lauren and Katherine Hamnett Limited. Special thanks is due to the GTZ projects ISAT/GATE, PSM Service Project, TOEB, and Protrade which supported the book project specifically and to IT Publications for their sympathetic collaboration.

Finally, we would like to thank colleagues at the Pesticides Trust and within the Pesticides Action Network, and Equilibrium Consultants for their support and encouragement over the past two years of work on this project. Our hope is that this first book on organic cotton will lead to further expansion of the work and publications on the topic.

DOROTHY MYERS, *The Pesticides Trust,*
and SUE STOLTON, *Equilibrium Consultants.*

1
Organic Cotton: A more sustainable approach

DOROTHY MYERS

'Alternative production methods are needed which entail distinct environmental benefits which can be defined in transparent terms and which can be made attractive to producers. . . . A production method designed for the economic, ecological and socio-political conditions of a producing area would be ideal. The ultimate goal of complete sustainability will not be easily attained, but organic cotton growing comes close to this goal.'

de Vries and Kox (1995)

Textiles, cotton and organic cotton

TEXTILES FULFIL a basic need, and textile production is as old as history itself. Cotton has always been a major part of the textile industry, and today provides about half of all global fibre requirements. By comparison, wool, silk and flax together provide only about 10 per cent. Cotton has a very long history as a source of fibre for clothing and other textiles, going back several thousand years in parts of the world such as India, the Nile valley and Peru. Two centuries ago, the mechanized cotton textile industry was the prime mover in the Industrial Revolution, with all the problems and possibilities that this created. Although it has a reduced relative significance in most of the industrialized economies today, it continues to play a very important role in the economies of the developing and newly industrializing countries.

Despite inroads made into cotton textile production by synthetic fibres, cotton has been successfully promoted in many countries in recent decades as a 'natural' fibre. The conditions of production and processing are often far from 'natural', however, and are largely unknown or ignored by the consumers of textile products.

The catalogue of environmental, health and economic problems described in the following chapter has become increasingly recognized. Conventional cotton production is now often viewed as a risky business. Efforts to tackle the problems inherent in conventional cotton production have focused on ways of reducing pesticide resistance in insects and minimizing the environmental impacts of chemicals rather than on eliminating them through alternative production systems. Organic production offers several advantages to farmers in industrialized countries and especially to small farmers in developing countries. It is a safe and environmentally responsible production method. Organic production is a system that can provide not only export crops for cash, but also good quality food for household and local consumption through the use of rotations (see Chapter 3). In this way food security issues are also addressed. The output can be judged and measured according to clearly established standards and can, on this basis, be sold as a certified product, often for a premium (see Chapter 6).

By comparison with these immediate cash benefits, the environmental and health benefits are less readily quantifiable and much longer term, and include improved health of soil, plants, animals and people. Improved knowledge and experience of the management of agricultural ecosystems and of the production-processing-manufacturing-distribution chain are also reported benefits of organic systems.

Movements for change

Interest in organic cotton has been fostered by a growing appreciation of the problems of conventional production and a wider recognition of the potential benefits of organic production. Opportunities for change have been created in several ways in the past decade, and momentum has been generated by a wide range of concerns. First, and most important, there are those involved in actual production in the field who are concerned about the effects of what they do on health, the environment of their communities and on their household economy. Secondly, there are those involved in the textile industry who are concerned about the polluting nature of the processes they carry out, and are under increasing pressure from environmental regulators (Chapters 5 and 6). Thirdly, there is a growing body of informed consumers who are ready to take environmental and social issues into account in their buying preferences (Chapter 8). Finally, having seen the failures and limitations of modern, conventional agriculture, there are groups involved in promoting alternative, more sustainable forms of agricultural at both a practical and policy level.

Expanding technical knowledge and expertise has also increased opportunities for change. Knowledge of biological pest control methods, for example, is expanding in some regions because of farmers' improved confidence in using their own traditional methods. Efforts are being made to exchange information and disseminate knowledge for the benefit of a wider audience.

Farmers' choices
Farmers can benefit in many ways from organic production systems. Especially in the South, they gain an improved understanding of agricultural ecosystems and the opportunity to draw on traditional farming knowledge, a good level of support from new and more supportive extension arrangements, help with capacity building and reduced dependency on

2

An organic cotton boll
Credit: *Verner Frang AB. Photo by Stephan Bergman*

state systems, premium prices, and improved environmental and working conditions—safer for themselves and their animals. Removal of input subsidies in many countries has led to increases in the cost of pesticides and fertilizers, which are not necessarily offset by increased income. Experience to date shows that farmers are more than ready to contemplate new systems if they are not locked into a state production system and are thus able to make their own choices, receive the support they need when converting, and find new markets. Organic systems can be of special interest to women farmers who often lack access to financial resources necessary for the purchase of inputs (see box).

Economic reasons are central to farmers' decisions to convert to organic systems. Provided that premiums can be passed down to their level, .farmers appear to be ready to make changes in spite of increased risks in the short term. In the open economies, notably the USA, cotton farmers are excessively dependent on pesticides and are seeking ways of reducing the spiralling costs that they entail.

Companies

Companies are increasingly being called to account for their social and environmental performance through consumer pressure. They also face increasingly stringent environmental regulation. Engaging in the organic sector provides an opportunity to companies in the North to respond to increasing environmental and social demands.

3

Acknowledging gender in the cotton chain

Some of the groups involved in organic cotton projects are attempting to look at the development from a gender perspective. Participants in the Pesticides Action Network (PAN), for example, have committed themselves to strengthening gender awareness in the work they do and are actively seeking ways to put this commitment into practice. It has been increasingly recognized in development work in recent years that women's issues cannot be considered separately from those of men, for to do so can sideline the interests of women. Both must be looked at together.

It is important to try to establish the different gender roles in relation to access to resources, reproduction, production, community activities and decision-making processes. In seeking to implement gender-awareness in relation to organic cotton production and processing, it is necessary to look at the whole chain. For example, many women are cotton farmers and are heavily involved in manufacturing, in designing, in the fashion industry and in retailing.

A start has been made in implementing gender awareness at the field level in Senegal and in Zimbabwe (see Chapter 14). First, it is necessary to build documentation systems which are gender sensitive. This means collecting data in a gender-disaggregated way, and requesting information from men and women separately. A gender perspective can be included in terms of the management of various aspects of projects. Many farmers are women and the needs of women farmers for extension advice and assistance, for credit and other services, and for training, should be given equal priority to those of men. In Zimbabwe, for example, AIDs widows are joining the organic cotton project because they do not have to buy inputs, use less labour and want to attend the farmer field schools because it provides an opportunity for learning, joint decision-making and other kinds of support.

Although still at a very early stage with much work to be done, a gendered approach to projects will ensure that social, as well as environmental considerations are taken into account in organic production and processing.

In the debate about trade and environment, developed countries are often seen as protectionist, applying increasing environmental regulation as a way of keeping out developing country exports. Textiles is one such sector. A recent report by the International Institute for Environment and Development suggests, however, that developing country producers can also benefit from increased environmental expectations in their export markets if they are able to adapt. The export of organic cotton fibre, yarns and textiles is an example.

In seeking to source environmentally responsible products in countries of the South, companies are looking to countries where open economies permit their trading partners to fill their requirements. Until fairly recently, the level of state involvement in cotton production in most Southern countries would not have permitted the development of organic cotton projects. Trade liberalization has provided export opportunities which did not previously exist. At the same time, textile companies in the North, especially in Europe, are seriously threatened by competition from countries of the South, especially Asia. They are being forced to streamline their operations and become more specialized in order to survive. Becoming involved in organic cotton is one way of creating a comparative advantage.

Consumer pressure
In the North, consumers are increasingly concerned about the environmental impact of their lifestyles and consumption patterns. This growing awareness is being translated into changes in buying patterns and demands being placed on companies through the market place. The burgeoning demand for organic food in supermarkets in Europe and the USA is an example. Consumers are not only interested in the environmental impact of the goods they consume, but also about their social impact, which is expressed through a growing interest in fairly traded goods. The approaches taken in many organic cotton projects are intended to create a more equitable distribution of benefits, including better returns at the farmer level. There is much interest among the Fair Trade organizations in including organic standards within their criteria.

Promoting change

Having understood that existing cotton production systems have serious limitations, many organizations both North and South are interested in change. The organic movement is interested in expanding new areas of organic production. Environmental groups are interested in pesticide reduction or elimination and development agencies are expressing their interest through support for environmentally responsible and economically viable forms of trade, development and agriculture.

NGOs have already played an important role in some countries by working with other sectors to stimulate markets and policy change. They also have an important role in keeping information flowing, especially where there may be tendencies, for commercial reasons, to inhibit information availability.

Progress in organic cotton developments

The first serious attempt at organic cotton production began in Turkey in the late 1980s, by a European co-operative of five organic food importers called the Good Food Foundation (GFF). Farmers were already active in organic food production (chickpeas, durum wheat, soya) and, familiar with cotton production, had wanted to expand their rotation to include organic cotton. The GFF wanted to demonstrate that organic farming need not be limited to food production and the farmers were ready to experiment.

A Dutch company, Bo Weevil, was formed to deal with the organic cotton production on GFF farms and to develop and market a range of products. A year later, two further initiatives were started in Turkey. The three projects set up specialist organic cotton companies which became involved in the cotton chain from farm production to garment manufacture, and even created their own outlets. Further developments took place quite rapidly when environmentally responsible textiles became fashionable in the early 1990s, coinciding with the high profile of environmental issues in many countries. The fashion fad changed—as fashion fads must—but interest in organic cotton continued in what many would regard as a more sustainable way, with many actors committed for the medium to long-term.

European companies in Peru and India set up similar projects. These companies had not been involved in organic food production, but were prompted by increasing environmental regulation and the need to develop new specialist markets in the face of increasing pressure from mass textile production in low-wage countries. Some companies were also interested in improving the social conditions of producers.

At the same time, large cotton growers in the USA (mainly California, New Mexico, Arizona and Texas) were looking for ways to reduce or eliminate pesticide costs. Arable crops were already being grown without pesticides and fertilizers, so why not cotton? A market was developed in California, where fashion houses quickly recognized the market potential and were soon demanding organic cotton. The Texas Department of Agriculture established the first organic cotton certification programme in the late 1980s.

Organic cotton production and processing is still mainly at the experimental level. It currently occupies a niche market, but there are signs that it is moving into the mass market, with large companies taking an interest such as Coop in Switzerland, and Nike and Levi Strauss in the USA. The Coop, for example, which began selling organic fabrics in 1993, sold one million organic items in 1997.

The niche market provides the opportunity for learning through action and building capacity. The number of projects and experiments has continued to expand in the 1990s in all continents in both large-scale production systems (Australia and the USA) and small-scale (Egypt, India, Brazil, Peru, Uganda, Tanzania, Zambia, Zimbabwe, Senegal and Benin). In less than 10 years, organic cotton production has spread to more than 15 countries. However, it still remains a tiny fraction of global cotton production. In 1995, when production was over 12 000 tonnes, it still represented only 0.06 per cent of total global cotton production. Table 1 gives estimates of organic cotton fibre production in 1997.

Table 1: Estimates of certified organic cotton fibre production for 1997, in tonnes

Country	1997 output in tonnes	Source of information	% of global total
Africa			
Egypt	500	ECOA	
Uganda	800	Agro Eco	
Tanzania	200	Bioherb	
Mozambique	50	IAM	
Zimbabwe	5	ZIP Research	
Benin	5	OBEPAB	
Senegal	10	ENDA-Pronat	
Total:	1570		19
India			
Maikaal	900	Remei AG	
Srida	30	Remei AG	
VOFA	105	Agreco	
Ginni Project	240	Schmidt & Bleicher	
Total:	1175		15
Latin America			
Peru	700	Per Jiborn	
Argentina	70	Pyma Cotton	
Brazil	5	Richard Charity	
Nicaragua	20	Ecofiber Index	
Paraguay	50	Ecofiber Index	
Total:	845		11
Turkey			
Bo Weevil/GFF	500	Bo Weevil	
Rapunzel	100		
Others	1200	Bo Weevil	
Total:	1800		22
Israel	50	IBOAA	minimal
Greece	110	Classico	1
USA	2600	Organic Fiber Council	32
TOTAL:	8150		100

2

The problems with conventional cotton

DOROTHY MYERS

Introduction

COTTON IS GROWN in a wide range of climatic conditions and agricultural systems, from smallholder agriculture typical of developing countries to large-scale, highly mechanized, industrial systems typical of countries like the United States, Australia, Sudan or Uzbekistan.

Cotton fibre production and consumption rose steadily in recent decades to nearly 19 million tonnes in 1990 and levelled out at around that figure for the rest of the decade. In addition to the five big producers (the USA, China, India, Pakistan, Uzbekistan) which accounted for almost 70 per cent of global production in 1998, cotton is grown in more than 60 countries. The total global cotton area fluctuated at around 33 million hectares during the years 1981–1998, and has in fact not changed substantially since the 1930s. Total production of cotton fibre has, however, increased steadily from a little more than 6 million tonnes to around 19 million tonnes, indicating a threefold increase in the average yield of seed cotton per hectare from around 200kg to 600kg. During the 1990s, yields have remained fairly constant at around the 570kg/ha level. Table 1 shows total production of cotton fibre in tonnes and yields in kg/ha for selected countries and years. It includes the top five producers, most of the countries described in this book, and the countries with the highest and lowest yields for purposes of comparison.

International trade

Only about one-third of cotton fibre produced is traded internationally and there are sharp contrasts within the producer group. The USA along with six others (Australia, Pakistan, Paraguay and countries of the Former Soviet Union) accounts for 70 per cent of world trade in cotton fibre. All other countries are very small exporters, but the exports may nevertheless be significant in terms of their national economies. In Benin, for example, cotton fibre accounts for 35 per cent of export earnings. In the other large producer countries (India, Pakistan, China), most of the output is consumed domestically or is exported in processed and manufactured form. Global trade in cotton fibre tended to fall between 1983/4 and 1992/3, as the trade in processed cotton and cotton textiles increased.

Table 1: Total production and average yields of cotton fibre in selected countries, 1990/1991 and 1997/1998

Country	Yield (kg/ha) 1990/1	Total production (in thousand tonnes) 1990/1	Yield (kg/ha) 1997/8	Total production (in thousand tonnes) 1997/8
USA	712	3376	696	3200
China	807	4508	917	4400
India	267	1989	314	2700
Pakistan	615	1638	560	1658
Uzbekistan	870	1593	746	1125
Turkey	1021	655	1056	750
Peru	647	77	548	46
Egypt	709	296	897	288
Benin	482	59	388	155
Senegal	420	18	340	20
Uganda	91	8	174	30
Mozambique	187	14	178	34
Zimbabwe	262	72	357	100
Tanzania	161	51	162	57
Australia	1603	433	1473	545
Israel	1668	52	1833	55
Kenya	86	6	109	5
WORLD	574	18 970	568	18 888

Source: International Cotton Advisory Committee (ICAC), 1998

Problems with conventional cotton production

Throughout the countries of Asia, Africa and Latin America, cotton is a major cash crop, and cotton production and processing is an important source of income at household level for many millions of small farmers—as well as being a source of foreign exchange at national level. In many countries therefore, strenuous efforts have been made to increase production, mainly by increasing yields through the intensive use of chemical inputs, irrigation and the use of higher-yielding varieties.

Improvements in cotton fibre output have generally been regarded as beneficial by those involved, including the farmers, but they have also involved costs, both environmental and social, which have not been reflected in cotton pricing and which have seriously affected people's livelihoods, health and environment. Indeed, despite its 'natural' image, cotton production has become increasingly associated with severe negative environmental impacts which include reduced soil fertility, salinization, a loss of biodiversity, water pollution, adverse changes in water balance, and pesticide-related problems including resistance. Social costs include, for example, severe health problems related to the heavy use of acutely toxic

9

pesticides especially in countries where regulatory systems are weak or unenforceable and safe use almost impossible. Even economically, farmers are not necessarily better off due to high production costs, and in some situations they are unable to select alternative crops or production systems.

Environmental and health costs also arise at other stages in the cotton chain. Cotton processing is a very resource-consuming, polluting and unhealthy industry. Large amounts of water, energy and chemicals are used at the different processing stages. Inputs required for processing usually find their way into the local waste water systems, resulting in highly contaminated effluents. Most effluents from cotton processing arise in the finishing stage and are characterized by their highly polluting load, high solid content and high temperature. In Sweden, for instance, every kilogram of textiles manufactured uses almost half a kilogram of chemical, most of which ends up in waste water. Chemicals can also remain in the final product, which can cause health problems. In the user or consumer phase, environmental problems arise from the use of energy, water and chemicals for washing, drying and ironing. Further environmental damage occurs in the transportation stages of the cotton chain as fibre, yarn, fabrics and finished textiles are moved around the world at different stages in production (see Chapters 5 and 6).

Pesticides in conventional cotton production

Amongst the catalogue of problems associated with conventional cotton production, excessive use of pesticides is perhaps the most serious and is the main motivation for many people and organizations to seek changes in current production patterns. Large quantities of the most acutely toxic pesticides are used in conventional cotton production. Cotton is very prone to insect infestation, partly for the reasons described in the box and also because it is often grown as a monocrop which, by its very nature, cannot be sustained without high levels of fertilizers and pesticides, because the natural systems of nutrient cycling and pest control have been subverted.

The proportion of global pesticides sales used for cotton has averaged 11 per cent over the decade to 1994, with a total world-wide sales value of over US$2800 million. The sale and use of pesticides in cotton production is increasing. These chemicals account for more than 50 per cent of the total cost of cotton production in much of the world. The USA is by far the biggest user, with 24 000 tonnes of pesticides used on close to 5 million hectares of cotton.

The use of insecticides predominates, with cotton accounting for about 24 per cent (US$1776 million) of the US$7400 million global insecticides market in 1994. Again the US is the predominant user, with 35 per cent of total global use. India, the former Soviet Union, Pakistan and Egypt together account for another 30 per cent.

The origin and development of cotton

Heavy use of pesticides is an inevitable consequence of the domestication and widespread cultivation of cotton. Cotton, which belongs to the family Malvaceae, bears the generic name *Gossypium*. *Gossypium* is a large genus containing more than 30 species, including a large number of wild relatives of domesticated cotton varieties. All wild cottons are drought-tolerant, hairy-leafed, perennial shrubs, with no serious pest problems and are indigenous to arid areas of sub-tropical regions of Africa, Asia, Australia and America. In fact, wild cottons continue to persist along desert fringes, in dry river beds and on rocky hillsides, in different parts of the world. Most wild *Gossypium* cottons are lintless. Only one type of wild cotton, which is known scientifically as *G. herbaceum* var. *africanum*, bears lint which can be spun and woven into cloth. This linted wild cotton is considered to be the common ancestor of all cultivated cottons and is still found growing today, in its centre of origin: arid parts of southern Africa, between Angola and Mozambique.

The wild lint-bearing cotton either was transported or floated across the Atlantic ocean to America, where it crossed with the New World lintless cottons, forming a new species of lint-bearing cotton, known as *Gossypium hirsutum*. *G. hirsutum* has since been used by plant breeders to establish commercial cultivars and these are now used in most of the world's cotton production. Years of careful selection by plant breeders has led to higher yields, longer staple, better spinning quality, improved yarn strength and adaptation for growing in cooler, more moist conditions. Commercial cotton can be grown as far north as the Ukraine and as far south as Argentina. Cotton is thus exposed to a range of tropical, sub-tropical and warm temperate environments which harbour alien pests and diseases with which it has no inherent ability to compete. Furthermore, instead of reaching its potential as a hardy, perennial shrub, commercial cotton is cropped during its most vulnerable stage—during the first year of its growth. As a result, commercial cotton is attacked by more than 46 different pests from 32 different countries. Most losses are due to six different species of bollworm.

Sam L.J. Page

The most important groups of insecticides used on cotton are pyrethroids and organophosphates. Those most commonly used are all classified by the World Health Organisation (WHO) as at least 'moderately hazardous'. Methamidophos and monocrotophos, both organophosphates and both widely used, especially in developing countries, are classified as 'highly hazardous'. Over 100 organophosphate compounds are in use, mostly as insecticides, in both industrialized and developing countries. They are generally acutely toxic and are nerve poisons. They work by inhibiting the enzyme cholinesterase, which can have severe effects on the central nervous system. Death can result from severe poisoning.

In addition to insecticides, significant amounts of herbicides, fungicides and defoliants are also used in cotton production. Synthetic fertilizers are also heavily used.

11

Discarded pesticide containers in cotton-growing area of California, USA
Credit: Dorothy Myers, Pesticide Trust

Table 2: Important insecticides used in cotton production

Chemical name and trade name	Chemical group	WHO toxicity class	Percentage share of global cotton insecticide market
Deltamethrin (Decis)	pyrethroid	II: moderately hazardous	12
Lamda cyhalothrin (Karate)	pyrethroid	II: moderately hazardous	9
Monocrotophos (Azodrin)	organophosphate	Ib: highly hazardous	9
Alpha-cypermethrin (Fastac)	pyrethroid	II: moderately hazardous	8
Chlorpyriphos (Dursban, Lorsban)	organophosphate	II: moderately hazardous	7
Esfenvalerate (Sumi-alpha)	pyrethroid	II: moderately hazardous	7
Methamidophos (Tamaron B)	organophosphate	Ib: highly hazardous	6
Dimethoate (Rogor, Perfekthion)	organophosphate	II: moderately hazardous	5

Source: Allan Woodburn Associates, 1995.

12

The heavy use of pesticides has given rise to widespread and serious concern for several reasons, including health and environmental effects, problems of resistance and resurgence, and secondary-pest development. These have caused economic losses in the short term and, in the long term, effects which are generally not quantified or internalized.

Information gathering in cotton-producing countries as diverse as Egypt, Senegal, Sudan, India, Nicaragua and the USA by Pesticides Action Network (PAN) participants indicates that acutely toxic organophosphates are much in use on the cotton crop and that their use has been reported to cause health and environmental risks. Problems easily arise in conditions where people are illiterate or unaware of dangers, where proper equipment is unavailable or too expensive, clean water is absent or in short supply, and where medical help is remote and costly. Figures for poisoning and deaths related to pesticide use reflect these problems. In developing countries, up to 14 per cent of all occupational injuries in the agricultural sector and 10 per cent of all fatal injuries can be attributed to pesticides. However, pesticide-related health problems are not restricted to developing countries. In one study in California, cotton ranked third among California crops for total number of worker illnesses caused by pesticides.

Application methods compound the problem, especially where spraying from aircraft is involved, as in the USA, Australia, Egypt or Uzbekistan. The environmental and health effects of massive pesticide use in cotton are perhaps most dramatically demonstrated by the situation in Uzbekistan. Intensive pesticide use and poor irrigation practices have led to such a high level of contamination that fields have become totally barren. Drinking water supplies over vast areas have become polluted, and there has been a frightening increase in the incidence of childhood blood diseases and birth defects. The most visible effect has been the reduction in the size of the Aral Sea which, because of changes in river flows for large irrigation projects, has lost 60 per cent of its water in 30 years. On the dry lake bed, a salt desert has been created, with dust storms threatening crops and human health in neighbouring areas. The sea itself, once the fourth largest body of freshwater in the world, is too saline and polluted with pesticides to support fish.

Pest resistance to certain overused pesticides is also a serious problem which in some places has caused cotton production to be abandoned altogether. This situation has occurred in parts of Nicaragua and Guatemala, Pakistan, Sudan, Egypt and India.

Many examples of the so-called pesticides treadmill have occurred in cotton production. Farmers starting out in a low-input/low-yield type of production are tempted to use higher inputs in the hope of higher yields and income. Pests are reduced and production is good, and easy, for a few years. Then pests develop resistance to pesticides or beneficial pest controlling organisms are destroyed, leading to more and more applications of increasingly toxic products, often in combinations, as farmers try to gain control. The 'treadmill' develops to the point where cotton production becomes uneconomical and may cease altogether unless alternatives are found. The box graphically testifies to the human devastation that such a situation can cause.

Integrated Pest Management (IPM) programmes have been initiated specifically aimed at the management of pest resistance and reduction in pesticide use. There are many differing definitions of IPM, but it generally consists of a combination of measures including cultural, biological and mechanical controls, supported by careful monitoring and regulation as necessary. The definition by the Food and Agriculture Organisation (FAO) is acceptable to many organizations (see Glossary).

Nicaraguan cotton production also illustrates many of the problems related to the heavy use of pesticides in cotton. In 1977, the area under cotton reached its peak at 220 000 hectares. Massive use of pesticides led to many problems. Several minor pests became major pests as a result of the elimination of the natural enemies which had held them in check. Many species became resistant, and many pesticides were no longer effective. Farmers

---

Pest resistance leads to desperate measures

In the state of Andhra Pradesh, South India, at least 80 cotton farmers committed suicide between June 1997 and January 1988 by taking the pesticide which they were using on their cotton crop.

Cotton was introduced in Warangal District, Andhra Pradesh 20 years ago as a cash crop and more than 1000 hectares are now under cotton, nearly a quarter of all the arable land. The crop has no government price support and increasing yields drove prices down. Farmers used massive amounts of fertilizers and pesticides in efforts to raise their output and eliminate the pests and diseases. Inputs were supplied on credit at interest rates as high as 36 per cent.

The crop was already in a precarious state when a massive infestation of Cotton leafworm, *Spodoptera littoralis* brought devastation in November 1997. This was followed by an attack of American bollworm, *Heliothis armigera*. Farmers resorted to desperate measures: spraying every other day instead of the recommended twice per season. The pesticide commonly used was methomyl, an organophosphate. But the pests had become resistant and attacked food crops, leaving farmers with no food for their families and no prospects of income. Farmers were heavily indebted to pesticide suppliers, landlords and moneylenders. After much criticism, the state government stepped in with support for the farmers. Officials of the local agricultural research station believe that cotton will continue to be cultivated in the area, but that farmers must be introduced to non-chemical pest control techniques, and the value of diversification.
Goldenberg, 1998

became locked into the 'pesticides treadmill' to the point where, in the late 1980s, pesticides accounted for half of their production costs, making cotton production no longer economically viable. Farm workers were poisoned, fish poisoning was recorded, wells and water courses were contaminated. The area under cotton had fallen to 35 000 hectares by 1990, and now stands at around 2000. A United Nations study estimated that the social and environmental costs of pesticides in Nicaragua during the cotton boom approached US$200 million per year, with the income from cotton production put at US$141 million.

Residues

Pesticides used on cotton can also enter the human food chain through cottonseed oil used in processed foods. Pesticides used in cotton production often end up in non-target species and result in contamination of, for example, meat and milk from cows fed on cotton products. In the late 1970s, beef imported from Guatemala was found to be contaminated with cotton pesticides and was refused entry into the USA. More recently, meat and milk in Australia were found to have been contaminated by pesticide-laden straw eaten by the animals. The pesticide was identified as chlorfluazuron. Several countries suspended beef imports from Australia. One year later, farmers discovered that newborn calves were also contaminated through their mother's milk. In a similar case, farms in New South Wales and Queensland were placed in quarantine after inspectors discovered high levels of endosulfan in beef cattle, probably due to spray drift contaminating grazing areas. Australian beef exporters have suffered substantial losses on account of pesticide contamination.

Loss of soil fertility

Reduction in soil fertility is also a problem. The application of high doses of nitrogen fertilizers speeds up mineralization processes in the soil which leads to a breakdown of organic matter in the topsoil. Organic matter is vital in order to maintain a proper soil structure and biological activity. As synthetic fertilizers are easier to apply, farmers often stop using organic fertilizers, going against age-old traditions. Especially when heavy mechanization is used, or heavy irrigation, loss of soil structure leads to a reduced capacity for the root system to penetrate the soil, making the plants more dependent on the easily soluble nutrients from synthetic fertilizers, and also more dependent on the regular availability of irrigation water.

Synthetic fertilizers are often limited to just a few elements. Nitrogen is always used, phosphate and potassium are sometimes used and calcium, sulphur and magnesium are less often used. The plant needs an array of nutrients in order to grow which may be available in the soil, but not in a soluble form. Organic matter, humus and micro-organisms play an active role in making these nutrients available for the plant.

15

Irrigation and water pollution

Problems associated with cotton production range from contamination of irrigation ditches by spraying or washing equipment, to contamination of ground water supplies from leaching out of pesticides. The use of nitrogen fertilizers especially at the time of irrigation leads to an increase of nitrates in ground and surface water. This can cause serious health problems when this water is consumed. Phosphate fertilizers in run-off water cause eutrofication of surface waters. This is a process where algae, feeding on phosphates, use so much oxygen from the water that fish may die.

Cotton is grown under irrigation in many countries, including Turkey, Egypt, Sudan, Pakistan, India, China, Australia and the USA. Large-scale (and sometimes small-scale) irrigation creates problems of salinization, especially when the water used is high in salts, the quantity of water is not high enough to match evaporation, and field drainage does not allow salts to be washed away. Water used for irrigation invariably contains some salts. When not leaching into the ground water, irrigation water evaporates, leaving salts on the surface. Salts can only be removed by regularly 'washing' the soil by applying a surplus quantity of water, usually outside the growing season. If this is not managed well, it may lead to irreversible damage, as has happened, for example, in Pakistan.

Loss of biodiversity

A variety of flora in production areas provides refuges for beneficial insects and diverts pests away from crops. Where this is reduced in monocultures or industrial cropping systems, diversity and the attendant benefits are lost. Many farmers try to control weeds, usually with herbicides or plastic mulching and are usually concerned about potential weed competition in terms of space, nutrients and water. Where cotton is grown in rotation with other crops, as in organic systems, biodiversity is increased.

The diversity of cotton itself has also been lost. Until a hundred years ago, farmers selected and bred the best varieties for their own use. This role has been taken over by private companies and government agencies which heavily regulate the supply of seed, often for phytosanitary reasons. In many countries, the traditional and regional varieties have been wiped out and replaced by varieties of foreign origin. Usually three to four varieties only are available to growers. Currently with liberalization, a few big companies are taking over the role of providing seed and can inhibit or even prevent on-farm breeding and seed exchanges. This may lead to a situation where a single company is providing one or two varieties to groups of countries and adaptations to local conditions are not possible. As discussed below, genetically engineered cotton is being introduced very rapidly in several countries, which could lead to further reductions in varieties.

16

Genetically engineered cotton

As concerns have increased about the health, environmental and pest resistance problems caused by the synthetic chemical inputs, and profitability is often in question, companies have responded by promoting genetically engineered cotton which is claimed to be 'environmentally safe'. Two types of genetically engineered cotton have been introduced in the United States and other countries around the world in the past two years: *Bt*-cotton, which contains a gene that enables the plant to produce its own pest-killing toxin, and herbicide-resistant cotton which has been developed to tolerate specific herbicides, glyphosate and bromoxynil. Both types come with their own set of problems (see boxes).

Bt Cotton

Bacillus thuringiensis (*Bt*) is a naturally occurring soil bacterium that has been used safely as a biological pesticide by both conventional and organic farmers for many years. Scientists have taken a gene that produces an insect toxin from the bacterium and inserted it into cotton plants. These plants and their offspring then produce their own *Bt* toxin. *Bt* cotton ('Bollgard') has been developed and produced by Monsanto. In 1996, *Bt* cotton was grown on a commercial scale for the first time in the United States. However, problems with the engineered cotton forced farmers to turn to chemical pesticides to save their crops from the very insects that *Bt* cotton was supposed to kill.

There are two major concerns about *Bt* cotton. First, that pests will develop resistance to *Bt* toxin, and secondly that the *Bt* gene will become established in wild relatives of *Bt* crops.

Insect resistance to Bt
The use of natural *Bt* exposes insects to the toxin only when it is applied and resistance has developed only rarely. But insect pests feeding on transgenic *Bt* crops are exposed to toxins continuously and are likely to evolve resistance quickly. *Bt* toxins in sprays, now commonly used by both organic and conventional farmers, would become ineffective and farmers would lose an important pest management tool.

Bt gene flow to wild relatives
Where *Bt* crops are grown near the crop's wild relatives, it is highly likely that the *Bt* gene will transfer to the wild populations as a result of the movement of pollen from the crop to the relatives. This could pose a serious threat especially in centres of diversity. For instance, the resultant wild plants may produce enough *Bt* to ward off insects that normally feed on them which could have implications for natural ecosystems. In some cases, the new gene may strengthen the wild plant, allowing it to become a weed in farmers' fields. With the *Bt* advantage, some plant populations may be able to displace other plants in natural ecosystems, altering local biological diversity. There has been little research in this area.

Jane Rissler, Union of Concerned Scientists

In 1996, US farmers planted 700 000 hectares (12 per cent of total cotton area) with *Bt* ('Bollgard') cotton. Bollgard was expected to control cotton bollworms but farmers were having to spray as well. Bollworm populations were reported to be 20–50 times the level that requires insecticide treatment. Monsanto claims that the damage in 1996 was due to unusually high pest populations and not to *Bt* resistance, and that where infestations exceed economic thresholds, spraying may be necessary.

The first commercial season for Roundup Ready (a glyphosate-resistant cotton) was 1997. About 250 000ha were planted in the mid-south region of the United States. Crop failures due to cotton bolls dropping off plants were reported in several cotton-growing states including Mississippi, Arkansas, Tennessee and Louisiana. It appears that the abnormal cotton boll development was not detected under the USDA's oversight programme when transgenic crops are tested to ensure that they are safe for agriculture and the environment before allowing them to be commercialized.

Monsanto dominates the market in genetically engineered cotton with its Bollgard and Round-up Ready varieties and profits are soaring as contracts are agreed in many cotton-producing countries, including China and Australia. The Monsanto approach is characterized by aggressive marketing strategies and public relations exercises. Genetic engineering is being promoted as the route to expanded and sustainable production. Under the terms of their contracts, farmers are required to pay licence fees and are not able to save their seed for following seasons, for example. Contracts are very actively enforced.

The economic context of cotton production

The previous section has dealt in some detail with the environment and health-related problems associated with conventional cotton production. Economic factors are also crucial in determining whether farmers are interested in seeking alternative production methods.

Taxation and subsidies
Cotton is traded in the world market despite great differences in the circumstances of production, costs and yields. Some producers can produce at or below the world market price, and others cannot. Cotton-based textile industries have been vital in the industrialization of major cotton-producing countries of the South. For these and other reasons, cotton production has been characterized by a high level of government intervention. Governments have often been heavily involved in determining where cotton should be produced, providing subsidies for agrochemicals, supplying seeds and irrigation, setting prices and providing information and extension. Farmers in almost all countries receive some form of subsidy or

Herbicide-tolerant cotton

Herbicide-tolerant cotton is a cotton plant that has been genetically engineered to be resistant to a herbicide that would kill a normal cotton plant. As a result, the herbicide can be applied while the plant is growing to control broadleaf weeds without killing the cotton plant itself. Developers of these plants maintain that by making cotton plants resistant to specific herbicides, overall herbicide use will decline. These claims are still unproven and unlikely in the long term. Currently, there are two types of herbicide-tolerant cotton available on the market: BXN cotton (tolerant to the herbicide bromoxynil) and Roundup Ready cotton (tolerant to the herbicide glyphosate). In addition to the many problems associated with the herbicides themselves, there is a danger that the genes for herbicide tolerance from the crops could be transferred to closely related weeds growing nearby. Such a development would make controlling weeds even more difficult for farmers than it is now.

Bromoxynil-tolerant cotton
Rhone-Poulenc and Calgene (a biotechnology company) have jointly developed the bromoxynil-tolerant cotton that is currently available to farmers. Bromoxynil is a toxic herbicide produced by Rhone-Poulenc with numerous adverse health and environmental effects. It causes cancer and birth defects in laboratory mammals and is toxic to fish and plants. In May 1998, the United State Environment Protection Agency (EPA) approved the use of bromoxynil on cotton, including genetically engineered cotton.

Glyphosate-tolerant cotton
Glyphosate (Roundup) is a broad-spectrum herbicide used to kill weeds. In California, for example, glyphosate exposure was the third most commonly reported cause of pesticide illness among agricultural workers. Monsanto, the US-based multinational agrochemical company, developed and is marketing 'Roundup Ready' cotton. Roundup is the world's largest-selling agricultural chemical and is estimated to account for up to 17 per cent of Monsanto's total sales.

Jane Rissler, Union of Concerned Scientists, Washington DC, USA.

preferential allocation of inputs. Marketing systems have often been highly centralized through state- or quasi-state-controlled bodies, for which cotton production has generally been a profitable business, while prices at farm level have not necessarily reflected world cotton values.

Market information is generally unavailable to the primary producers in developing countries and farm-gate prices declared by the government do not necessarily reflect world cotton values. For example, in the late 1980s, Kenyan cotton farmers received about 60 per cent of the world market price; Tanzanian farmers received about 40–45 per cent. The opposite effect is achieved by subsidies to EU and US cotton producers. Between

1988 and 1992, the US cotton programme cost US$1.13 billion per year or US$0.15/lb averaged over all production, while subsidies for EU producers averaged US$2.00/lb per year, although EU cotton production is very small. Other incentives and disincentives are also used by governments, such as access to irrigated land and extension support. Failure to pay promptly has been a disincentive to farmers to continue production in some countries of Africa. These complicated economic structures make clear comparisons between conventional and organic production systems problematical, but an area that must be addressed (see Chapter 7).

Production structures in Africa, for example, have been firmly in the hands of state monopolies intent on maximizing revenue for the government by paying the lowest possible prices to the farmers and selling at the highest possible prices in the international market. At the same time they have controlled the ways in which the cotton is produced and insisted on heavy use of chemical inputs which were often subsidized by the governments or aid programmes. In some African countries, taxes may offset subsidies. However, liberalization is creating opportunities for change in many African countries.

Conclusion

This chapter has attempted to describe some of the problems associated with the current dominant cotton production system. In the search for safer, healthier and more profitable alternatives to the cotton production system, the organic option is a way forward.

The rest of the book describes progress to date in creating a new system of responsible production and processing which is environmentally and economically viable and socially acceptable.

3
Organic cotton production

BO VAN ELZAKKER with contributions from TADEU CALDAS

Introduction

GIVEN THE SHORT history and diverse nature of organic cotton production, the techniques of organic cotton growing are still developing. It is, however, possible to review some preliminary results of field research and to identify priorities for future study. This chapter is not intended to repeat orthodox wisdom on cotton growing which is already well served by a number of excellent publications (see Further Reading section at the end of the book).

The diversity of cotton production world-wide makes generalization difficult. Cotton, both conventionally and organically produced, is grown on all continents under a wide range of agro-ecological conditions. Climates vary from the monsoon tropics through a Mediterranean climate to virtually desert conditions. What works in one situation does not always work in another. Cotton is also grown under different farming systems, from smallholders to commercial farmers or estate systems. The intensity of the system and whether the crop is rainfed or irrigated are also important factors in the production process.

Organic production has led to a wide range of options with which farmers, agronomists and scientists can experiment, outside those offered by conventional 'chemical' approaches. It is these processes which are reviewed here. Further production information is given at the end of the book in the series of case studies where more detailed information on the key organic cotton areas is given.

The organic farm system

Cotton is grown in a *farm system*. However obvious this statement may be, it is an approach that is much neglected by cotton specialists who tend to concentrate on cotton alone. Success in organic cotton growing is influenced by the other crops in the rotation, by the presence of farm animals, by the availability of land and labour and by the level of training of the farmer, his or her family and other workers. Growing cotton as a single or monocrop has created many of the problems associated with conventional cotton production.

Successful farming requires a holistic approach—a systems approach. This is where the word 'organic' originates. Sustainable organic farming is not just about organic fertilizers—and certainly not about organic pesticides. Many define organic farming by a simple formula:

No synthetic fertilizers + no synthetic pesticides = less yield × higher price.

Such an approach, experience has shown, can still lead to unsustainable farming systems. Organic farming is better defined by a formula such as:

The use of locally adapted varieties + the reduction of nutrient losses + the use of locally available organic material and green manuring + a wide rotation + fostering natural balances + mechanical and manual weed control = no need for synthetic inputs.

Although this formula is simplistic, it does indicate where the farm systems design should lead.

The conversion issue

In many cases, farmers convert to organic production because they are offered better prices for their produce. They substitute synthetic inputs with organic alternatives. This type of system is often referred to as 'organic by substitution'. Although it represents a move in the right direction, such farms are just as imperfect as their conventional counterparts. They do not systematically prevent problems, they have to troubleshoot, or fix them as they go along. For a true organic farm the focus of the conversion period should be to get the farming system in balance, so that substitutes are not required.

As smallholders tend to farm closer to organic principles than specialized large commercial growers, it would perhaps appear to be simpler for them to convert their farms to organic systems. The poorer farmers may even be 'organic by default'. These farms may not, however, be as sustainable as the romantics amongst us would like to believe. Experience shows that systems nearly always need some adaptation. The role of appropriate extension approaches, such as participatory technology development, is of great importance in these situations if farmers are to understand and internalize changes.

The farms of often better-educated commercial farmers may be a far cry from the organic ideal. These farmers may have better access to training and information and are, therefore, often better able to adopt new ideas. Once the management decision is made, these farms have to go through an ecological conversion period. In this case, converting to an organic production system nearly always has financial implications, as yields decrease initially and premiums are not always available during the conversion period.

In general terms, conversion to an organic cotton system results in more diversity: in the rotation, in the type of activities, and in the solutions to

22

problems. Although some believe that organic farming can only succeed on mixed farms, research into stockless systems is being carried out in some countries and specialized crop farms can co-operate with nearby animal units. In such an arrangement, fodder grown on the organic farm is exchanged for manure from the animal unit.

Finally, it should be noted that conversion to an organic farm system is not only a technical issue. It also has equally important social and economic implications.

The rotation

Cotton is often known as a monoculture crop, but in organic systems it is very likely to be grown in a wider rotation with other crops, such as cereals and legumes. Organic farming systems aim to increase the diversity of crops, in time (through three to four-year rotations) or in space (through intercropping or growing several crops in the same season in different fields). The rotation design is an important tool in reducing the build up of pests, diseases and weeds, balancing the rates of extraction, and replacing nutrients and maintaining a proper soil structure. A wider rotation also reduces the economic risks for farmers, and usually reduces labour peaks.

Even small-scale organic cotton farmers, cultivating up to five hectares, are able to create very diverse rotations. Kenyan coastal farmers, for instance, intercrop chickpea after every row of cotton and the annual rotation can include cotton and sesame with an intercrop of maize and beans. In India, cotton can be intercropped with pulses and a range of legumes one year and maize and sorghum another, and then be followed by a second crop of irrigated wheat. Although this reduces the yields of cotton, the overall farming system can be more profitable and more suited to producing both food and cash for the farmer.

Traditionally, nitrogen-fixing crops (i.e. legumes) are a key part of the organic rotation. After a number of years, soil nitrogen is built up to levels which allow sufficient vegetative growth, with composts only being applied to the crops with the highest needs. When legumes are grown as a cash crop, the crop residues are either fed to farm animals or composted, thus allowing nutrients to be returned to the fields. Legumes can also be grown as forage for farm animals, whose manure is an important composting ingredient, or as a winter cover crop, which is ploughed-in the next spring. Under mixed farming conditions, forage production is an important ally for farmers in avoiding weed problems, soil-borne disease and in building up organic matter levels, soil structure and soil life.

In some organic systems, mainly in the South, land returns to fallow after a couple of years of crops. This practice is becoming less and less common as population pressure grows. Fallow does not necessarily mean the land is unproductive. In mixed farm systems, farm animals can graze. If farmers sow leguminous seed mixtures at the start of the fallow period, the 'improved fallow' provides better-quality feed for animals, improves the soil and provides a vegetation structure that is easier to handle when taking the land back into arable production.

The diversification of crops and inclusion of animals into a farming system also depend largely on the production context. Organic farmers cultivating large surface areas will need to use different strategies in order to make their systems more diverse and sustainable. Large-scale farmers, for instance, may not be able to count on animals for the fertility of the land, and therefore rely more on the use of green manures and crop rotations. Leguminous plants such as clovers and alfalfa are used in the US and Australia, for example. Soya beans are used in sub-tropical and tropical climates such as Brazil, India and Argentina. Some American organic farmers cultivate maize undersown with legumes and leave the stubble as mulch and fertilizer for the cotton crop. Similarly, large-scale farmers in the US will sow strips of maize, beans or plants of the carrot family, such as coriander and fennel, to attract and feed predators.

Cotton

Varieties
In the past, cotton has usually been bred for higher potential production and improved fibre characteristics, leaving the secondary breeding objectives such as problems of pest, disease and drought resistance to be dealt with by the use of inputs. Nowadays, interest in reducing inputs, for cost reasons if for no other, is resulting in these 'secondary' goals being given greater importance.

Cotton breeding programmes have resulted in a wide range of varieties. However, government programmes often dictate to farmers which variety growers should use. In all cases, growers tend to be choosy, or even emotional, about the varieties they grow. Apart from the market price of their crop, few cotton topics draw such heated debate in the local bar, café or marketplace as the selection of varieties.

Government restrictions usually mean that organic farmers have to grow the same variety as in conventional systems. In some organic cotton projects, however, older varieties are being re-established, as they are better adapted to the local situation.

It is recommended practice for any organic cotton project to carry out on-farm research to compare varieties. On-farm, because very few research stations have compared varieties under proper organic conditions, and because the research stations do not adequately reflect the conditions of the farms where the cotton is actually grown. The next step should be to initiate specific 'organic' selection, breeding and multiplication schemes, but in many countries government regulations prevent farmers retaining their own seed. Organic standards require farmers to use organically grown seed (see Chapter 6) which can be a problem for cotton producers where restrictive government regulations exist. Fortunately, requirements to use organically grown seed can be introduced over a period of time. This may well become one of the most difficult problems facing organic cotton growers in the longer term.

Seed treatments
The treatment of seeds with fungicides or insecticides is not allowed in organic farming, although for the 'substitution' organic projects, alternative treatments can certainly be found. Seed treatment has become unquestioned standard practice in the conventional system, so it may be helpful to re-examine the need for such treatment. Of course, bacteriologists can tell horrifying stories of what can happen if seed cotton is infested with the bacterial blight, *Xanthomonas malvacearum*, whilst a phytopathologist will point to the havoc wreaked by soil-borne fungi like *Fusarium oxysporum*, *Verticillium dahliae* and *Rhizoctonia solani* on germinating plants, and an entomologist will extol the benefits of seed treatment in the control of the pink bollworm, *Pectinophora gossypiella* or cutworms *Agrotis* sp.

However, we need to ask if seed treatment is necessary in an organic situation. A healthy soil, healthy rotation and natural balance, combined with proper supervision in an organic cotton seed multiplication scheme, including proper storage, should largely avoid these problems.

If seed treatment does become necessary, a number of alternative treatments are available. For instance, in India, a traditional practice is to 'pill' or encase the seeds in cow dung, the fungicidal properties of which have been known for centuries. *Trichoderma* spp. are used in Egypt, the spores of which are able to compete successfully with those of potentially harmful fungi present on the seed coat. Although restricted in organic production, cuprous oxide may be allowed in cases where there is a danger of bacterial wilt. Copper is known to reduce growth, notably of germinating seeds, so it should not be used unless absolutely necessary. In some situations, seeds are inoculated with *Azotobacter*, *Azospirillum* and phosphate-solubilizing bacteria. The bacteria work in association with the plant and increase nutrient uptake.

Seeds can be treated to reduce the small fibres that remain attached to the seed after ginning ('linters') to facilitate sowing operations. In many countries the main treatment is acid delinting. However, small farmers in the tropics have developed a range of natural methods. In Senegal, for example, farmers use the juice of the Baobab tree (*Adamsonia digitata*) mixed with manure, which produces a fermentation which burns the hairs from the seed. In India, farmers' use of termite clay and cow dung to 'pill' the seed not only incorporates natural fungicide, as already mentioned, but also eases sowing and stops the seeds from sticking together.

25

Soil management and fertility

Fertilizers
Farmers use fertilizers to improve their yields, seldom caring about actually replacing the nutrients used by the crops. In conventional cotton growing, fertilizers are applied at sowing and once or twice after the crop has established itself. They are intended to maximize the yield of the particular crop. Farmers do not necessarily follow the recommended practices, however: they often prefer to see a strong nitrogen-stimulated vegetative growth, despite the fact that this does not necessarily lead to higher yields and can create additional pest problems.

In the case of 'substitution organic', farmers often try to copy the conventional application rates. However, it is often very laborious and inappropriate to copy the application of a nitrogen fertilizer like urea or an NPK composite fertilizer with a compost made from cow manure or chicken dung.

In general, organic farmers should not try to copy conventional fertilizer applications. In organic farming, soil fertility is more a long-term, system issue. In the first place, as few nutrients as possible should be lost. Growing nutrient catch crops outside the main season reduces the leaching of nutrients. Use is also made of crop residues. In organic farming, the burning of crop residues is generally regarded as bad practice. However, in the case of cotton, this is a matter of some debate, as it is acknowledged that cotton stalks may carry over pests and that incorporation in the soil, or composting, may increase pest infestations. Furthermore, cotton stalks are (in unmechanized situations) difficult to shred, incorporate or compost. However, it has been shown in Mali, for example, that cotton stalks can be properly incorporated in some manure-producing systems. This is an area that requires further study.

Cotton fibre is a simple construction of carbon, oxygen and hydrogen. The fibre itself does not contain an important quantity of nutrients. These are all in the seed. If the farmers returned the seed to the field, nutrients would be preserved in the system, and a very sustainable situation in terms of soil fertility would be achieved. However, the seed is a valuable economic output in itself. It is pressed for cotton-seed oil, which is an important cooking oil in many developing countries. The residual cotton seed cake is important as animal feed. If the cake is fed to a farm's chickens or cattle and the manure is collected, composted and applied to the fields, nutrients are recycled back into the system. In this way, nutrient loss is minimized and the need to 'import' nutrients into the farm system is substantially reduced.

Soil fertility strategies are based on proper rotation design, with nutrients in an organic form being added usually only once or twice throughout the rotation. The top soil should contain sufficient nutrients for the crop to take up when needed. This is related to characteristics such as water retention and rooting depth.

Preparing for cultivation, the Maikaal project, India
Credit: Jörg Böthling, Agenda, Hamburg

The use of nitrogen-fixing plants to increase and then maintain soil-nitrogen levels has been mentioned before as a rotation issue. Soil pH and the presence of *Rhizobium* bacteria may need attention. Green manures do not have to be leguminous plants, they can also be grown for their biomass. A grass ley, or a crop of sun hemp (*Crotolaria juncea*) can, for example, improve soil properties like organic matter and internal drainage.

The basic fertilizer in organic farming is compost. Organic materials from different origins, including external sources, are composted, usually on-farm. An important ingredient of composts is animal manure. The technique of composting is described in various publications (see References and Further Reading). Applying rock phosphate or other natural materials rich in the relevant nutrient can alleviate structural deficiencies, such as a lack of phosphate. Rock phosphate is ideally applied through the compost heap as the acids available assist in making the phosphates available in a soluble form. There is a discussion going on in the organic movement about whether to allow, for example, superphosphate in those areas where rock phosphate is contaminated with heavy metals (which are removed when making the fertilizer). This move would be especially relevant during the conversion period to load the system.

With regard to fertilization, it is not enough to think only in terms of quantities of nutrients to be added to the field, but also of measures to improve the absorption of the nutrients already available in the soil. Although healthy soils should not need any extra assistance in this area, in some cases it may be worthwhile inoculating the soil with bacteria and fungi, which enhance nutrient absorption. The use of *Azotobacter* and *Azospirillum* bacteria can, for example, be used to improve nitrogen fixation and *Mycorrhizae* fungi and *Bacillus flavus* to improve the absorption of phosphorus.

Organic cotton-growing systems allow the use of natural fertilizers like bonemeal, castor cake or wood ash as supplements. This may appeal to those looking for materials to substitute synthetic fertilizers, but in practice they are seldom used. Often these materials are not easy to come by in large quantities, they are laborious to produce, unpleasant to handle, and relatively expensive. Experience shows that yields are increasing more through a revitalized soil life, a better soil structure, a proper pH, and sufficient moisture retention, rather than the availability of nutrients *per se*. In this sense, the focus of conventional agricultural science seems very narrow.

Soil preparation
In organic cotton production, soil and seedbed preparation is generally the same as in conventional cotton growing. However, as soil structure is more important in organic farming, heavy equipment is used more carefully than in conventional systems, because of the possibility of compaction when used on wet soils and because the use of diesel fuel is an important issue in a system designed to be less dependent on external inputs. For some organic cotton growers in the South, this means that the balance tilts back in favour of animal traction. This not only has advantages for the quality of the soil, but can also improve the nutrition of the farming family. Farmers are able to sell animals as a contribution to their household income. Animals also produce manure, a grossly undervalued input in conventional agriculture.

Sowing
As in conventional cotton growing, sowing should be done at the optimum time to guarantee good germination and early growth, giving the crop an advantage over weeds. Although pest pressures are not that high in organic cotton projects, recommended practice includes synchronizing sowing to reduce the potential build-up of pest populations throughout the season. However, consequent peaks in weed control and harvest can be a more important disadvantage.

Generally, the same 'good farming practices' are followed in organic as in conventional systems. It is possible to establish more plants in the row and use wider spacing to facilitate easier weed control, but this is generally not done in practice. Ideal plant density is sometimes disrupted by farmers growing, for example, beans between the cotton crop, which obviously reduces cotton yield per hectare. Organic cotton growers in Uganda carry out another technique where a number of maize or sorghum plants are planted every few metres in the row. These plants are known to attract the natural enemies of a range of pests, but do not significantly lower the planting density of the cotton.

In California plant densities are considerably lower in organic than in conventional systems. The resultant changes in the microclimate around the plants reduce pest populations and improve plant growth parameters.

Weed, disease and insect pest management

Weed control
In well-established organic fields, the variety of weeds is greater than in conventional fields that are treated with herbicides. Few conventional farmers realize that herbicides favour the most noxious weeds because they are the ones that are able to maintain themselves. In organic farming, a diverse population of weeds exists which is easier to control.

In organic farming, weeds play an important part. They contribute to a more favourable microclimate in the stand, they harbour natural enemies for the pests, and they may even attract pests away from the cotton plants. Of course, there should not be too many weeds, but cleanweeding is certainly not necessary in the organic system.

Weed management strategies are primarily determined by the rotation. It is possible, for instance, to adapt a rotation to control those weeds which may be particularly troublesome in cotton by the selection of crops which either allow a more intensive weed control or suppress weeds by their dense foliage.

Although outsiders may expect organic cotton growing to need more weed control than conventional systems, this is not always the case. It may be true during the first years of conversion, but once a proper rotation is in place the need for weeding declines.

Disease management
Usually, local cotton varieties have been bred with some disease resistance, for example against bacterial blight (*Xanthomonas malvacearum*) and *Verticillium* or *Fusarium* wilt. If the soil is well drained, the crop is grown in a rotation, sown into warm soil and if weeds are kept under control then disease should not pose any great problems in organic cotton growing.

For preventing seed-borne diseases, rogueing of fields intended for seed production is important.

The number of curative treatments in organic farming is extremely small. This is a great motivation for farmers to prevent disease outbreaks. Nevertheless, breeding for disease resistance remains an important issue.

Insect pest management
Conventional cotton growing has a history of problems in pest management. Cotton is still the crop on which most pesticides are used. There is therefore curiosity, and even scepticism, as to how pests are managed in organic

systems without synthetic insecticides (see Table 1 on page 33). The processes are not as difficult as might be expected, partly because in organic cotton growing, there are fewer pests to deal with than in conventional systems. This is due to the simple fact that in organic systems no chemical sprays are used. Many pest problems originate because their natural enemies are decimated by insecticide applications, and by stresses created by nitrogen applications and excessive irrigation. In none of the current organic cotton projects are pests, or the cost of controlling them, a major issue.

Breeding is one of the first approaches to reduce pest damage. In tropical countries, breeding for leaf hairs has improved the ability of the plant to ward off *jassids*. Breeding for early maturity also reduces insect damage.

Insect pest management in organic cotton growing starts with the monitoring of pests and, to a lesser extent, their natural enemies. As natural enemies are important in pest management systems, techniques to monitor them need to be further developed. Monitoring can be carried out using traps to which insects are attracted by a food bait or pheromone, or through sweep sampling or leaf sampling. Monitoring can alert farmers to the possibility of sudden outbreaks and help in determining whether, and when, curative treatment is needed.

Pest management strategies are directed at enhancing and restoring natural balances. This is done in the first place by creating a good habitat for natural enemies. Trees should be conserved in the field boundaries, or be planted. Hedges, bushes or strips of uncultivated areas should also be left as field boundaries. The extent to which they contribute to a good microclimate in the field and offer refuge to natural enemies is often underestimated.

Although seldom attempted, another insect control strategy is to encourage natural enemies by sowing host plants, termed 'insectary plants', on which they feed. Chickpea, maize and *Malvaceae* vegetables can also be effective 'trap crops' for attracting pest species away from the main crop. Weeds can also be important in promoting natural enemies. In Turkey, for example, it is clear that lacewings (*Chrysoperla sp.*) develop more quickly in spring when they can feed on flowering wild carrots and other *Umbelliferae*. Good farmer training is called for in implementing these techniques.

A next step is to review, and reinstate where possible, traditional and cultural methods to reduce pest incidence. In a number of cotton-growing countries, the collection of leaf worm eggmasses by hand is still practised on both conventional and organic systems. In Egypt, the collection of eggmasses has been abandoned in organic cotton-growing areas, as their low incidence does not warrant this expenditure on labour, but is still standard practice in conventional cotton areas. Synchronized sowing and a closed season, i.e. a period of 4 to 5 months without cotton, or residues, in the field, are examples of cultural practices. In Uganda, all pests except the cotton stainer are controlled through ants of the *Acantholepis* family. The farmers who rear them in their backyards actively promote their presence.

Fighting the boll weevil

The boll weevil (*Anthonomus grandis* Boheman) is a native of Central America. Upland cotton (*Gossypium hirsutum*) is the most significant host, with other cotton varieties also becoming a host if grown within its range. The boll weevil is a key pest in about half the total US cotton area and its effects are also felt in Central America, Colombia, Venezuela, Brazil and Paraguay. The boll weevil is the most costly pest in US cotton production in terms of losses and insecticide control practices. About 30 per cent of all insecticides used in US agriculture are used on boll weevils, but current losses are still at around US$150–300 million annually. Control efforts cost about US$ 75 million annually.

There is evidence, however, that small farmer systems, using a combination of techniques, are able to keep boll weevil damage within acceptable limits.

In *Brazil*, infestation by the boll weevil has been so serious in some areas that cotton has ceased to be the main cash crop. The semi-arid state of Ceará has experienced a so-called 'cotton crisis' for more than two decades affecting different sectors of the state's economy, particularly the small farmers. In an attempt to help overcome the crisis, ESPLAR, an NGO that provides agro-ecological research and assistance to small farmers, implemented a project with about 150 small farmers who planted 250 ha of organic cotton.

Boll weevil damage in the Ceará projects has been maintained at acceptable levels by taking precautionary measures. The most important may be the regulation of proteosynthesis, changing the ratio of sugar and soluble aminoacids in the cell so that the cotton plant becomes less attractive as a crop to feed on. A second measure is to introduce diversity into the field, for example, by planting of leucaena, sesame, sunflower, maize and vigna beans in rows parallel to the cotton. Thirdly, attention is paid to field sanitation. Fallen flower buds are collected and destroyed every third or fourth day. As a result, although boll weevils are present, they do not multiply to the point where they become a pest. Finally, it is important to sow the cotton early enough to escape the population growth curve.

In *Nicaragua*, cotton has been an important export crop for many years but was dependent on heavy investment in synthetic chemicals that resulted in pest resistance and heavier pesticide use. By the end of the 1960s, more than 30 per cent of foreign currency earnings from cotton was spent on importing pesticides. The high chemical usage led to contamination of beef and a US ban on Nicaraguan beef imports. By the 1960s and 1970s, Nicaragua and Honduras had the highest rates of poisonings and death from pesticides in the world. Production costs of cotton increased to a point where they exceeded earnings from cotton exports.

In 1995/96, 40 farmers with small to medium land holdings took part in organic cotton trials using plots that had lain fallow in the previous season. They were keen to join the trials because of the lower costs of production estimated at US$600/ha compared with US$1120/ha for conventional cotton. Several technologists from the cotton advisory organization, FUNDA also took part in the trial. The centre of cultivation was Posoltega, between Leon and Chinandega in northern Nicaragua, an area where cotton had been traditionally cultivated as a monoculture. The majority of the farmers own their own fields and therefore

It is common, however, in organic cotton growing, even in well-established farms, that one or two species still pose a threat. Here, more active prevention methods are needed. In a cotton project in Maharashtra State, India, farmers distribute Trichocards in the field at the rate of two per acre. These cards contain eggs of laboratory-reared *Trichogramma* spp., small wasps that lay eggs in the larvae of the bollworms. In Egypt, in the El-Fayum area, organic, and increasingly conventional farmers, use impregnated rings to control the pink bollworm (*Pectinophora gossypiella*). Adult males are attracted to the rubber rings that release the same smell as the females, thus confusing the male and reducing breeding success and therefore the size of future generations. In fact, the pink bollworm is the only remaining pest in that area, and monitoring shows that infestation levels are decreasing year by year. Although it may be too optimistic to think that this (and other pests) will ever vanish completely, it appears that once natural balances have been restored, only a few insect species continue to pose a threat to the crop and that these can be managed with biological control methods.

In the above situations, pest control is no longer based on curative treatments or sprays. However, to some extent microbial preparations like *Bacillus thuringiensis*, *Beauvaria bassiana* and Nuclear Polyhydrosis Virus (NPV) are used as entomopathogens. *Beauvaria bassiana* can be used to control boll weevil and NPV and Baculoviruses can be used to control caterpillars. Some of these microbials can be produced by the farmers themselves, thus reducing their costs.

Apart from *Trichogramma* wasps, lacewings and various *Coccinelid* beetles can also be reared in small laboratories and released in order to establish a better balance between pests and natural enemies. It is usually not possible to maintain these populations and it is necessary to re-release

Table 1: Main pests and their control without synthetic pesticides in African cotton

Pest	Control method
The American bollworm (*Helicoverpa armigera*)	Trapping of adults. Planting of trap crops (maize, pigeon peas). Establishment of ants like *Acantholepis* spp. Release of predators and parasites like *Chrysoperla* sp. and *Trichogramma evanescens*. Application of *Bacillus thuringiensis* and other microbials like *Metarrhizum* sp.
The spiny bollworm (*Earias* sp.) and pink bollworm (*Pectinophora gossypiela*)	Observation of a closed season to interrupt life cycle. Promotion of *Acantholepis* ants. Promotion of locally present *Trichogramma*, *Apanteles*, *Agathis*, *Rega*, *Netelia*, Bracon and *Trichospilus* spp. Release of predators like *Trichogramma evanescens*. Use of mating disruption pheromone. Application of microbials like *Beauvaria bassiana*.
False codling moth (*Crytophlebia leucotreta*)	No problem as long as insecticides are not used. Promotion of natural enemies. Application of granulosis virus.
Cotton leafworm (*Spodoptora littoralis*)	Manual collection of eggmasses. Application of baculovirus.
Stainers (*Dysdercus* and *Oxycarenus* spp.) with secondary infection by *Nematospora* sp.	Synchronized sowing to shorten harvesting season. Use of trap crops like of the *Malvaceae* family. Favouring of natural enemies like *Phonoctonas* spp. Trapping at out-of-cotton-season host plants. Post-harvest sanitary measures. Possibly pheromone to be developed for early season trapping.
Aphids (*Aphis gossypii*)	Avoid soluble N and excessive irrigation (excessive growth). Trap crops like maize and sorghum. Promotion of natural enemies, like *Chilocorus angoliensis* and *Chrysoperla* sp.
Lygus bugs (*Lygus* spp.)	Companion planting with sorghum. Cissus adenocaulis can be used as a trap crop. Promotion of natural enemies like spiders, predatory bugs and braconid parasitoids.
Jassids (*Empoasca* and *Jacobiella* spp.)	Breed for varietal resistance.

Note. This table provides an indication of the main pests and control approaches, and does not attempt to be complete.

them annually. Techniques to rear these insects are available and may provide a cheaper alternative to farmers than sprays.

The use of the organic equivalent to synthetic chemical sprays, the so-called 'botanicals' or plant extracts sprays is not widespread. Neem extracts (*Azadirachta indica* or *Melia azadirach*) in particular have, however, recently been used especially in some countries of Africa—Senegal, Tanzania, Mozambique and Benin—and in India. Others in use are rotenone (*Derris elliptica*) and ryania (*Ryania speciosa*). As with synthetic sprays, these materials are not very selective, and if used indiscriminately a 'pesticides treadmill' can be developed just as in conventional cotton growing. These natural insecticides may not be readily available, may not be permitted as an insecticide (if they have not been registered in the local regulatory system) and can be expensive if farmers do not produce them themselves. Some other organic pest control methods mentioned above may also introduce unacceptably high costs and may not reduce farmers' dependency on commercial external inputs.

Harvesting

Except in large estates that are highly mechanized, all cotton is hand-picked. Hand-picking ensures the quality and length of the fibres, as only undamaged and completely ripe cotton bolls are selected. Hand-picking can also result in lower percentages of litter, which makes the cleaning process easier and reduces the overall amount of waste. On the other hand, hand-picking is very time consuming, and is only advantageous where local social conditions permit.

Where mechanical harvesting is used, the crop must first be defoliated. In conventional agriculture, synthetic chemical herbicides are used to defoliate the crop, which is not allowed in organic farming systems. In Texas, some organic cotton-growing areas benefit from early frosts that defoliate the crop at an appropriate time. In California, foliar sprays of weak organic acids result in some leaf drop, but alternatives like the application of zinc sulphate which assists in boll maturation and opening need to be developed further. Other organic farmers are experimenting with tobacco toppers to remove late-season rank top growth that also encourages boll maturation and opening. Proper irrigation management is also a key factor in stimulating timely plant desiccation: curtailing the water supply at the right time at the end of the season enhances maturing and defoliation.

Organic agriculture allows for experimentation, but sooner or later new materials have to be officially approved. In Israel, for example, magnesium chlorate and detergents are used. Such materials are controversial because they have not been approved by standard setting bodies such as the IFOAM Standards Committee. Similarly, in California, salt solutions have been prohibited because of the danger of salinization.

When cotton is mechanically harvested it is important to develop techniques to separate the trash resulting from incomplete defoliation, as in organic cotton processing fewer treatments are available to cover up flaws in quality. As organic seed cotton is often stored longer while waiting for a separate ginning run, more attention also needs to be paid to the correct moisture content of the cotton.

Conclusion

In most countries where organic cotton is grown, the development of alternative solutions to the common problems of cotton production has been stimulated. Technically, organic cotton can be grown successfully: an array of techniques and approaches exist to tackle practical problems. Some of the solutions may appear to be very experimental or even 'amateurish', but that is how alternatives are initially developed. It is clear that successful organic cotton farming needs a different approach from 'recipe' farming. Above all, it needs ingenuity and innovation on the part of farmers, extensionists and scientists.

4
Creating structures for organic conversion
BO VAN ELZAKKER and TADEU CALDAS

Introduction

CHANGES IN AGRICULTURAL production, practices, processing and manufacture present a considerable challenge. The production chain of cotton products is long and complex. Those interested in converting to organic production have thus not only to research and investigate new production and processing techniques but also to create new institutional structures. Developments have included many new approaches and a wide range of new partnerships and linkages have been created. In this chapter, Bo van Elzakker looks at the development of some new organizational structures and at possible criteria for the establishment of new organic cotton projects. Tadeu Caldas goes on to discuss the components of the support systems required by small farmers if they are to change from a conventional to an organic system.

Frameworks for action
BO VAN ELZAKKER

Conversion to organic cotton production is a relatively recent activity and as such there has been little analysis carried out of the social and institutional aspects. In looking at the way projects have developed, it is nevertheless possible to identify certain patterns in the process.

The early organic cotton projects

The first organic cotton projects were initiated in the 1980s primarily by European and US clothing companies. As there was no organic cotton being produced, these companies had to organize each step in the production chain themselves, from the farmers to the ginner, spinner, weaver/knitter, dyer and finally to the manufacturing operation. They also had to organize the inspection and certification process, design the final product and experiment in retailing. Descriptions of the Maikaal project in India point to the importance of each actor's awareness of others in the chain as a factor contributing to the success of the project. Similarly in Uganda, the actors are all aware of each other and, for example, decisions about the level of premiums at each stage are agreed amongst the various parties (see case studies in Chapters 9 to 14).

In the experimental stages, it appears that an integrated production chain of the kind described above is not only beneficial but also perhaps necessary. In the longer term, however, such an approach may not be viable and may even hold back expansion. The dependence of the whole production chain on one clothing company which has set up the project may not be economically efficient, because farmers would not be free to sell to a wider market. Moreover, in order to guarantee consistency of quality in the garments, cotton from different origins and of differing qualities may need to be blended to balance out the irregularities that naturally occur in any harvest. Any company or organization involved from the purchase of raw cotton through the chain to the final retail outlets is faced with high capital overhead costs.

Examples of this 'first generation' of organic cotton projects include Bo Weevil (Netherlands) working in Turkey, Verner Frang (Sweden) working in Peru, Remei (Switzerland) working in India, Sekem in Egypt and Eco-sport in the US.

Recent organic cotton projects

The newer projects tend to take a much less structured approach, with perhaps only one or two parts of the chain being organized by a sponsoring agency or company, with smallholder co-operatives or individual estate owners, for example, producing organic raw material and marketing it on a non-exclusive basis. However, despite this more open approach, there is still a long way to go before clothing retailers can call upon their traditional suppliers to produce a range of organic clothing.

Although moving towards a more liberal, free-market situation can be beneficial for the participants in the chain, many companies still commit themselves to buying, perhaps not exclusively, from a specific source. Most of the steps between the farmer and the clothing company, like ginning, spinning, knitting/weaving and manufacture can be carried out by companies based on seasonal contracts. When quantities of organic cotton are large enough and distances travelled not too great, this processing does not, in principle, have to be more expensive than processing conventional cotton. Spinners are, however, often the bottleneck. They require large volumes (200 tonnes) to spin separately, and they usually produce only a limited number of different 'counts' of yarn. Dyeing may also be difficult, as it requires a modern dyeing plant to meet high environmental standards. The supply of buttons, zippers and other haberdashery suitable for organic manufactures is also likely to remain a specialist business for some time to come.

Farmer support and extension is essential in organic cotton projects
Credit: Dorothy Myers, Pesticide Trust

Organizations involved

One of the noticeable features of the development of the organic cotton sector has been the array of different groups involved in setting up and supporting projects. These include Non-Governmental Organizations (NGOs) and government agencies in the North and South, and as noted above, the commercial sector.

In the South, projects have been set up by local rural development NGOs such as ENDA-Pronat in Senegal, Organisation Beninoise pour la Promotion de l'Agriculture Biologique in Benin, and the Lower Guruve Development Organization in Zimbabwe working closely with local farmers' groups. Generally, these initiatives are in contact with organizations based in the North who provide assistance and information about growing techniques, marketing and other aspects. Participants in the Pesticides Action Network (PAN) promote and support pilot conversion projects, network and facilitate exchanges of information and experience, provide assistance with marketing, and raise awareness amongst consumers in the north. In Greece, the World Wide Fund for Nature (WWF) initiated the first organic cotton production in the country and, when it became successful, handed it over to a commercial company which produces T-shirts for, amongst others, the WWF catalogue. The Swedish Society for Nature Conservation has been instrumental in developing standards for the

38

Some criteria for developing an organic chain

Some possible project requirements, which may be applied when investigating organic cotton conversion projects, are described below. The criteria are indicative and the list is not intended to be exhaustive.

At the farmer level

o In areas without a recent history of cotton monoculture or heavy and indiscriminate use of pesticides, conversion to organic will be more rapid.
o In areas where pesticide use is high, organic fields must be separated from those treated, in order to prevent drift of pests and pesticides.
o Government tolerance towards the project should be secured and, for example, aerial spraying programmes in the area should be stopped.
o As cotton is grown in rotation, a market for the organic rotation crops should be investigated and, if possible, secured.
o Farms should be diversified or should at least have ready access to organic matter for composting/fertilization.
o Good farmer support and extension should be in place or set up early in the project.
o Overheads (organizational, technical advice, education, and certification) should not add more than 10 per cent to the cost price after 2–3 years.

At the processing level

o To avoid the higher cost of separate ginning, the minimum volume of organic cotton should be determined. This volume (usually 100–200 tonnes) should be reached within two to three years.
o Smaller processing units should be selected, as they can be more innovative and are used to dealing with special quality requirements. If the confidence of the mill manager is gained and there is interest in innovation, he or she may agree to invest in a new product by processing smaller volumes in the first years, by accepting that organic cotton may spin differently and by investigating the technology of low impact dyeing, etc.
o Most innovative technology is developed when those involved are enthusiastic and committed, and are not only motivated by immediate financial returns.

For the whole chain

o When necessary, longer conversion periods may have a dramatic impact on the availability of marketable cotton and the profitability of the operation.
o The impact of small volumes in the first years should be calculated and, if necessary, means of financing established.
o The certification requirements of the final market should be investigated.

processing of organic textiles and has been certifying organic cotton products. Farmers' organizations have also been involved in initiating projects. In the USA, for instance, a group of organic cotton farmers formed the Texas Organic Cotton Marketing Co-operative (see US Case Study, Chapter 9), which is very vocal in representing members' interests.

Special programmes of bilateral aid agencies such as GTZ or Sida in co-operation with governments and the private sector have sponsored several projects (see Appendix 1: Sources of Support, at the end of the book). GTZ is involved in promoting several organic cotton projects at field level with technical and managerial input, and at the same time helps to market the organic cotton produced. Sida also has an organic trade promotion programme, EPOPA, which initiated organic cotton production in some African countries: Uganda, Mozambique and Zimbabwe. In some cases, governments or government agencies initiate organic cotton production in their own country or are supportive of the idea. The organic cotton project of the Instituto do Algodao Mocambique (IAM) is an example. Following years of spending hard currency importing agrochemicals, it was concluded that pesticides and fertilizers were too expensive for smallholder farmers and that instead, organic production should be promoted. In Egypt the government has been granting exceptions from its otherwise strict regulations to experiment with alternative seed treatments and pest control measures (see case studies in Chapters 9 to 14).

It is unclear so far in what directions organic cotton production and processing will develop but it seems highly likely that financial, technical, managerial, marketing and institutional support will continue to be necessary in the foreseeable future, especially in those areas where lengthy conversion periods are required (see box on page 39).

Structures to serve small-scale organic cotton farmers

TADEU CALDAS

Conversion to an organic cotton system is a complex and risk-prone process, especially when small-scale producers are involved. It is easier to serve one 1500ha organic farm in Texas, for example, than a project involving 700 small farmers in 85 villages in an area of 100 square kilometres in India. The first involves a change in the management system of one farmer, whereas the second involves hundreds of farming families.

Although large areas of mechanized farms exist in developing countries, most cotton produced in the countries of Asia, Sub-Saharan Africa and Latin America is grown on small- and medium-sized holdings. The reality is that servicing large numbers of small cotton growers requires specific mechanisms which are very different from those required for middle- and large-scale farmers, and has different technical and capital needs to initiate production. Organizational requirements are complex since farmers need more individual monitoring and control in order to fulfil specific managerial and technical requirements and to satisfy international certification standards.

Developing alternative services

New systems are required for small farmers to support their conversion efforts to organic production. This support system might include:

○ extension through research, experimentation and technology development;
○ credit, input procurement and supply;
○ documentation;
○ collective certification and marketing;
○ mutual agreements, control and monitoring;
○ price support; and
○ producer-processor-manufacturer-retailer links.

Some of the current organic cotton projects have been able to develop most of the elements listed above, whilst others may not be able to develop all the elements or indeed may not need to do so if structures already exist in relevant and satisfactory forms. For new projects the elements can serve as a checklist which can help ensure success.

Extension through research, experimentation and technology development
In the context of organic cotton, experimentation is aimed at developing practices that are compatible with each farmer's level of risk and management. Farmers act as researchers and are encouraged to answer specific questions through simple experimentation which they evaluate themselves together with their peers and trained extensionists. Results are disseminated to other farmers by extension teams trained in organic or biodynamic agriculture and participatory research methods. This type of approach has already proved useful in generating new information on botanical pesticides, intercropping designs, composting practices, rotations and pest monitoring methods. On-farm research also generates confidence in the farming community. It focuses attention on the value of farmers' own solutions to problems rather than on their being the passive recipients of knowledge, developed elsewhere and often handed down by outsiders, which is geared only to the commercial interests of the cotton industry. Gaining confidence in their own capacities takes time, but farmers gradually demand less of technicians and instead become providers and evaluators of innovations which can quickly be put into practice. Responsibility for the outcome is shared between farmers and advisers. Farmers exchange visits are useful in complementing the training of project extension workers, and innovative farmers can be involved as 'resource persons'.

Operating manuals or handbooks can be useful, particularly for project staff, where large numbers of staff and farmers are involved. They can include technical information about conversion to organic agriculture in the context of local agronomic and economic needs and practices. Continuous updating is, however, important to incorporate new experiences and farmer innovation.

Credit, input procurement and supply
Credit and subsidies provided by government bodies and agencies are normally used as a means of promoting the use of chemical inputs such as pesticides. Credit can, however, also play a useful role in the development of organic systems. Although one of the aims of conversion is to reduce dependency on external resources, off-farm inputs obtained within the region or country can be helpful to farmers during the conversion period. In countries where these are available, sponsoring organizations can support farmers by establishing bulk orders and distribution systems. These facilities can, in the medium term, develop into independent retailing operations for the sale of bio-inputs or into co-operatives. For example, extra soil fertility inputs such as de-oiled seed cakes (castor, neem, etc) can be a good way of providing extra 'organic' nitrogen to the system in addition to animal manures and legumes. Other important off-farm inputs could be pest predators, especially in areas where the ecological balance has been severely damaged. In most cases these alternative inputs are not available from local traders, making access to them impossible if they are not provided by a sponsoring organization.

Small farmers are usually short of cash during the growing cycle and it is therefore often necessary to make these inputs available to farmers through credit. Credit can be provided by a sponsoring organization, that may be a company such as a local spinning mill or an NGO or aid agency. Over time, local banks or farmers' credit associations could also be involved. Recovery of loans in cash or in kind will depend on the system of repayment, the organic fibre premium, the size of the debt against the yields and on the relationship of the extension team to the farmers. Careful monitoring by project staff should result in better productivity and loyalty to the project, which in turn can result in a lower default rate. Credit schemes could in time be extended to cover loans for animals or farm implements.

Documentation
The need for documentation in organic cotton production is primarily to provide data upon which better advice can be based as well as for the organic certification process. The latter requires, for example, information on the past and present use of the land, rotations, last date of chemical application, use and source of organic inputs and farm maps. Every farm requiring certification must be documented in this way. The process of assessing a wide range of information about the farms and farmers also brings the extensionists into closer contact with the farmers and leads to a better understanding of the problems and potential of the farms they serve. The process of documentation can therefore have a broad application, being useful for the

project managers, decision-makers, advisers and technical personnel, as well as for the inspectors and certification bodies.

Collective certification and marketing
Inspection and certification costs can also be reduced when groups of smallholders join together, such as in a co-operative (see Uganda case study). Such central organization can develop an internal quality control system in which the agronomists can take over some of the external inspector's roles. The foreign inspector then merely checks whether the internal control system works well, instead of inspecting all the individual farms (see Chapter 6).

Mutual agreements, control and monitoring
Monitoring mechanisms are required to assess levels of compliance with mutual agreements established by the promoting organizations. The agreements normally incorporate the basic requirements of the organic standards as well as guarantees to deliver the cotton crop and penalties for any lapses in following the organic standards. Agreements include the services that will be offered in return, such as guaranteed purchase, technical advice and premiums.

It is not easy to monitor large numbers of small-scale farmers and no amount of penalty will bind a farmer to an agreement if it is felt the crop, and subsequently his or her income and livelihood, are at risk. The best way to reduce cases of lapse is to ensure that farmers are given as much support and information as possible to cope with any problems that occur.

Although this type of support goes a long way towards reducing the possibility of lapses, monitoring still has to be carried out and suspect situations investigated. Several possibilities exist for monitoring. One is to have staff performing random checks on the farms, the other is to instruct the extension team to carry out spot checks, and sample soil and leaf material as well as cross check the information supplied by the farmer with farm workers and neighbours.

Price support
Farmers' income and the capacity of the traders to sell the final product at a competitive price are both crucial elements in ensuring the success of an organic cotton project. Premium prices for farmers can therefore be important in the early stages to cover the conversion period, when farmers cannot sell their products as certified organic, and to encourage farmers to convert (see Chapter 7). The level of premium should take into account the possible decline in yields (and therefore income) in the conversion phase, local prices in relation to international prices, production costs, and the quality of the cotton. Sometimes, the prospect of reduced costs and a guaranteed market is enough to convince farmers to commit their land to

organic production. Farmers also value the intensive technical support and monitoring. High premium levels can compensate farmers, especially where price levels have been kept low by state monopolies.

In general, premium levels are 10–30 per cent above the local market price. The best way to ensure that this level is adequate is by carrying out a gross margin analysis for the whole farm to determine the impact on income level both before and after conversion. Production costs are the key element in this analysis. If production costs are too high then adjusting incomes through premium pricing is difficult without making the selling price uncompetitive. However, in the initial stages, setting up the required range of services is capital intensive, yields are likely to be low and the market is largely unknown to traders and manufacturers.

Producer–processor–manufacturer–retailer links
Links between producers and consumers have been a characteristic of organic agriculture. They are a necessary part of the structure if consumers are to be confident about the nature of their purchase. In this type of system the consumer is encouraged to consider not just the quality of the garments, but also the impact of his or her purchasing decisions over the lives of farming families and environmental conditions in the production area.

Thus a range of institutional structures involving a number of players providing a variety of services for very different reasons, have evolved in relation to organic cotton production and processing. The range, quality and scope of services vary enormously depending on the size of the project, the situation of farmers, market availability and capital resources of the implementing organizations, as well as on technical advice available.

5
Creating a final product

KATE FLETCHER, NICOLE WAAYER,
JAMES M. VREELAND Jnr, LYNDA GROSE

Introduction

THIS CHAPTER provides an introduction to cotton textile production—
from fibre to fabric. The major environmental and health impacts associated with textile processing are discussed in the context of the product
lifecycle and more environmentally responsible alternatives are introduced. The first part of the chapter is devoted to the textile industry's
response to environmental pressures and to the textiles-environment debate. The chapter then looks at cotton textile production, including discussion of key impacts at each stage and environmentally responsible
alternatives, where they exist. The chapter includes information on naturally pigmented organic cotton and ecological design.

Cotton textile processing lifecycle and design
KATE FLETCHER and NICOLE WAAYER

Transforming a cotton crop into a textile fabric involves many stages of
processing, often in a number of different countries, with a variety of skills
and technologies. An organic cotton crop does not necessarily produce an
organic fabric, as the sequence of fibre to fabric processing involves chemicals as well as water, energy and waste. Production and processing systems
which take account of the environmental, social and economic health of the
entire system are important for the organic movement. It is not enough for
a product to be produced organically and then processed in a conventional,
polluting system.

The product lifecycle encompasses all activities from raw material
cultivation, processing, transportation, distribution and use to final disposal. There are environmental impacts at each stage of the cotton textile
lifecycle which vary according to how the fibre is cultivated, the way the
fabric is made and how it is used. Overall environmental impact is also
related to cultural factors, product type, length of product life and dis-
posability. In endeavouring to create a lifecycle which is as benign as
possible, all these factors must be taken into account and plans made to
reduce the total environmental impact.

Impacts vary at different stages in the lifecycle for different types of end-product. Clothing textiles, for example, have far higher environmental costs in the consumer 'use' stage than furnishing textiles, as they are laundered more frequently. The main environmental impacts for furnishing fabrics is in fibre cultivation and processing, and for carpets, it is processing and disposal. In comparing impacts for different fibre types, synthetic fibres use more energy in their initial extraction than natural fibres, but less in subsequent processing and, while they are not biodegradable, synthetic fibres are usually recyclable.

There is also a North–South dimension to the differential importance of environmental costs. In the use stage, for instance, the rich Northern community usually wash and dry their clothes in high-energy and water-consuming machines, with an associated high impact, whereas in the poorer South it is far more common to wash clothes by hand and dry them outside. Thus the environmental impacts for a textile garment used in the South can be very different from one that is used in the North.

The use stage in the North has major environmental impacts. A lifecycle study by the American Fiber Manufacturers Association of a synthetic fibre blouse showed that as much as 88 per cent of atmospheric emissions, 86 per cent of energy and 68 per cent of solid waste attributable to the total textile lifecycle are amassed during washing and drying. These results, however, should be placed in context. Only garments were studied and results could be significantly affected by a change in laundering habits. If the garment is washed at cold temperatures and dried on a line, total energy consumption is reduced by 78 per cent, and the bulk of the environmental impacts would be in production rather than in use.

The complicated nature of environmental impacts associated with the textile lifecycle means that interpretation is highly problematic. For clothing textiles in the North, most environmental damage is caused during use (as with many consumer products). This is not an indication that production is necessarily environmentally responsible, but rather an acknowledgement of a *comparatively* low impact. It is important, therefore, to work towards the continued reduction of overall impacts which can be achieved by improving the environmental responsibility of production, while simultaneously promoting greater efficiency in consumer use and lessening the environmental burden of disposal.

In the search for 'solutions' to complex environmental problems, there is great reliance, from industry and the public alike, on science and technology. There is a generally accepted belief that all environmental solutions are technical rather than social, cultural, structural or design-related. While scientific research and development has a crucial role to play in reducing the environmental impact of the product lifecycle, a shift in consumer demands, design specifications or structural relationships can also bring environmental benefits. Technical developments can, for example, make the

Naturally pigmented organic cotton

Introduction

Naturally pigmented cotton, i.e. cotton which has a botanically formed pigmentation lodged in the centre, or lumen, of the fibre, is as old as the plant itself. Archaeological evidence indicates that the oldest cotton remains so far examined may not have been white but brown. Domesticated independently some 4500 years ago in at least four areas—Central America, Peru, Northern Africa and Central Asia—these primitive cottons survive today as distinct land races. Conserved by traditional peoples for craft and medicinal purposes, indigenous or 'native' cottons have a range of natural colours, including beige, brown, green and mauve.

Ancient cotton land races have been almost entirely displaced or replaced by modern cultivars, all white in colour, developed essentially to facilitate the take-up of dyes, and designed to provide users with an unlimited range of textile design possibilities. However, interest in more environmentally responsible fabrics has seen a revival in interest in naturally pigmented cottons. Naturally pigmented cotton applications are, however, limited for modern textile production usage on account of the short-staple length, extremes of fineness and thickness of the fibre wall and brittleness. Recent responses by farmers to market demands for organic and naturally pigmented cotton thus appear to be restricted to regions where germplasm resources have either been conserved by indigenous peoples (Peru, Guatemala and Mexico) or regenerated from seedbank collections in other countries (United States, Israel, Australia, India and Russia).

Coloured cotton in ancient America, Egypt and China

Fibres and fabrics made by Andean weavers five millennia ago show that two distinct colours, light brown and chocolate brown, were in use through the entire pre-colonial period. The colours were intentionally differentiated by ancient Peruvian fisher folk who made nets and lines from the darker shades that apparently are less visible than lighter ones to fish swimming near the surface of the water.

With a finer, longer and stronger lint than either of the two old world cotton species, *Gossypium herbaceum* and *G. arboreum*, the two new world cultivated species, *G. barbadense* and *G. hirsutum*, soon displaced all African and Asian cultivars, altering the distribution and range of cotton cultivation in entire subcontinents (see also Chapter 2).

In Guatemala, several varieties of perennial and naturally pigmented cottons were described over a hundred years ago by Pastor. In 1905, Guatemalan white and brown dwarf cotton landraces were grown by the USDA in southern Texas, Kansas, Maryland and Southern California in a series of experiments to determine boll weevil resistance. Other pigmented varieties introduced to the American south during the nineteenth century included 'Week's Guatemala', 'Lane's Yucatan', and a Mexican-Egyptian hybrid.

Modern Egyptian cotton was ostensibly derived from a South American, probably Andean (*G. barbadense*), progenitor which had a long, strong golden-brown lint. This quality was much used by hand-spinners and transferred to subsequent commercial selections, such as the Ashmouni and Mit Afifi varieties. The latter had richer, darker brown lint, averaging 34 mm in staple length, and gave rise to American–Egyptian Yuma in 1908 and Pima in 1910.

In China, so-called 'Nankin' varieties, like the early Egyptian ones, appear to have yielded a short-staple, pigmented fibre, but use of the fibre was restricted to the noble classes. Widespread cotton cultivation is recorded by Chinese writers by about the thirteenth century. Upland *G. hirsutum* and long staple *G. barbadense* cotton varieties have now almost completely displaced the aboriginal central Asian and African perennial species and now constitute the genetic base for modern organic cotton fibre production in these countries.

Naturally pigmented cotton textiles

Naturally pigmented cotton fabrics were among the first artifacts of Amer-Indian manufacture collected as tribute and shipped to Spanish courts after the 1492 colonization. Naturally pigmented cotton lint was still widely cultivated and spun by female Indian artisans in coastal villages of northern Peru during the past century. At that time some 12 shades of natural brown cotton were identified, and coloured lint was routinely blended with sheep's wool by English manufacturers to lower the costs of producing fine woollen fabrics, reduce shrinkage, increase durability and give better lustre and finish.

In Colombia, the revival of native cotton spinning and weaving is now being undertaken by a small group of student-led peasant producers as a rural development alternative in the hills of Santander. Natural variation in colour was maintained by hand weavers in Mexico and Guatemala, where attempts to bring pigmented forms under intensive cultivation were undertaken during the American civil war. In 1936 it was reported that in Haiti, naturally pigmented fibre for commercial garment production was obtained from a native, perennial form. The lint was ginned and woven industrially as an attractive, khaki-coloured fabric in a factory in Port-au-Prince.

Naturally pigmented cotton fabric was also common in the United States; probably being introduced from its presumed centre of origin in highland Mexico. Cultivated by subsistence farmers and on large plantation estates, spun and woven by hand and by machines, naturally pigmented cotton was traditionally made into attractive, homespun cloth in several southern states. In the heart of the Mississippi delta region, a golden-brown linted cotton has been cultivated by rural spinners and weavers for more than two centuries.

Revival of interest in the twentieth century

Due to petroleum-based dye shortages during World War II, Soviet textile engineers resorted to the use of naturally pigmented fibres to add colour to otherwise undyed cotton fabrics. In 1945, the Soviet Embassy in the US offered for sale some 700 tonnes of naturally pigmented fibre, which was woven into some one million yards of brown cloth.

In California, Gus Hyer, a USDA cotton geneticist, worked with coloured lint lines, largely of upland varieties, for several decades. According to California cotton seed distributors, it was Hyer's seed stocks that formed the basis for contemporary brown and green linted commercial fibre production that began in California in the 1980s under the direction of Sally Fox. The project was abandoned in 1997 after nearly a decade of experimental production in the plains of Texas and Arizona.

The 1990s witnessed acclamations of the environmental and commercial benefits of naturally pigmented cotton, which was used by several major garment manufacturers including Esprit, Fieldcrest-Cannon and Levi Strauss. These projects were discontinued, however, probably because the American consumer is not enthusiastic about clothing in such a limited colour range. Sally Fox argued that brown cotton yarn is cheaper to produce than dyed yarn on an industrial scale, but production never really got off the ground as modern spinners could not accommodate the poor quality of the fibre.

After briefly booming in the early 1990s, naturally pigmented cotton in the United States has once again ceased to attract serious farmer/converter/consumer interest. However, production in other countries has grown significantly. Naturally pigmented cottons have been introduced in Israel, India, Australia and other countries, largely with government support. In Peru, expansion of this crop has been led by a single company, without any local or external subsidies, and is now cultivated on over 3000 hectares annually. Most of the production is used in national markets for inexpensive school athletic uniforms, distributed by the government. As such, the school uniform programme represents the largest single use of naturally pigmented, organically cultivated cotton world-wide, restoring Peru's pre-eminent status as producer of this unique fibre. The native cotton project of Peru, for example, has stimulated a revival of interest in the species, which is now protected by law as a natural and cultural resource. Pakucho brown and white fibre today is obtained from many hundreds of small indigenous producers using traditional, organic agricultural methods.

James M. Vreeland Jnr

dyeing process more resource efficient (see box on naturally pigmented cotton, page 47). At the same time, if consumers and designers demanded fewer dark shades, resources could be saved and levels of dye in effluent reduced.

Design is an integral part of lifecycle thinking (see box on ecological design, page 51). The position of design at the beginning of the lifecycle has the potential to bring a high level of environmental responsibility in production, use and in disposal. The use of design as a co-ordination mechanism, planning for impact reduction across a product's entire life, is however, only possible if the designer has experience of industry practice and knowledge of the associated environmental impacts and if industry, in turn, appreciates the solutions that good design has to offer.

Textiles can be designed and produced to be durable, although this is largely at odds with the demands of the Northern-based fashion industry, which promotes stylized products which quickly becoming obsolete as fashion cycles change. In practice, the useful life of a textile can extend over a number of decades and the creation of products with a long and durable existence saves valuable resources. Some steps in the chain of cotton processing which affect the durability of cotton products are, however, likely to present difficulties for the environmentally responsible processor. For example, it is conventional practice for cotton to be treated with caustic soda (mercerizing), to increase fibre strength, lustre and dye absorption, with the result that in dyeing, less dye is needed to reproduce the same depth of shade (see below). The negative environmental effects of mercerizing may well be compensated for by the environmental benefits of reduced resource consumption at the dyeing stage and increased durability.

It is also important that the physical life of a product is compatible with the needs of its useful service life, i.e. it should have *appropriate* durability. There is no environmental benefit to be gained from developing products that persist in the environment after their useful life is over. Cotton fabrics do not readily biodegrade after being treated with process chemicals, such as dyes and those used to give special finishes.

As with cotton growing, the scale and degree of mechanization of cotton processing can vary greatly, as can environmental impacts. Processing can be carried out in a range of situations from small, locally based units to state-of-the-art mills, each having differing degrees of resource efficiency, local pollution loads and socio-economic impacts in the surrounding area. Pressure to develop more environmentally responsible techniques of textile processing has led to the development of new and, in some cases the reassessment of old, technologies. Hi-tech, fully integrated processing plants have super-efficient machines and improved health and safety conditions compared with traditional processing. At the other end of the spectrum, simplifications made to the production process also bring environmental benefits. The market for organic products can also help preserve traditional forms of cotton processing, such as the traditional labour-intensive textile techniques like piece-dyeing, block and screen printing, hank-dyeing, hand-winding and hand-weaving.

The textile industry is very complex and disparate. Traditionally, different stages of production have been carried out at different geographical locations favoured because of their close proximity to natural and labour resources. Merchants transported first the yarn and then the fabric between spinners, weavers, finishers and the market place. As each step in the cotton production chain evolved into a separate industry, so the overall costs, both social and environmental have become increasingly obscured. Globalization has exaggerated the geographical separation between different stages in the processing chain and adds to the confusion about costs.

Ecological design and organic cotton

Ecological design is an approach which integrates ecological considerations into the design process. Though the concept is simple, the implementation is complex. In most industries today, including the textile industry, infrastructure has not been based on ecological principles and therefore, in order to integrate ecological consideration, designers have to step beyond the conventional arena of aesthetics and involve themselves in the complete supply chain of textile and product development. An understanding of the ecological impact of a design decision is the first requirement, investigating alternatives the next step. The ultimate goal is to develop products which have less ecological impact through integrating and expressing the alternatives.

Conventional design

Conventional designers work within the confines of the existing industry infrastructure, which is linear. Conventional designers are at one end of the chain focusing on market trends, ensuring an acceptable price for the product, achieving desirable quality and designing garments within the company image. They are completely disconnected from the supply chain of the product. They usually select fabrics and yarns from a sales person and specify colours or patterns, but generally have no contact with the growing, harvesting, cleaning or processing of the fibre into finished fabric nor with recycling later on.

They are therefore totally unaware of the ecological ramifications of their design decisions. Furthermore, if and when they do become aware of the impacts of their decisions, they are still powerless to investigate and implement alternatives. They simply do not have access to experts and information that would help them to make the necessary changes.

Designers face a series of challenges when designing a commercially successful product including: price, production, aesthetics, quality, target market and competition. All these elements are interconnected and are essential ingredients in the commercial success of a given product. If any one of the elements is neglected or pushed too far, the commercial success is limited. When the 'worth' of a product is analysed inside a company, the discussion will often erroneously isolate two elements of the design: do we want a good price or high quality?—we cannot have both. Do we want something easy to produce or something unique and ahead of the competition?—we cannot have both. The reality is that *all* elements must be taken into account. When a product is well designed with a good balance of all the elements, criticisms do not usually arise. Most people respond well to the product and it will sell well.

Ecological design

In addition to these challenges, the ecological designer must also consider the 'ecological' aspects of the product. Not surprisingly, there are similar commercial critiques of organic products which isolate certain elements of the design process. Questions arising can include: do we want an organic product or a good price? We cannot have both because organic fibre is expensive. Do we want an organic product or an aesthetically pleasing product? We cannot have both because organic fabrics look dull. Or do we want an organic product or an easily produced garment? We cannot do both because organic cotton is in too short supply. As before, the reality is that we need all elements of design in the appropriate balance, and when we have a well-designed organic product, it sells well.

Examples of the ecological design process

In the early 1990s, in the organic cotton industry in the United States, all the elements that a designer has to balance presented difficulties: organic cotton fibre was at least twice the price of conventional; available fibre was limited due to the small number of farmers growing cotton organically; the variety of fabrics and therefore finished products was limited by the small number of mills involved and the high minimum amounts needed to develop new products; and quality issues in yarn production included uneven spinning, which led to breakages during weaving. Some of this was traced back to stickiness of the fibre caused by secretions of the *Lygus* bug (see US case study): the limited supply of organic fibre meant that mills could not blend the fibre as thoroughly as they might have wished in order to offset the stickiness. The organic market was completely new and unpredictable. The so-called 'green' trends in fashion led to a plethora of ecological claims including 'natural', 'hand-picked', and 'chemical-free'—none of which helped communicate the significant benefits of organically grown cotton.

The organic industry at that time relied on communicating the message of organic agriculture to justify the higher price of a lower-quality, poor-looking garment. No wonder there was limited commercial success! The message could not carry the product.

In 1991, through a series of organic cotton conferences in the US, organized by the Sustainable Cotton Project, interested parties across all sectors of the cotton industry came together to discuss how to bring organic cotton to the commercial marketplace. These conferences brought together designers, farmers, mills, manufacturers and retailers.

As a result of these meetings, the designers involved began to work completely differently from conventional designers (see the US case studies in Chapter 8). With access to experts all the way through the supply chain, designers began to find new solutions to the challenges arising with organic cotton. Understanding the difficulties of making the transition from conventional to organic farming and that certifying agencies required a three-year period before the 'organic' label could be used, manufacturers bought transitional fibre at reduced premiums. Designers became aware of different fibre types and shifted from higher priced *Acala* cotton to *Texas Upland* cotton for knitted products. This brought knitted product prices down. More mills became involved, and increased competition further reduced fabric prices. Manufacturers made unprecedented pre-harvest commitments to farmers, thereby securing the market for the farmer, which reduced risk and resulted in lower fibre prices. Then, as the market increased, more farmers became involved and shared information on organic techniques. Increased farm efficiencies brought fibre costs down and increased the amount of fibre available to the industry. As manufacturer interest increased, more mills became involved and a greater variety of fabric types became available. This increased the visual appeal and value of the final product. The arrival of organic woven fabrics enabled designers to develop products with greater retail price elasticity: shirts and jackets can absorb the higher fibre costs more readily than a T-shirt, for example. Finally, as more fibre was produced, more thorough blending was possible to offset potential stickiness and maintain consistent yarn quality.

Since the first of the organic cotton conferences, the market has often fluctuated. However, the new model of communication has remained in place, and key companies and individuals in the industry have continued to form partnerships and commitments which have steadied both the market demand and the supply of organic fibre.

Conclusion
Designers are the orchestrators of a commercially successful product. By becoming 'ecological' designers, involved in the supply chain, they can have access to experts to help make necessary changes upstream and further increase the commercial viability of organic cotton. Designers know best how to create a product with high visual appeal which can successfully carry the message of organic cotton. With a potentially more stable organic industry infrastructure in place there are greater opportunities for ecological designers to build upon the limited successes of the early 1990s and create a powerful organic market into the next decade.

Lynda Grose

As a fabric is transported around the world, from processor to processor, it uses local resources and causes local pollution, both of which normally do not impact upon and are not paid for by the consumer. These costs are external to the product. Environmental responsibility is not well served by the industry structure. The isolation of different sectors within the industry is also reflected in the fibre producing and fibre reclamation industries. Both are well established but remain unconnected. With little history of communication between the two ends of the lifecycle, producers do not design fabrics to be easy to reuse, and in turn recyclers do not request fabrics to be so.

The next part of this chapter examines the processing stage of the lifecycle and the development of more environmentally responsible practices. In the North, textile processing—and especially the processes involved in fabric finishing—have been a target for environmental legislation, leading to the restriction of emissions and some process chemicals. The industry has been obliged to pay attention to treating the symptoms of environmental damage, such as contaminated effluents and waste generation with much emphasis on chemical processing. Environmental damage associated with mechanical processing has been largely ignored and often assumed to be benign. Issues such as energy consumption, dust, noise and waste creation must be considered.

The cotton fibre to textile fabric processing chain involves three major steps: yarn manufacture, fabric manufacture and fabric finishing (see Figure 1). This section introduces these processes, the major environmental problems associated with them, and the development of more responsible practices. These practices are then elaborated on in Chapter 6, where the requirements of environmental standards and labelling in the textile sector are discussed.

Yarn manufacture

Cotton, like all natural fibres, contains many impurities (seeds, dirt and plant residues) and in order to convert the cotton crop into useful textile fibres which can then be spun into a yarn, it requires initial processing. All the processes in yarn manufacture are mechanical and produce large amounts of dust. Dust can cause eye irritations and lung problems such as byssinosis. Developments to reduce this include the introduction of more sophisticated machinery with dust extractors. Energy efficiency and waste minimization are also important at the yarn preparation stage.

Ginning
After harvesting, the cotton fibre is firstly separated from the seed, a process known as ginning. About one-third of the raw material is cotton fibre, the rest is seeds and impurities. Hand-picked cotton contains considerably fewer impurities than cotton which is machine picked. The cotton plant is valued for its seeds, which can be stored for the following season, sold for additional income, or made into by-products such as oil and animal feed. In an organic system care must be taken not to mix organic and conventional cotton fibres, thus requiring separate, or carefully cleaned, storage and ginning facilities.

Opening, blending and spinning
It takes several steps to turn the raw cotton fibre into yarn. First, several bales of raw cotton are opened and the contents mixed together so as to ensure consistent fibre quality. Next, the fibre mass is unravelled and cleaned by carding, a process which combs the fibres and lays them parallel in readiness for spinning. For a fine, high-quality yarn, the fibres are also combed to remove shorter lengths. The short fibres are used for spinning into bulkier yarns or as filling material. Good blending and carding is instrumental in producing a yarn of uniform strength and thickness and an overall quality product.

There are two ways to spin a yarn; rotor and ring spinning. The rotor

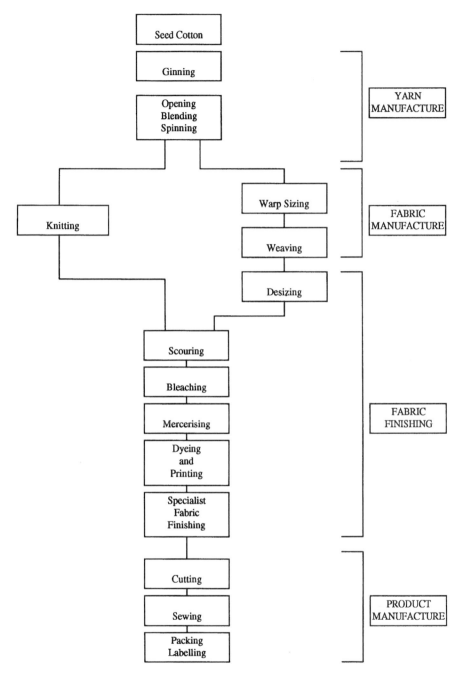

Figure 1: The fibre to product manufacturing chain

Towards the final product: spinning organic cotton in India
Credit: Jörg Böthling, Agenda, Hamburg

processing method is cheaper, but gives a lower quality yarn. Both processes are high speed, and in ring spinning lubricants are sometimes applied to protect the fibres from the stresses they experience during spinning, enabling the yarn to run more smoothly through the machine. A common lubricant is paraffin oil, however synthetic oils are also used. Synthetic oils biodegrade most readily out of the two, and are washed out of the fibre during fabric cleaning (scouring), prior to dyeing. All additional fibre treatments, such as the application of lubricants in spinning, add to the chemical complexity of the waste water arising from fabric scouring and make it more difficult to neutralize.

Fabric manufacture

The two most common methods of processing cotton yarn into fabric are weaving and knitting. Fabric manufacture, like yarn manufacture, is dominated by mechanical processing and similarly the major environmental burdens are related to energy use, waste production and the generation of dust and noise. These burdens vary between different knitting and weaving machines, technologies and processors.

Weaving

Weaving involves the interlacing of yarns in two directions. The warp, which runs the length of the fabric, is first wound onto a beam and fed through the loom. Weaving exerts considerable stresses and strains on the warp and in order to give it extra strength and minimize yarn breakages, it is coated with size. Starches, such as potato starch, are often used as a cheap way of sizing the warp in cotton production. Alternatively, more expensive synthetic sizes such as polyvinyl alcohol can be used. Size does, however, cause environmental problems in its removal (as discussed in 'Fabric finishing'). The yarn running perpendicular to the warp, across the fabric width, is the weft. The weaving patterns created by the warp and weft together influence fabric strength, weight, and wrinkle properties, as well as fabric aesthetics.

Knitting

There are two methods of knitting: round and flat knitting. Round knitting produces a tube and is commonly used to produce jersey fabric for items such as T-shirts. Flat knitting creates fabric widths or pieces. Unlike in weaving, yarns used in knitting do not have to withstand such high tensions and are not sized. They are, however, coated with an oil (which is injected into the needles) to facilitate their movement through the machine. The knitting oil is normally a mineral or vegetable oil, is soluble in water and is washed out in scouring. Overall the environmental impact of knitting is lower than that of weaving, because of the absence of size.

Fabric finishing

This is the final stage in fabric processing and includes preparation of the fabric to be dyed or printed, fabric colouration itself and the application of any specialist fabric finishes such as water repellents or those used to resist creasing. This stage has major environmental impacts and includes the use of vast quantities of water, energy and chemicals and the production of substantial amounts of effluent. Most of the effluents from cotton processing arise in this finishing stage. According to the United Nations Environment Programme (UNEP), effluents from the textile processing chain are characterized by their grey colour, high polluting load which includes heavy metals, high solids content and high temperature.

The majority of processes in fabric finishing cannot be avoided. While some processes, such as colouration, can be dispensed with, most other processes are essential. In such a situation, the most environmentally responsible route for the processor to take is therefore one of energy efficiency, waste minimization and effluent treatment. A standard sequence of effluent treatment for woven and knit fabric finishing includes: screening, to remove fibrous waste from the effluent; equalization, to mix waste in order to achieve a fairly standard effluent for downstream processing; and biological treatment, to lower the effluent's polluting load. In biological treatment, micro-organisms are cultivated which feed on the substrates in the effluent. A typical aerobic system consists of a sedimentation tank, followed by an aeration tank and a second sedimentation tank, and requires a treatment time of between 24 and 48 hours.

Environmental impacts in fabric finishing can be reduced by a careful selection of processing chemicals. These chemicals have a range of potentially hazardous properties relating to their toxicity and to the health and safety effects of prolonged exposure to them, and can often be substituted by less hazardous ones, although it is often the case that the substitutes are more expensive. Reducing environmental impacts arising from the finishing stage can also be achieved by reducing water consumption, which in turn leads to lower volumes of effluent. Modifications to processes and equipment also have the potential to bring environmental benefits, such as, the merging of the three process stages, desizing, scouring and bleaching, into a single process.

Desizing
For woven fabrics, it is an imperative that after weaving, size is removed. Size is a process chemical and there are obvious financial and environmental benefits in reclaiming it. When natural starches are used, the size is removed by washing the fabric with water containing starch-degrading amylase enzymes. No recovery is possible because the starch breaks down during the desizing process. As the starch degrades, it uses up large quantities of oxygen (i.e. it has a high biological oxygen demand, or BOD), significantly affecting oxygen levels in waste and river water and posing a hazard to aquatic life. Desizing accounts for a large proportion of the BOD polluting load from cotton fabric finishing, making some form of biological treatment of waste water essential. Alternative sizes, such as synthetic, polyvinyl alcohol, can be reclaimed and reused. Synthetic sizes are more expensive than their natural starch counterparts and their use is not as widespread, mainly because it is only when sizing and desizing take place on one site, i.e. when a weaver reclaims its own size, that their use is financially viable. Whether size is natural or synthetic it should be readily biodegradeable and waste treatment plants should be able to biodegrade it effectively. The recovery of size in cotton processing is one of the most important areas where effective chemical recovery and reuse (using ultrafiltration technologies) is possible.

Scouring
After fabric production and prior to dyeing and/or printing, the fabric requires thorough cleaning. Small particles of seed are removed by scouring, along with the cotton fibres' natural wax coating and other impurities which may have been added to aid processing. The result is a fabric which absorbs water easily and can be bleached and printed or dyed to a uniform colour. For the scouring of cotton, boiling and water-

based solutions of caustic soda (sodium hydroxide) are used. Although the scouring process uses relatively little water, the waste water is rich in organic compounds, is characterized by a high polluting load and needs to be treated before being discharged.

Bleaching

Most cotton has an off-white colour, so bleaching is necessary to produce white fabrics and those that will be dyed or printed to pale colours. Bleaching also enhances colour brilliance after dyeing; improves colour uniformity, even for dark shades; and removes the last traces of residual impurities. On the down side, bleaching weakens the strength of the fibres and thus the durability of the textile product. The oldest known method of fabric bleaching is sun bleaching. Nowadays in Europe, it is common practice to bleach with hydrogen peroxide in a wet process. Hydrogen peroxide is active only at temperatures above 60°C, resulting in a fairly energy-intensive bleaching process. Chemical additives are needed in the bleaching bath to stabilize the hydrogen peroxide and optimize the bleaching process, giving a fabric with uniform appearance. One of these additives (sequestering agents) counters the effect of reactive metal particles present in the bath which otherwise would act as a catalyst for the bleaching agent and cause it to attack and break down the cotton fibre. Special care therefore needs to be taken in bleaching cottons grown on soils with a high metal content, such as those in Brazil.

Cotton can also be bleached with sodium hypochlorite and sodium chlorite. During bleaching, a number of chlorine-based products are formed, including the highly toxic chloroform, which pass into air and waste water and which then have to be carefully treated. The continued acceptability of chlorine as a bleaching agent for cotton is being questioned due to concerns about the negative environmental and carcinogenic effects of chlorine substances.

Mercerizing

Mercerizing greatly increases the lustre, strength and dye absorption properties of cotton yarns and fabrics (knitted and woven). It involves treating the material under tension with a strong aqueous solution of caustic soda (sodium hydroxide). The fabric then has to be chemically stabilized and washed. During the process, the cotton fibres swell, untwist slightly and become more parallel in the yarn structure—giving a more regular arrangement of fibres, so changing the fabric's appearance and increasing its strength by up to 100 per cent. Mercerized yarns and fabrics also benefit from improved dye absorption, allowing the same depth of shade to be achieved with between 30 and 50 per cent less dye. After mercerizing, it is often possible to reuse the dilute caustic soda solution in other processes, such as in scouring or dyeing. Caustic soda from waste water can also be recovered and recycled using membrane technology or by effective evaporation. When no reclamation system exists, it is important for the mercerizing effluent to be treated to neutralize the pH of the waste water.

Dyeing and printing

Textiles can be dyed as fibres, yarn or fabric. Different fibres have an affinity for different dyes. Similarly, different colours and shades of colours use different dye classes. The dyebath contains processing (auxiliary) chemicals as well as dye, and these chemicals vary by dye, dyer and machine, as does liquor ratio (the ratio of water to chemicals), water temperature and dyeing time. After dyeing, the yarn or fabric requires intensive washing to remove auxiliary chemicals in addition to any unfixed dye.

The colouration process is very resource intensive in terms of water, energy and chemicals, and produces effluent which is often highly coloured, but rarely toxic. In countries with poor working conditions and few environmental protection measures, dyeing and printing can nevertheless pose a serious threat to human and environmental health. Steps are being taken to reduce the wide-ranging environmental impacts attributed to this stage. Waste-water treatment is becoming more widespread. The recovery and reuse of dye solutions from the dyebath, for instance, is proving effective in reducing both volumes of effluent and the use of chemicals. Likewise, alternative processing methods have brought a greater degree of environmental responsibility. 'Pad-batch' dyeing, suitable for cellulosic fibres like cotton, for example, saves energy, water, dyes, chemicals, labour and floor space. It involves steeping the fabric in dye liquor, 'batching' it into rolls, covering it with plastic film and storing for up to twelve hours, after which it is washed. The simplicity of the process is matched by the quality of dyeing it provides.

Cotton dyeing is dominated by the use of synthetic dyestuffs, although natural dyes have become more popular recently as a result of public concern associated with the health and environmental effects of synthetic dye chemicals, such as azo dyes, which have been banned in some Northern European countries. No one dyestuff can be seen to provide the 'best answer' to environmentally responsible colouration, and there is a wide variability in impact associated with different dyes depending on depth of shade, method of application and the concentration of dye and process chemicals (auxiliaries) in the dyebath. Similarly, no one colour can be singled out as having the best or the worst environmental impact, although the darker the shade, the greater the amount of dye lost to effluent. Therefore some scope for environmental improvement exists by dyehouses avoiding (and designers and consumers not specifying) dark, heavy shades, such as navy and black.

60

Traditional dyeing of cotton material in India—an environmentally responsible alternative to conventional dyeing
Credit: WWF Switzerland

Cotton has an affinity for a number of dyes, such as the following.

Natural dyes. These are made from plants, animals and shells such as: indigo, madder, walnut shells and cochineal insects. Natural dyes have no built-in affiliation for the fibre and so fixing agents, normally polluting heavy metals (such as chromium and tin), called mordants are used. In comparison to synthetic dyes, natural dyes have poor light and wash fastness and have large variations in colour tone, making colour matching difficult. In addition, large quantities of resources are needed for a small amount of dye—as concentrations of dye found in nature tend to be extremely low—making their widespread use impractical. For example, the annual demand for indigo is 14 million kilos, which if produced naturally, would require 400 million kilos of indigo leaves, 98 per cent of which would become acid waste.

Reactive dyes. Around half of all cotton is dyed with reactive dyes. While they have good fastness and produce bright shades, reactive dyes have an especially poor exhaustion rate and can, in the worst case, leave up to 50 per cent of the dye unfixed, which is then flushed away. These losses are an integral part of the dyeing process and are not a result of poor dyeing. After dyeing, a thorough wash-off is necessary to remove unfixed dye and other chemicals. High salt concentrations are required to fix reactive dyes to the fibre, up to 100g of salt per litre of water, which can prove to be an environmental hazard if discharged untreated, as can the presence of heavy

61

metals and chlorine in the dyestuff. Considerable work has been done to introduce reactive dyes with improved exhaustion and lower salt concentrations.

Sulphur dyes. Relatively cheap, with deep colours and good light and wash fastness, sulphur dyes are the second most popular dye for cotton. Sulphur dyes are water-insoluble compounds which have to be chemically 'reduced' by a two-stage process before they show an affinity for the fibre. The original dye is dissolved in a solution of caustic soda and then reduced to a form which allows the dye to penetrate the fibre. After dyeing, it is then converted back to an insoluble form (by oxidation) which prevents the dye molecule from leaving the fibre. The traditional method of reduction involves treatment with highly polluting sodium sulphide, the release of which is normally restricted because if introduced into a water course, it severely depletes oxygen levels. An alternative reduction technique uses an alkaline solution of glucose, which significantly reduces concentrations of sodium sulphide in effluent while slightly increasing the BOD load.

Direct dyes. Direct dyes are water-soluble and use polluting copper salts as fixing agents. The dye gives a full range of shades and leaves between 5 and 30 per cent of dye unfixed, to be washed away.

Vat dyes. Similar to sulphur dyes, vat dyes have to be reduced by chemical process before they can be absorbed by the fibre. The agent typically used is sodium hydrosulphite, which if discharged untreated, can cause environmental problems.

Printing is one of the most chemically complex areas in textile processing. It is possible to print with almost all classes of dye needing a wide range of chemical auxiliaries. Textile printing involves the accurate application of a colour paste, made up of dye, a thickening agent and other chemicals, onto a fabric. Unlike in dyeing, colour is applied to specific, selected areas of fabric, which reduces resource consumption. There are many different methods of printing, such as flat screen or roller, each with different demands on resources.

Fabrics can be printed with dyes or pigments. When printing with dyes, fixation normally occurs by steaming, after which thorough washing has to remove any residual dye and all the other auxiliary chemicals. Pigment printing is cheaper, only involving three processing stages: print, dry and bake, and unlike printing with dyes it does not involve a final washing-off stage. Although no washing-off is necessary, print pastes still end up in waste water as machines are cleaned. In pigment printing, all auxiliary chemicals and dye remain on the fabric and in drying and curing some volatile substances in the auxiliaries can be emitted to air. The presence of pigment and auxiliary chemicals on the fabric throughout its use and disposal means that the environmental and toxicological effects of these substances are especially important.

Specialist fabric finishing

Cotton textiles can be given a range of additional treatments, some of which are done for reasons of aesthetics and others for improving fabric performance. Some treatments are mechanical, such as calendering, where the fabric is pressed between rollers, giving it a glaze and increasing its density. Others are chemical, such as those providing water repellence and crease resistance (easy-care). Easy-care has traditionally involved a treatment of urea and formaldehyde which when baked onto the fabric forms a resinous polymer and makes the fabric less prone to creasing. The use of formaldehyde is now restricted, it is a skin irritant and is linked to the production of carcinogens. Conventional treatments for water repellence made use of paraffin wax coatings. More durable finishes which withstand washing and repel oily stains as well as water are based on fluorocarbons, the use of which has been linked to atmospheric ozone depletion. It must be noted, however, that the negative environmental effects of applying such finishes should be traded off against the environmental benefits that the finish brings, such as a reduced need for washing or additional durability.

Product manufacture

Creating a final product, whether it is clothing or furnishings, involves some form of product manufacture. The fabric is cut out and assembled, normally by sewing. Waste is a major issue in pattern cutting and its minimization is important for financial as well as environmental reasons. To reduce cross-contamination of fibres in recycling, sewing threads of the same fibre type as the product should be selected. Similarly, buttons and zip closures added to textile products should be chosen with care so as to minimize toxicological effects and to maximize ease of recycling. Zips made from plastic offer an improved alternative to nickel-plated metal fasteners, as do buttons made from materials such as shells, nuts and wood.

Conclusions

The fibre to fabric processing chain is complex, resource intensive and environmentally damaging. The majority of processes in the chain are unavoidable and in such cases, best environmental practice can be achieved by focusing on reducing water, energy and chemical consumption to a minimum and treating wastes before discharge. Some of the environmental problems caused by the activities of the textile industry are highly avoidable, however, and a high profile for both technical and non-technical alternatives could lead to large reductions in impact. Cotton is but one of a wide variety of fibres processed by the textile industry and while intrinsically, it is not one of the most environmentally friendly fibres, its continued popularity makes it necessary to minimize impacts associated with its production. Future research and development should be directed towards reducing impacts across the entire lifecycle, including reductions in energy, water and chemical consumption, substitution of hazardous chemicals with less harmful ones, entire product biodegradability, a more empowered role for design, reduced impacts in consumer use, and, improved communication between different producers in the lifecycle, so that resources are used more efficiently. The future provision of textiles will require a new, more integrated system which will produce economic and environmentally responsible solutions: fibres and fabrics which do not waste the resource base, reflect the real needs of society and are part of a materials-efficient economy.

6
Certifying organic production and processing

GUNNAR RUNDGREN and SUSANNE HAGENFORS

CERTIFICATION OF organic cotton production and processing adds credibility to the final products and promotes marketing at a premium price.

At the production level, there are over 100 certification agencies for organic agriculture worldwide—far too many to be discussed in this chapter. Certification programmes and standards vary, especially in response to regional differences, although there are general underlying concepts. Certification of organic agriculture focuses on the production system rather than the products and organic cotton fibre production should therefore be viewed as part of a wider system. This chapter begins with an introduction by Gunnar Rundgren to the principles of certification systems in general and then highlights the special needs for certifying the production of small-scale organic farmers.

With regard to the processing of organic cotton far fewer systems exist. Textile processing standards only began to appear in the early 1990s and are still being refined and developed. As processing standards are therefore still in the early stages of development, the second part of the chapter provides a comprehensive review by Susanne Hagenfors of progress to date.

An introduction to organic certification

GUNNAR RUNDGREN

Certification provides a comprehensive system for ensuring that certain standards of organic production and processing are met. The system includes:

○ developing rules or standards (standard setting);
○ verifying and evaluating performance against those standards (inspection);
○ recognizing producers who successfully meet the standards (certification).

In this chapter the term 'certification agency' and 'certifier' are used to describe the organization that performs certification. 'Certification programme' is used to describe the activity of the certification agency (which might include certifying not only organic, but also other types of production). 'Certification system' refers to all the elements of the programme, including the standards, the documentation and the operators of the system themselves.

As shown in the previous chapters, cotton production and processing are complex processes. They therefore require highly efficient and professional certification mechanisms. Certification provides the product with credibility, assures the buyer that the product has been produced organically, and enables organic products to be marketed at a premium price. This is particularly relevant for organic fibres where the market has been flooded by products described in vague terms such as 'green' and 'eco'.

There are several important features of organic certification. Each actor in the chain has to fulfil certain requirements in order to be certified. Producers must know the production standards and be contractually bound to follow them, accept inspection and certification procedures, have a system of record keeping which is acceptable to the certification agency, and be capable of implementing a certifiable system. The consumer then buys certified products which are identified by a certification mark or label.

Criteria for a certification system

A certification system should be objective, independent, transparent, competent, credible, voluntary, non-discriminatory, confidential, cost-effective, goal-orientated, and easy to communicate. The importance of each criterion should be determined by both the production conditions and the certification system itself, as well as by the expectations of the market and any legal requirements. Independence, competence, and objectivity are usually seen as the most essential features.

The certification system should be handled by a body which is both legally registered and has ownership of its certificate or mark. This can be a company, trust, NGO or governmental body. Independence is essential and the certification agency should operate without undue influence from any interested party. In the case of a certification programme administered by a producers' association, other interested parties should also play a role to reduce possible conflicts of interest.

Elements of a certification system

The basic elements of the certification system are the setting of standards, carrying out inspection, the certification process and providing information.

Standards form the basis of the system and should be clearly written and presented to operators and other interested parties. They should comply with existing regulations within both the producer and consumer country. They need to reflect progress and new information through revisions and improvements. The IFOAM Basic Standards (see Appendix 3 at the end of the book) provide a common world-wide definition of organic agriculture and processing. They are minimum standards which provide a basis for developing more detailed production standards at national or regional level.

At least a hundred regional or national production standards have been developed so far. They usually belong to organic farmer associations or to certification agencies and are adapted to local social, cultural, economic and ecological conditions. In European Union countries, the Regulation (EEC) 2092/91 has set the principle standards for organic farming and food processing. As a result of the economic dominance of Europe in organic markets, this regulation has also been widely used in international trade. Standards proposed at the federal level in the US for organic production and processing have proved to be highly controversial and have not yet been approved. (Table 1 gives details of the main certifiers of organic cotton and the standards they use.)

Inspection verifies and evaluates the system according to the standards, and reports in a clear, objective and transparent way to the certification agency. Inspectors can either be employed by the certification agency or work as independent contractors. The inspections cover agricultural production, transactions between participants in the chain, storage and processing, labels and certificates and documentation. Producers will normally be inspected at least once a year.

The certification process is often complicated and procedures cannot be reduced to a simple checklist. A certification committee has responsibility for final decisions, which can be linked to the producer making further improvements to the system within a certain timeframe. Producers usually have the right of appeal to a third party in the case of disputes.

Information for consumers and producers is a vital element in any certification system. Since organic certification is complex and labels seldom provide consumers with much information, certification programmes usually provide details of standards, procedures and of how certificates are issued.

International recognition

There is no single process for giving a certification system international recognition. Buyers and consumers must trust the certification procedure. Regardless of whether a certification programme is legally approved or accredited, it is still the market that finally decides if a certification is recognized or not.

Accreditation establishes three tiers of assurance: the operator assures that the product is produced according to the appropriate standard; the certification assures that the producer is meeting the standards; and the accreditation recognizes the competence of the certification programme (see Appendix 3 for details of the IFOAM accreditation system).

Mutual recognition is important among organic certifiers. If certified cotton is sold to a spinner, the spinner's certification agency has to accept the certification of the lint in order for the yarn in turn to be certified. Without this acceptance, the certification of the lint has little value. It is

Table 1: Organic certifiers, and standards used, in key organic cotton projects

Country	Project name or state	Certifier used	Standards in use for inspection and certification
Egypt	Sekem/Cotton People Organic	IMO	Demeter and AKN
India	Maikaal bioRe	IMO	EU
	Srida bioRe	IMO	EU
	Vidharba Organic Farmers (VOFA)	Agreco	EU
	Ginni project	SKAL	SKAL
Turkey	Rapunzel	IMO	EU
	Cotton Country	IMO	EU
	Hess Futur	IMO	EU
	Emrullah Tanriverdi	Ecocert	Turkish/EU
	Yilderim Project (Bo Weevil)	SKAL	SKAL
Peru	Verner Frang	KRAV	KRAV
	Tiendas Unidas	OCIA	
		SKAL	SKAL
USA	California	CCOF	California State
	Texas	TDA	Texas State
	Arizona	OCIA	OCIA
	New Mexico	OCIA	OCIA
Senegal	ENDA-Pronat,	Ecocert	EU
	Koussanar;	Ecocert	EU
	Vellingara	Ecocert	EU
	Kongheul	Ecocert	EU
Uganda	Lango Union	KRAV	KRAV
		SKAL	SKAL
Tanzania	Tansales Limited	IMO	EU
Mozambique	Instituto do Algodao do Mocambique (IAM)	KRAV (Discont.)	KRAV
Zimbabwe	Lower Guruve Development Association	KRAV	KRAV
Nicaragua	Prolana	IMO	EU
Paraguay		SKAL	SKAL
Argentina	Pyma Cotton	Argencert	Argencert

therefore essential that mechanisms for regulating this are in place. Mutual recognition or reciprocity describes a situation in which two certification agencies recognize each others' competence, and accept that raw materials certified by one certification agency can be used in products certified by the other. This is particularly important in the case of cotton, since trade and production are complex and globalized.

Cost and benefits of certification

Costs of certification can be high in relation to the value of the product and thus can become prohibitive. This is especially true for textiles because of the number of processes from producer to consumer. It is not unusual for up to 10 different production units to be involved in the production of a single shirt. There are few certification programmes in developing countries, even though this is where the production and processing of organic cotton is increasingly concentrated. Most organic cotton certification is carried out by international agencies which make for increased costs compared to local certification. Some international certification bodies use local inspectors to help reduce costs, but the final certificate is provided by the agency itself.

The main objective of certification is to gain access to the market for certified organic products, but there are other positive benefits which include:

○ Better planning: certification requires producers to have documentation and production planning, which can increase both efficiency and profits.
○ Better marketing and extension: data collected in the process of certification can be very useful for market planning as well as for extension and research.
○ More transparency: the basic principle of transparency requires certification programmes to say who and what is certified. This facilitates more direct contacts between producer and consumers.
○ Credibility and visibility: certification improves the 'image' of organic agriculture and increases its credibility and visibility.
○ Access to support: certification can also help introduce support schemes for organic agriculture, since it defines a group of recipients. Without certification it is difficult to implement special support for organic farms.

Certification of smallholder groups in developing countries

Current international standards are mainly influenced by the practices and ideologies of organic agriculture in the industrialized world, especially in Europe. This can cause problems for emerging organic production in developing countries, or those with different agricultural traditions and

Lucy Kidaga Larubi, a local inspector in Uganda scanning for insects
Credit: Gunnar Rundgren, Grolink

conditions. Using European standards imposes high costs on developing country production, especially where there are many smallholders producing relatively small quantities of organic produce.

Normally, certification requires an annual inspection of each farm and of its written records. This is a reasonable procedure for the average producer in the North, but difficult and possibly unnecessary in situations where thousands of smallholders are involved. Many certification agencies are responding by designing special programmes to suit these situations. Smallholder groups need to be large enough to support a viable internal control system which assures compliance of individual farmers. Such systems are in place in the Maikaal project in India and in Uganda (see case studies in Chapters 11 and 14).

Annual inspections of the smallholder group are carried out by the certification agency, which consists of inspection of a proportion of individual farms and an assessment of the internal control system.

In evaluating the internal control system, the certification agency must ensure that:

○ internal inspection of all farmers is carried out annually;
○ new operators are only included after proper inspection;
○ internal inspections adequately address the compliance of farmers;
○ instances of non-compliance are appropriately dealt with;

○ adequate inspection records are maintained by the internal control system; and

○ internal records match the findings of the certification programme.

The internal control system will assist farmers in understanding certification and will help to address problems raised by requirements for documentation in situations where many people may be illiterate or where there is a language barrier between producers and certifiers. The system can also fulfil several other functions for production and marketing planning, and extension and data collection for research. In this way the costs of the system will bring other benefits and in any case should be less than inspections by an external, usually foreign, certification body.

Development of local certification programmes

The establishment of local certification schemes is needed to help promote organic agriculture and to reduce certification costs. In most cases, such programmes will also have a better understanding of local conditions and share a common language with farmers. To establish a local certification programme is an expensive and lengthy process. Local programmes are faced with the problem of achieving international recognition. Generally, an established certification programme from the North trains the local certifier who then gradually takes over the running of the local programme. In most cases it will take at least two to three years before a new certification programme gains international recognition.

Conclusion

Certification of organic products is a new field, with even the oldest systems only having a history of twenty years or so. As such it is still constantly developing and adapting to solve a range of new challenges. The expansion of organic markets, including organic cotton, has involved the creation of new areas of certification. This has created new opportunities but also some potential new problems. Certification systems can provide producers with valuable new markets but could also, if not properly controlled, stifle the very systems they are supposed to be encouraging through increasing costs and bureaucracy.

Certification, standards and labelling for textile processing
SUSANNE HAGENFORS

The development of eco-trends in fashion sought to satisfy the demand of the growing number of consumers whose purchasing choices were directed as much by environmental and health effects as value for money and the dictates of fashion. But many clothing manufacturers' attempts to satisfy the ecologically conscious consumer have paid scant attention to the realities of environmental problems inherent in the production of clothing for the mass market. In many cases environmental concerns were seen purely in terms of a company's marketing strategy. A profusion of clothing and household textile products appeared, bearing labels made of recycled paper printed with the manufacturer's own eco-logo and a short text proclaiming ecological virtues such as 'hand-picked', 'non-chlorine bleached' and 'benzidine-free' or 'heavy metal-free'. To most consumers these claims made little sense as few people know much about the complexity of the various processes involved in the manufacture of textiles.

Even supposedly useful information about the raw material ranged from the confusing to the spurious. Claims of products being made from 'natural cotton', for instance, are meaningless—for is not all cotton natural? The claims '100 per cent cotton' or 'pure cotton' equally have no environmental credentials. Also, for example, products claiming to be made without chlorine bleach had obviously not been bleached at all, whilst those which claimed to be free of azo dyes were undyed products. 'Closed' dyeing systems were also heralded, despite the fact that the textile industry has not succeeded in containing their use of water and chemicals except in a few very special cases. A dyeing machine is no more closed than an ordinary washing machine. It might look like a closed system during the dyeing and washing process, but afterwards the dirty water is flushed away.

Without clear definitions, labelling schemes or legislation even well-known terms can be misleading. When the term 'organic' is used without any information on control or on the certification organization, the possibility of fraudulent claims are more likely. 'Sustainable' and 'Integrated Pest Management (IPM)' can also be used to indicate farming practices with lower environmental impacts than conventional practices, but the terms have no clear definition or certification system.

In an international market, confusion also exists when the same terms are used for clearly different procedures and products. In the US, for example, 'green cotton' often refers to cotton that is neither bleached, dyed nor chemically treated during manufacturing. In Europe, however, Green Cotton is the brand name of the Danish company Novotex whose products are made of bleached and dyed conventional cotton although some organic cotton is used.

Although for most the eco-trend was merely a passing phase, a few companies did take these new ecological concerns to heart, trying to trace where and how their products were produced. The multifaceted and fragmented nature of the textile industry, however, made this task difficult. Even when their questions were answered, interpreting the results proved no easy task. Literally thousands of chemicals seemed to be used, and their trade names reveal nothing of their content or environmental effect. To determine what was environmentally responsible and what was not, was clearly no easy task.

Two fashion companies in particular, Esprit and Steilmann, put considerable effort into ensuring the environmental provenance of their products. They banned some chemicals, set up restrictions for others and tried to find organic fibres. After a year of favourable publicity and considerable interest in their products, they both added dyed and printed clothing to their 'eco-collections', claiming that environmentally responsible clothing need not look different from other collections. A big step from the raw-cotton concept. But interest in their eco-collections decreased when fashion moved on from a natural look to strong colours and synthetic fibres.

Today, these companies no longer make eco-collections and most of the manufacturers' eco-logos have disappeared. The new trend is for textile companies to make environmental quality a part of their overall image. The popular Swedish furnishing company, IKEA, has announced that they will take ecological quality into consideration in their manufacturing process. The company's decision has, for example, led production sites in Turkey, Portugal and India to invest in waste-water cleaning plants to ensure continued orders from IKEA. The company has also shown interest in organic fibres, but so far claims difficulty in finding the large quantities they require at acceptable prices.

For companies to move from merely following a fashionable eco-trend to a more thorough environmental assessment of their products requires considerable investment and detailed information on the areas they should be considering. Ideally, their production claims should be independently verified.

Textile standards and labels
One of the results of the eco-trend of the early 1990s was an increasing interest in environmental labelling, an interest which soon extended to textiles. By 1992–93, textile eco-labels were being initiated in several European countries both within the organic farming movement and in new eco-labelling organizations.

In comparison with the manufacturers' labels which suddenly appeared during the early 1990s, these labels aim to fulfil four key criteria:

○ they are intended for use on products with a considerably lower environmental impact than their conventional counterparts;
○ the label is administered by a body which is independent of the textile industry;
○ the criteria have to be presented openly so that everyone knows how they can be met and what actions have to be taken for compliance; and
○ inspection of the producers should be in the hands of a third party.

Differences in experience and attitude towards labelling and environmental aspects of production have led to the development of two distinctly different groups of criteria by the organic movement on the one hand, and the eco-labelling organizations on the other.

The organic labels

The organic movement has already developed a range of standards for the production and processing of foodstuffs and beverages. The different organic labelling organizations, however, have had more problems defining what is meant by the 'organic' processing of textiles. This is not surprising, as the modern textile industry is dependent on parts of the chemical industry.

The Dutch EKO. This label is administered by SKAL, the Dutch inspection organization for organic products. Their entry into organic textile production resulted from their long-standing involvement with organic food production in Turkey. In the late 1980s farmers asked if they could add cotton to the crop rotation and sell the cotton as organic. This request resulted in the development of organic textile standards, which were agreed in September 1994. The criteria allow for only organic natural fibres, and the production methods require the final product to be fully biodegradable or recyclable. All production sites are inspected and some additional analyses of chemical residues and qualities of the final goods are required.

TDA. In the USA, the State Departments of Agriculture control the inspection process for organic food governed by the Organic Food and Production Act of 1990 and administered by independent and state-level certification agencies. In the early 1990s, the Texas Department of Agriculture (TDA) developed their own standards for growing and processing organic cotton. The standards may in the future be approved at federal level. Monitoring is carried out through on-site inspection at both farms and processing plants. Chemical analyses are not used.

KRAV. KRAV is the main Swedish inspection organization for organic farming and processing. Grolink, a subsidiary of KRAV, carries out international inspections and is licensed by KRAV to certify textile production. Since 1994 KRAV has been certifying production of organic cotton and flax. KRAV standards for all processing of textiles were developed in 1996 and will be revised to conform with the newly adopted IFOAM Textile Standards. KRAV's standards are for products made from organic natural fibres, but allow up to 5 per cent of synthetic fibres. Using a different label, there is also the possibility (the equivalent of the IFOAM food standards) to allow up to 30 per cent synthetic fibres, in which case the product may not be called 'organic'. Inspection of all production sites is obligatory. Chemical analyses are used for spot checking or if there is cause for suspicion.

The German AKN. Arbeitskreis Naturtextil e. V. (AKN), a consortium of small companies, was established in Germany in 1991. Prior to this, four companies belonging to AKN had been producing natural textiles since 1982. The standards have two levels: the first requires natural, but not organic, fibres and is regulated by a system of self control; the second is solely for organic fibres and was drawn up with co-operation from the Swiss Institute für Marketkologie (IMO) in 1996. Only products conforming to the second level are allowed to use the label, and it is only this second level which is reviewed in this chapter. On-site inspection by IMO and chemical analyses are both required prior to approval. The AKN standards are also used by the biodynamic organization Demeter.

Many of the organic farming certification organizations are accredited by IFOAM and most are members. The IFOAM International Organic Accreditation Service Inc. (IOAS) (see Appendix 1 at the end of the book) is a third party carrying out audits and evaluation of the certifier's activities including standards, inspection and documentation practices. Apart from annual reporting, the certifier is re-evaluated every three to four years.

The IFOAM Standards Committee began developing standards for the processing of organic fibres in 1996 and these were added to the IFOAM Basic Standards in 1998 (see Appendix 4). The IFOAM standards are in effect minimum requirements, and IFOAM accredited certifiers are allowed to set more stringent standards if they wish. The development of widely accepted IFOAM standards will also lead to mutual recognition, meaning it will be possible to sell imported textiles labelled by the organic logo well known in the marketing country, whoever made the inspection of the farming and manufacturing.

Step-by-step eco-labels
By 1996 four big national/international eco-labelling organizations in Europe had developed textile criteria. They all shared the idea that an eco-label should reward the best products currently available whilst recognizing that research and technical developments will allow the criteria to be revised and improved. Labels based on this view take a step-by-step approach to environmental improvements, taking the modern textile industry as a starting point and then promoting gradual change to more environmentally responsible production.

The EU eco-label. The EU's work on environmental labelling tends to be a compromise between the interests of politicians, industry, unions, environmental and consumer organizations. At present the criteria are mainly based on parameters which can be checked by chemical analyses of the final product, but random inspection of wet-processing plants will also occur. The EU textile criteria were agreed in May 1996, and took effect in 1997. The EU has chosen to look only at a narrow range of products, i.e. T-shirts and bed linen made of cotton or blends of cotton and polyester.

The Nordic Swan. The Nordic Swan label is a collaborative effort of the governments of the Nordic countries. It is mainly recognized in Sweden,

Norway and Finland, with Denmark joining the process in 1997. Textile criteria were agreed in December 1994. Products made of natural and synthetic fibres are included in the criteria. Inspection consists of chemical analysis of raw material and final products, as well as visits to farms and processing plants.

The Swedish Bra Miljöval (Good Environmental Choice). The Swedish Society of Nature Conservation (SSNC), the biggest environmental organization in Sweden, has operated a private eco-label on a wide range of products since 1989. The SSNC collaborates with the three leading grocery retailers in Sweden, thus ensuring a strong demand for labelled products. The criteria are drawn up solely by SSNC. Textile criteria for viscose, reused, natural and synthetic fibres were added in November 1994. Inspection of manufacturing is carried out by spot checks. The inspection has so far been carried out by the SSNC, but other monitoring organizations are accepted. Chemical analyses are not obligatory, as the SSNC consider it more useful if money is spent on improvements.

The Dutch Milieukeur. Stichting Milieukeur is an independent foundation established in 1992 as a joint venture between the Dutch Government, manufacturers, consumers, the retail trade and environmental organizations. The textile criteria were agreed in March 1995. Milieukeur asks for declarations from the producers in combination with inspections at least once a year.

Other textile labels

A range of health-related labels, such as Öko-tex 100, TOX PROOF and GuT, have been developed in Germany. These 'health labels' all have similar criteria based on the chemical analyses of the final product. Heavy metals, formaldehyde, pesticides such as pentachlorophenol (PCP) and carcinogenic azo dyes are subject to monitoring. The maximum levels set for chemicals are not hard to keep below and their usefulness as an indicator of a healthier product is questionable. The labels do not provide any environmental impact information. Environmentally damaging chemicals and processes, such as chlorine bleaching, are allowed as they do not leave traces in the final products. There is also no inspection of waste-water treatment.

New laws and regulations

Considering the large amount of chemicals used in textile production, relatively few health and environmental problems have been registered. The main areas of concern to date have centred on the adverse health effects of chemicals such as formaldehyde and some dyes and textile dust. Formaldehyde is a well known allergenic substance which in textile manufacture is released from cotton treated for 'easy care'. In a few countries like Japan and Finland maximum formaldehyde content in textiles has been regulated.

Carcinogenic azo dyes and PCP are banned in all textiles and products with skin contact in Germany and the Netherlands. PCP was banned due to its environmentally hazardous properties like persistence and bioaccumulation and because of dioxin contamination during the PCP production process. A German study has shown that half of the dioxin content in household waste water could come from textile washing. Probably the main source is the anti-mould treatment of textiles by dioxin-contaminated PCP. Exceptionally high levels of dioxin and PCP have also been found in waste water from wet-processing plants washing raw cotton fabrics.

Brominated flame retardants have also been identified as persistent, bioaccumulating substances. In some countries the use of these chemicals in the textile industry has been increasingly restricted. Despite the restrictions, research in Sweden has revealed that levels of the chemical are increasing in birds, fish and animals all around the country and in the seas nearby. Two explanations are that the substances are continuously released from old products still in use or that flame retardants are still present in new imported goods.

Criteria for awarding labels

The award of the different labels reviewed above for textiles is primarily dependent on the methods of agricultural production and chemical use during manufacture. Energy consumption, waste-water treatment and emissions during processing are seldom included although they often have major environmental impacts. This is clearly a deficiency in the labelling systems. The criteria for the award of labels are discussed here in more detail and summarized later in Table 2.

Production of fibres
All the organic organizations' labels require that the fibre is produced under certified organic farming systems. This is also the case for the step-by-step SSNC label (see Table 2). The rest of the step-by-step labels give some economic incentive for the use of organic fibres. For example, the cost of pesticide analyses may be lower.

Manufacture
Most of the label requirements during the manufacturing process deal with chemical residues. Toxicity and biodegradability are the most important factors when chemicals are judged. Test methods have to be defined, and most labels rely on the OECD's system of tests for the classification of chemicals. Some labelling organizations have drawn up lists of chemicals which are allowed during production and those which are not and some define which tests the chemicals have to pass.

Spinning, knitting and weaving. The use of spinning and knitting oils are restricted by most labels, with some labels requiring biodegradable oils which can be eliminated in the waste-water treatment plant. Oils made from native (e.g. vegetable or animal fats) sources are always allowed, whereas mineral and synthetic oils might be restricted.

Biodegradable naturally based sizes are allowed by all labels, whilst some labels accept the biodegradable synthetic sizes. Some manufacturers recycle sizes. Although this requires non-biodegradable synthetic size, the system is accepted by some labels if more than 50 per cent of the size is recycled.

Bleaching and washing. All labels consider the formation of unknown organochlorine substances during chlorine bleaching as an important environmental problem. The criteria allow a variety of bleaching treatments, from accepting no bleach at all (AKN), to no chlorine bleach (most labels), to an acceptance of emission of certain amounts of organochlorine substances from chorine bleach (EU).

Hydrogen peroxide has to be combined with a sequestrant to give proper bleaching. EDTA (ethylenediaminetetraacetic acid) is a commonly used but persistent (slow to biodegrade) sequestrant, and put on negative lists by some labels. This means, however, that similar chemicals like DTPA (diethylenetriaminepentaacetic acid) are allowed, although they can be as persistent as EDTA.

Sequestrants are also used in combination with surfactants during the washing, before and after dyeing and printing. Most labels use positive or negative lists of surfactants.

Dyeing. More than 99 per cent of the dyes used in the textile industry are synthetically produced from mineral oils and sometimes metals. All these dyes are suspected to be environmentally harmful as they are persistent and sometimes also toxic. As dye production methods are patented and there are literally thousands of different dyes there has been no investigation of their environmental effects and no label has imposed any restriction on the dye manufacture.

Some labels forbid all kinds of metal in dyes, whilst some allow defined amounts. No label allows the use of synthetic azo dyes made from the carcinogenic amines.

The residues of unfixed dye, after the dyeing process has been completed, vary considerably. Few labels, however, restrict the amount of unfixed dye in spent dyeing liquid. During dyeing many auxiliary chemicals are added to give special qualities. Some labels do not mention these chemicals, whilst others provide positive lists or criteria for allowable auxiliaries (see Table 2 to identify what can be used for 'organic' textiles).

Printing. Pigment printing is the most commonly used textile printing method. The pigment printing paste contains pigments, solvents and binder. All ingredients except the solvent will be fixed in the final textile. In some countries the use of the most harmful and ozone-forming organic solvents has been restricted. In other countries printing pastes can contain up to 70 per cent of white spirit. Some labels accept only water-based methods, some allow solvents or water, and one organic label tries to regulate the emission.

Mechanical and chemical finishing. All labels accept mechanical finishing methods, including steam and hot air. But the use of chemical treatments for easy care, fire resistance or as dirt or water repellents and so on are not accepted by the organic labelling organizations, except KRAV. The step-by-step labels allow chemicals which have less dangerous effects on health and the environment.

Pesticides are sometimes used during the manufacturing process, for example, as an anti-mould agent used for cotton clothing which will be transported long distances by sea. PCP, often used for this purpose, is prohibited by all labels.

Energy, water use and emissions. Water consumption can vary from 30 to 200 litres per kilo of cotton fabric, depending on the number of processing steps and the standard of the machinery. Considerable energy is used when heating water, so high water consumption leads to high energy use. Only SSNC and KRAV have a limit for energy consumption and none restricts water use.

In Sweden, the average chemical use in textile manufacturing is 0.4 kg of chemicals per kg of textile. A small part is left in the final fabric. Most of the chemicals will be found in the waste water, and this mixture of hundreds of different chemicals calls for careful waste-water treatment. Only some labels have quality limits on the waste-water treatment, other labels have no restrictions at all.

Atmospheric emissions from the textile industry include exhausts from the heating system and organic solvents from pigment printing. Exhaust from heat production is not at present regulated by any of the labelling systems. Milieukeur is the only system with restrictions on organic solvents to the air. The limit is 150mg/m^3 air, but states no maximum amount per kilo of textile. The other labels restrict the use of solvents instead, probably a simpler method to achieve the same result.

Quality. Most labels have some requirements concerning the quality of the final product. Colour fastness to light and washing is usually included as well as low content of formaldehyde. Shrinking properties might also be subject to a maximum. Products which require dry cleaning are not usually allowed. Textile quality is not easy to define, however, and involves many aspects. A high-quality fabric can be made into a low-quality dress if the sewing thread is weak or the seams are badly made.

Social conditions during production. Working conditions and other social aspects during farming and textile manufacturing are mentioned in two labels, but their formulations are vague. The draft versions of the EU and the Swan labels included plans to ban child labour, these criteria were however abandoned on account of the difficulties of verification. In the EU criteria, Denmark tried to include limitations on the amount of textile dust in factory air but failed for the same reason. IFOAM has discussed these issues in its Basic Standards for Organic Agriculture and Processing, and the general principles and minimum requirements of Chapter 8 of the *Basic Standards* are being developed into some key guidelines for ensuring social justice in organic agriculture.

Monitoring and verification. Detailed information about the product is asked for during application. Inspection and residue analyses are the main monitoring methods to check the statements made by producers. Obligatory site inspections during all production steps are usually required by the organic certifiers; this gives a high standard of reliability and allows those statements made which cannot be confirmed by chemical analysis to be checked. Inspection is, however, expensive. Production sites in different countries are common, which raises costs even higher. To reduce the cost, some organizations have chosen to institute random inspections and inspect only a few steps in the production chain.

Chemical analyses of the final product is obligatory under most of the labelling systems. Heavy metals, formaldehyde, pH-value and azo dyes are common tests. The price of each analysis is usually reasonable but, of course, costs build up depending on requirements. Pesticide analysis is expensive and can generally only be carried out for organochlorines and organophosphates. The number of pesticides to be analysed is often influenced by the total cost, and the value of pesticide analysis is questionable as the results are often difficult to interpret. For example, there has not yet been enough research to prove whether a pesticide-free sample of cotton fibre might indeed have been sprayed during an early stage of growth.

Several chemicals are difficult to trace. The bleaching method, efficiency of waste-water treatment and choice of surfactants, for instance, cannot be determined in the final product. Such parameters can only be checked by site inspections.

Comparison of labels for eco-textiles

Table 2 gives a comparison between standards for a simple product, bed linen. The bed linen examined is made of dyed unprinted cotton or cotton/polyester. The comparison should not be considered as complete but shows the main restrictions.

It is clear from the table that the final products differ. This may well not be noticeable in shops but is apparent in use. There will, for instance, be variations in the colour charts and some of the products will need ironing if the consumer does not like creases after washing. Some dyes might also have less light and washing fastness. The products with step-by-step labels have about the same colour and crease-proof treatment as the standard bed linen. Only some really dark colours or blue/green colours are missing. TDA and SKAL do not allow crease-proof treatment, but allow the same dyes as step-by-step labels. If metal complex dyes are restricted, then colour fastness in light might be reduced, but this has little importance for a product like bed linen.

The production requirements for raw fibres are certainly different. The organic labels require 100 per cent organic cotton, except for KRAV which allows organic cotton to be blended with up to 30 per cent polyester (in which case the product cannot be labelled 'organic'). The step-by-step labels allow all kinds of cotton/polyester blends.

When we look at chemical use the differences are greater and the list of permitted chemicals differs. The Swan and SSNC declare that they mainly consider environmental aspects of the chemicals, but they have added a general restriction on all carcinogenic chemicals, whereas SKAL, AKN and TDA mostly consider human health aspects and prefer natural-based products. In some cases health seems to be the only concern. For example, TDA and AKN call for spinning oils and surfactants which are easy to wash away, but do not consider their environmental aspects.

All the step-by-step labels, except Milieukeur, have limits for emissions to water. Such limits are, however, not well defined by SKAL and AKN, and not even mentioned by TDA.

Even though this comparison is only made for a single product, some general conclusions can be drawn. It is clear that the EU and Milieukeur labels are easy to acquire without making major changes for many producers, as long as they simply choose non-metal dyes. Acquiring other labels will, in most cases, need modification in production methods. The main changes required are in chemical use and type of fibre used. Chemical shifts are easy to make if the motivation is there. Shifting to organic fibres is more difficult because of the limited supply. The Swan requires major changes in the chemicals used, but does not require organic fibres. To obtain certification from SSNC (higher level), KRAV, AKN, TDA or SKAL, organic fibres are required. They all demand changes in chemical use, with the AKN label being the most demanding.

The EU and Milieukeur have not been successful labels, maybe because their criteria levels are too low. AKN also have few products labelled, but here the reason might be the opposite: perhaps the criteria are too hard to achieve or the manufacturers consider the products too different or expensive to be attractive to enough consumers. The rest of the labels all have more products labelled, but none of them have such a wide range of products that an environmentally responsible consumer would be able to find labelled alternatives for most clothing and household textiles. T-shirts, underwear and towels made of cotton or sometimes linen are the organic products which are most frequently labelled.

Table 2: Comparison of textiles (bed linen) manufactured under various eco-textile labels

Step in the production	Conventional product	The EU eco label	The Nordic Swan	The Swedish Bra Miljöval
Raw fibre				
Cotton farming	Unknown origin but probably sprayed with pesticides and hand-picked.	Same as conventional product.	Fertilizers and some pesticides allowed. Farm inspected by the eco-labelling organization.	Inspected and certified organic cotton.[2]
Pesticide analyses	Probably not analysed.	Trace of 10 pesticides are banned.	Trace of 28 pesticides are banned	No analyses.
Polyester content	Most linen produced with 0–50% polyester.	All blends accepted	All blends accepted.	Max. 30% of virgin polyester
Polyester manufacturing	High energy consumption, atmospheric emissions etc.	Max. 1.2 g VOC/kg max. 300 ppm antimony in fibre[1]	Documentation of VOC and antimony emissions during production is required.	Documentation of VOC and antimony emissions during production is required.
Textile manufacture				
Spinning	Likely use of spinning oil made from slowly biodegradable mineral oils.	No restrictions.	Mineral oils are accepted if they are biodegradable.	Mineral oils are only accepted if they are biodegradable.
Weaving	All kinds of sizes can be used and size recycling is unusual.	Readily biodegradable sizes or size recycling.	Readily biodegradable sizes or size recycling.	Readily biodegradable sizes or size recycling.
Desizing and washing	Less biodegradable surfactants and sequestrants like APEO and EDTA often used.	APEO and EDTA not allowed.	APEO and several other not easily biodegradable surfactants not allowed, EDTA and other strong sequestrants are banned.	APEO and several other not easily biodegradable surfactants not allowed, EDTA and other strong sequestrants are banned.
Bleaching	Can be bleached with chlorine or peroxide.	Chlorine bleach is allowed as long as emissions are low.	Chlorine bleach prohibited.	Chlorine bleach prohibited.
Mercerization	In many countries waste water with high pH-value are emitted without neutralization.	pH 6.5–9 of water emitted to recipient.	pH 7–10 of water emitted to recipient.	50% of the alkali has to be reused.
Dyeing (dyes)	Synthetic and benzidine dyes might be used. About half of the dyes contain metals.	Metal and benzidine dyes are forbidden.	Limited use of metal dyes, benzidine dyes prohibited.	Limited use of metal dyes, benzidine dyes prohibited and dye residue in waste water is limited.
Dyeing (auxiliaries)	Heavy metals and other persistent auxiliaries can be used.	Metals not allowed, no restrictions on other auxiliaries.	Heavy metals not allowed, auxiliaries should be ultimately biodegradable.	Heavy metals not allowed, auxiliaries should be ultimately biodegradable.
Easy care treatment	Medium or high formaldehyde resins are common.	Only low or non formaldehyde resins allowed.	Non formaldehyde resins allowed.	Non formaldehyde resins allowed.
Formaldehyde in final product	Approx. 200–500ppm.	Max. 75ppm.	Max. 30ppm.	Max. 30ppm.
Waste water	No waste water treatment in most countries.	Max. 25 g COD/kg of textile.	At least 75% reduction of COD.	Max. 30 g COD/kg of textile.
Appearance of final product	Bed linen usually treated for easy care and produced in wide range of colours.	Bed linen in most colours can be easy care treated.	Bed linen in any colour, can be easy care treated.	Bed linen in most colours except dark blue, red and black can be easy care treated.

Notes: 1. VOC (Volatile Organic Carbons) are emitted during polyester manufacturing. Antimony, a very toxic metal, is used as a catalyst in processing requirements are the same at both levels. 3. COD: Chemical Oxygen Demand

Milieukeur	The German AKN	The Dutch Eco	The Swedish KRAV	The American TDA
Same as conventional product.	Inspected and certified organic cotton.	Inspected and certified organic cotton.	Inspected and certified organic cotton.	Inspected and certified organic cotton.
Maximum 1 mg chlorinated pesticides per kilo.	Trace of 43 pesticides are banned	Maximum 0.5 mg chlorinated pesticides per kilo.	Spot check analyses	No analyses.
All blends accepted.	Not allowed.	Not allowed.	Max. 5% polyester	Not allowed.
No restrictions.	Not applicable.	Not applicable.	No requirements on polyester production.	Not applicable.
No restrictions.	Mineral oils accepted if easy to wash away.	Mineral oils not accepted.	Mineral oils only accepted if they are biodegradable.	Mineral oils accepted if easy to wash away.
No restrictions.	Only readily biodegradable natural sizes or size recycling.	Only readily biodegradable and natural sizes.	Readily biodegradable sizes or size recycling.	Readily biodegradable natural sizes and one synthetic size (PVA) allowed.
No restrictions.	Most synthetic surfactants prohibited as well as several sequestrants, but natural surfactants with slow biodegradability accepted.	Ultimately biodegradable surfactants allowed. Zoelite, NTA and carboxylic acids allowed as sequestrants.	APEO and several other not easily biodegradable surfactants are not allowed, EDTA and other strong sequestrants are forbidden. Chlorine bleach prohibited. Mercerization: 50% of alkali has to be reused.	Processing aids accepted if easy to wash away, surfactants should be biodegradable.
Chlorine bleach prohibited.	Bleaching is not allowed.	Chlorine and perborate bleach prohibited.	Chlorine bleach prohibited.	
No restrictions.			50% of the alkali has to be reused.	
Metal and benzidine dyes prohibited.	Only natural dyes are allowed.	'Low impact' synthetic dyes and natural dyes allowed, benzidine dyes prohibited.	Limited use of metal dyes, benzidine dyes prohibited dye residue in waste water is limited.	'Low impact' synthetic dyes and natural dyes allowed.
Metals are not allowed, no restrictions for other auxiliaries.	Some auxiliaries are allowed, but no metals.	Few auxiliaries are allowed, but no metals.	Heavy metals are not allowed, auxiliaries should ultimately be biodegradable.	Auxiliaries accepted if easy to wash away.
Low or non formaldehyde resins allowed.	No easy care method allowed.	No easy care method allowed.	Non formaldehyde resins allowed.	No easy care method allowed.
Max. 75ppm.	Max. 30 ppm.	Max. 30 ppm.	Max. 30 ppm.	Analyses not required.
Minimum biological treatment or equivalent.	Minimum mechanical and biological treatment.	No restrictions.	Max. 30 g COD/kg of textile (usually need of at least two step treatment)	No restrictions.
Bed linen in most colours but some shades missing, can be easy care treated.	Bed linen not crease-proofed, colour chart is limited, no bright white products.	Bed linen is not crease-proofed, most colours but some shades missing.	Bed linen in most colours, but dark blue, red and black missing, can be easy care treated.	Bed linen not crease-proofed, most colours but some shades missing.

polyester manufacture. 2. Bra Miljöval can be attained at two levels. Organic fibres are only requested at the higher level. The

The future of eco-textile labels

None of the eco-textile standards and labels reviewed above have up to now been really successful. The reasons are manifold and can be found at all stages from farmer through production chain to consumer. They include:

○ low consumer awareness of the environmental problems connected with textiles;
○ the existing labels are not widely known or understood by most consumers and those who do know about them have difficulty finding products which have been awarded the label;
○ no matter how many labels a garment has, the consumer will not buy it if it is the wrong colour, size or style;
○ in most cases manufacturers are ignorant about how their products have been produced and of the environmental problems associated with the textile industry; and
○ manufacturers are reluctant to eco-label their products because they do not perceive a strong customer demand and certification involves considerable effort and expense.

As more products are labelled, awareness is likely to grow, involving more consumers, manufacturers and farmers. Organizations labelling eco-textiles, of course, have an interest in labelling more products, both to increase the labels' recognition and to receive income from licensees to recover development costs. These organizations which, through necessity, have contacts with all steps in the production chain are thus able to play an important role in stimulating contacts between farmers, yarn suppliers, weavers, dyers and so on, which in turn could stimulate the market.

The textile industry is an international business of huge dimensions. Several countries might have been involved before an ordinary T-shirt is completed and, once made, the same product will be sold in different countries. Manufacturers therefore ask for criteria which are internationally accepted. It would be even better if they could choose an internationally recognized label. A temporary solution would be to produce according to criteria accepted by the already well-known national labels in each country.

In the meantime, more co-operation between the existing labelling organizations would be helpful. If the organic organizations accepted each others' methods of control, costs would be reduced and new markets opened. Interpretation of the different criteria would have to be discussed, hopefully leading to clearer definitions of what is accepted and what is not. Co-operation between the step-by-step labels would also contribute to creative refinements of the schemes as they have better chemical knowledge and more experience in the placing of requirements on chemical use.

If the organic production certifiers' knowledge of organic farming could be amalgamated with the chemical awareness of those involved in the step-by-step labels, real progress could be made.

One way forward would be for the blending of organic and conventional natural fibre to be accepted (see Chapter 8). The organic textile market would be stimulated and blending would avoid the clean-out costs usually necessary when changing from conventional to organic raw materials in ginning, spinning and weaving. The organic labelling organizations are sceptical, as they generally do not accept the mixture of organic and conventional raw materials.

SSNC has tried a third way, with a two-tier label. Most manufacturers enter the scheme at the lower level with products made of conventional fibres but aim to find a source for organic raw fibres. Usually it takes a couple of years to find the organic fibres or yarns, and probably many of these manufacturers would have given up if they had not been able to use a label during this transition period. The two-tier scheme was specifically chosen to encourage manufacturers to start the conversion of their textile processing at a level where changes could be made relatively easily and quickly. So far the model seems to work. When organic raw materials are more readily available the lower level will be withdrawn.

As the environmental problems associated with textile production are both large and worldwide, all steps towards a more sustainable textile production system are welcome. The consumers in the future will show which labelling system is most reliable and successful.

7

Comparing the costs of organic and conventional cotton

BO VAN ELZAKKER

Introduction

ORGANIC COTTON production has many advantages, but apparently higher production costs over conventional seem to constrain wider implementation. Finished organic cotton products are also usually more expensive at retail level. The questions are whether organic production is more expensive than conventional in real terms, at what level and for whom, and also whether it is more expensive when environmental externalities are taken into account. How to take them into account is also a problem.

Very little work has been done to date on the economics of organic cotton production. This chapter draws heavily on a study by the United Nations Conference on Trade and Development (UNCTAD), which provides examples of cost-building of organic and conventional production and processing in smallholder systems in India, Egypt and Peru. Information is also available from California comparing the costs of organic and conventional cotton growing in large-scale commercial systems. Further information is available from the United States which gives an indication of relative costs when environmental externalities are incorporated into the retail price of a sample garment — a T-shirt. Reference may be made to these papers for more information (see Further Reading).

Comparing conventional and organic cotton production costs

Cotton production costs vary enormously from country to country and from one situation to another. As described in Chapter 2, cotton production has been heavily subsidized or taxed in most producing countries. This has led to price distortions and makes assessments of costs for conventional as well as organic production problematic. Trade liberalization and the imposition of structural adjustment programmes in many producer countries is leading towards a reduction in distortions. However, the fact that irrigation water is free or subsidized in one country, diesel fuel in another, synthetic chemical inputs in another, and farm income supported in yet another, contributes to a highly complex structure in which true comparisons are difficult to make. Organic cotton production is, however, very 'site specific', making comparisons within the same country or region more important than comparisons between countries.

One of the most important points to take into account in comparing conventional and organic cotton production costs is that organic cotton is produced in an organic farm system which produces many other crops in the rotation. If organic cotton growers are unable to sell their other crops at premium prices, then all the extra costs of the organic system are loaded onto cotton. Moreover, a single crop focus gives no indication of the level of diversification in the system and so does not differentiate between a farm that needs to buy in its organic fertilizers and one which produces them itself. A single crop focus is therefore a simplistic way of comparing costs but, in the absence of comprehensive farm system data, it provides indications of the comparative production costs of conventional and organic cotton.

A further problem is the transition or conversion period. Most organic standards request a three-year 'clean' period before the crop can be certified as organic. During this period, farmers must observe organic standards but may not be able to sell their cotton as organic and therefore may not be able to benefit from the organic premium which is usually paid by buyers. This requirement can be an obstacle to farmers wishing to convert unless some financial support is provided to bridge the gap. This then becomes a further charge on the project which should be earned back.

The following series of graphs and related discussions are based on specific situations in several countries: India, Egypt, Peru and the United States. They are not representative of the situation in the countries in general but only of the areas to which they relate. Hard data in most cases do not exist and figures, presented below in graphical form, are therefore indicative rather than quantitative. Much more data and further analysis are required. The present intention is to contribute to building a picture of cost comparisons so far as it is known and understood. Production is irrigated in Egypt, Peru and the United States, and so figures for use of water are included; production in India is rainfed. Costs of land are excluded in the calculations for India, Peru and the United States. The figures for the United States are noticeably different from those for the other countries, partly on account of the way the authors present their data. Farms from which data were collected (with the exception of India where the project was in its early stages) were fully organic but were not necessarily regarded as optimal organic systems.

The main differences between conventional and organic cotton production that emerge are in the costs of maintaining or improving soil fertility and in managing pests. It is recognized that certain important costs are not included and the importance of externalities was mentioned earlier. Farmers face variations in yields and therefore in risks. They also need to acquire the technical and other skills to manage the new system which imposes its costs.

India

A comparison between the costs of conventional and organic cotton production in the state of Maharashtra in India are shown in Figure 1. In this particular situation, important savings are made in organic cotton growing with the costs of seeds, fertilizers and pesticides. There is an increase in the cost of bullock labour and farmyard manure, and also a significant cost for certification which relates only to organic production. The overall outcome is that costs for cotton grown organically per unit of land are 16 per cent lower than for conventionally produced cotton. At the same time, yields are estimated to be 14 per cent lower. However, whether or not the farmer is better off growing organic depends on the absolute size of the yield, the level of organic premium, and the absolute size of the costs.

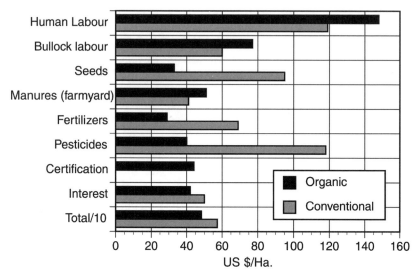

Figure 1: Comparison of costs of conventional and organic cotton production in Maharashtra, India, 1996, in US$ per hectare

Source: UNCTAD and IFOAM (in press).

According to the consultancy, Ecotropic, figures from the state of Madhya Pradesh (the Maikaal project) indicate a slightly different state of affairs (see Chapter 11: India case study). In the 1994–5 season, a preliminary study comparing 60 farmers growing part organic and part conventional plots revealed that, although organic yields were on average 14 per cent lower than conventional, production costs were 37 per cent lower. Fertilizer costs were only 17 per cent of those for conventional cotton (assuming that domestically produced farmyard manure was free in both systems). Pesticide costs were 42 per cent lower in the organic system.

In the subsequent seasons of 1995–96 and 1996–97, better soil fertility management and a higher investment in organic fertilizers have helped increase yields, reduce pesticide costs still further and increase incomes. It should be noted, however, that even in a relatively small area there can be major variations in yields, pointing to variations in farmers' management capacity and resources available, as well as to the expertise of the extension team and variations in soil fertility, pest pressure and the availability of water.

Egypt
An example of a comparison between the costs of conventional and organic cotton production in a specific situation in Egypt are shown in Figure 2 (see also Chapter 13: Egypt case study). In Egypt, fertilization in organic cotton production is more expensive than in conventional production but pest management is cheaper. Organic fertilization is more expensive because many farmers do not have their own animals and so have to buy extra manure. Total costs are slightly more for organic (2 per cent) and yields are reported to be, on average, 7 per cent lower.

Peru
Studies so far in Peru indicate that organic production costs are about 11 per cent higher than conventional, mainly because the costs of organic

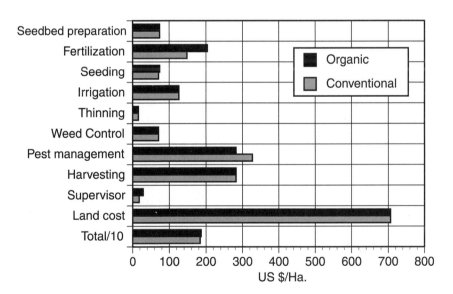

Figure 2: Comparison of costs of conventional and organic cotton production in Egypt, 1995, in US$ per hectare
Source: UNCTAD and IFOAM (in press)

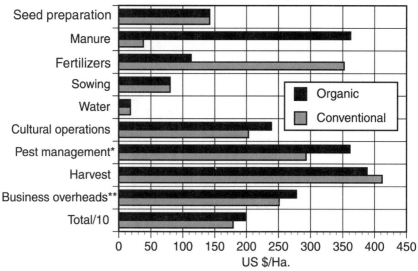

* includes growth regulators
** technical assistance, interest, management costs

Figure 3: *Comparison of costs of conventional and organic cotton production in cotton under conversion to organic, Valle Grande, Peru, 1995–6, in US$ per hectare*

Source: UNCTAD and IFOAM (in press).

fertilization are higher. Costly synthetic fertilizers are replaced by 'guano', a natural fertilizer of bird droppings. Several other costs are also higher, including pest management, cultural operations and supervision. Information available on yields indicates that they are about 20 per cent lower for organic than for conventional (see also Peru case study).

United States
The cost build-up for organic production in the United States, shown in Figure 4, is quite different from the countries described above. The categories in which costs are incurred are not the same, and within those categories there are significant differences between conventional and organic. The greater cost of organic is 11 per cent, and there are indications that yields are about 12 per cent lower.

To summarize the indicative information from the different countries, it seems that the costs of organic production can vary greatly depending on the country and project. In Maharashtra (India), costs can be 16 per cent lower, in Madhya Pradesh (India) 37 per cent lower, in Egypt they can be 2 per cent higher, in Peru and the United States they can be 11 per cent higher.

Information available at present is limited and does not provide a basis for drawing general conclusions, except to note that production costs and

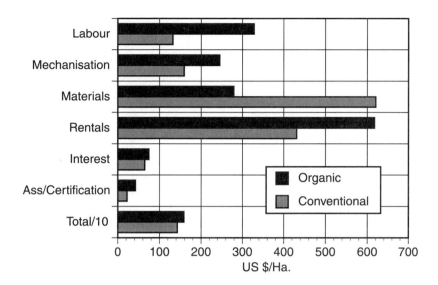

Figure 4: Comparison of costs of conventional and organic cotton production in the San Joaquin Valley, California, 1995, in US$ per hectare

Source: Klonsky et al. (1995)

differences between organic and conventional production are very variable and dependent on local conditions. Indeed, the conclusion of the study on International Commodity Related Environmental Agreements (ICREA) for cotton was that local conditions determine the viability or otherwise, of organic cotton production. The report also concluded that those countries or regions where conversion to organic production would not impose excessive costs are often those in which natural conditions are more suitable for cotton production. In areas where natural conditions are unsuitable, the amount of inputs has to be much higher in order to achieve good yields. In these circumstances, savings on inputs would probably be greater — but loss of yield may well be much greater.

Comparing the costs of conventional and organic cotton processing and manufacture

Processing
The earlier chapters of the book have described ways in which organically produced cotton is processed (Chapter 5) and also the complex situation that exists with respect to environmentally responsible standards in production and processing (Chapter 6). An assessment of the differences in costs between processing conventionally produced and organically

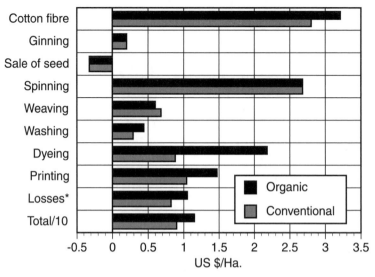

* Losses may be due to lack of uniformity of quality etc.

Figure 5: Comparison of costs for processing conventional and organic cotton in Egypt, 1996, in US$ per kilogram of cotton fibre
Source: UNCTAD and IFOAM (in press).

produced cotton fibre in an environmentally responsible way has been made using an example from Egypt (see Figure 5).

The costs for organic fibre are higher in most categories except ginning and spinning, and are significantly higher for dyeing and printing. For weaving, costs are slightly lower. The overall increase for the end-product is 28 per cent. Looking to the future, the textile industry is expected to phase out the use of cheaper and more polluting dyes and technology in favour of environmentally responsible dyes and auxiliary materials, and the modern equipment to use them. The costs of the new technology are expected to decrease with more widespread use. This will vary from one situation to another. For example in the United States, where cotton is machine picked and organic cotton has more leaf trash (on account of incomplete defoliation), the costs of ginning, and possibly weaving, of organic fibre may be higher.

Manufacture
In order make a comparison of the costs of manufacturing organic and conventional cotton, quotations for a specified garment were reviewed. Several factories in Egypt were asked to present prices for an order of 20 000 short-sleeved T-shirts, dyed and printed with button finish. Figure 6 shows the differences in costs of the manufacture of conventional and

organic T-shirts at each separate stage in the processing from the purchase of the fibre to printing.

All the costs for organic cotton manufacture are the same as for conventional manufacture apart from the higher cost of raw materials and the costs of buttons (bone, shell or wooden buttons are more expensive than plastic). It appears therefore that in this particular case, specially finished T-shirts are 24 per cent more expensive ex-factory than the conventional equivalent.

The question of premiums

At this point in the discussion, it is important to examine the question of premiums paid at various stages in the organic production and processing chain. The premium is not part of the cost price but is an amount paid to the farmer, processor or manufacturer as an incentive to convert to organic — often by sponsors of projects. Farmers are not usually willing to grow organic cotton (or any other crop) if there is not a clear positive price differential as a reward. A premium may be paid to motivate farmers to experiment, to balance a perceived risk or to make up the difference when other crops in the rotation, although grown organically, may have to be sold at conventional prices. The relationship between cost prices, yield and the premium paid to farmers is not always clear and may be arbitrary.

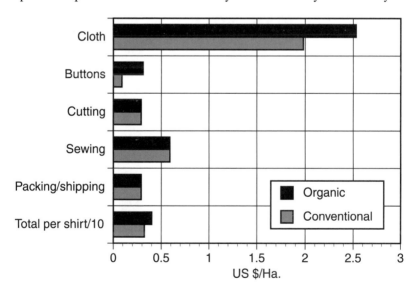

Figure 6: Comparison of costs for manufacture of conventional and organic T-shirts in Egypt, 1996, in US$ per T-shirt based on an order of 20,000 pieces

Source: UNCTAD and IFOAM (in press).

93

Experience shows that farmers are aware of the environmental improvements that organic production brings, but their main motivation is improved income in the short-term rather than concern about their environment in the longer term. Table 1 compares indications of increases and decreases in the costs of organic production in the examples described earlier in the chapter, the level of decrease in the yields and an indication of the premiums which are paid in these specific situations. It appears that in most situations, farmers are better off when the premium is taken into account, except in the case of Peru where they appear still to be worse off. It appears, however, that there is a wide variety of outcomes for farmers in these situations.

Table 1: Examples of premiums paid at farm level

Country/state	Cost price increase of organic production per unit of land	Yield decrease of organic production per unit of land	Premium paid
India	−16 %	14 %	25 %
Egypt	2 %	7 %	15 %
Peru	11 %	20 %	18 %
California	11 %	12 %	50 %

Source: UNCTAD UNCTAD and IFOAM (in press).

It seems that processors and manufacturers are not paid a premium, except when relatively small quantities are involved and they face significant extra costs for cleaning equipment, ordering special materials, or special storage for organic cotton. This is an economy of scale issue and relates to the need for projects to be of a certain size to accommodate extra costs of this kind. Questions of economies of scale, along with many other issues, need further investigation.

Calculating the economic feasibility should be based on an analysis of local conditions in order to predict correctly the impact of conversion and develop strategies which would encourage organic conversion. Different strategies would be appropriate for different areas. For example, premiums for farmers may be appropriate in some regions, improvements in agricultural extension in others, or environmental regulations and subsidies in yet others. An analysis of different conditions could be made which would lead to calculations of the level of premium required to achieve a certain level of conversion. It may mean that producers in some areas would be ready to convert (Egypt and India, for example) whereas those in others would not (Peru and California).

The importance of the price differential in the final retail price

Using the Egyptian example, Table 2 shows the ex-factory price for T-shirts and an average West European retail price for a similar shirt.

Table 2: Comparison of costs for Egyptian conventional and organic T-shirts up to retail price in Western Europe in US$ per T-shirt (in 1996)

Process	Conventional	Organic
Growing	0.68	0.78
Processing	1.30	1.76
Manufacturing	1.26	1.48
Total per shirt ex-factory	*3.24*	*4.02*
Distribution	11.26	19.49
Total US$ per shirt in Western Europe	*14.50*	*23.51*

Source: UNCTAD and IFOAM (in press).

Starting with *conventional* T-shirts and the costs shown in Table 2, Table 3 shows that a price increase of 20 per cent in the costs of growing (US$0.14) *and* a 30 per cent increase in the costs of processing and manufacturing (US$0.77) to cover the extra costs of organic quality would together (US$0.91) generate a price increase at retail level of only 6.2 per cent (assuming other costs remain the same). Table 2 also clearly shows that, in this particular case, the difference in price at retail level in Western Europe of organic over conventional is in excess of 60 per cent — a striking contrast.

The costs of cultivation of the raw material and the costs of its processing and manufacture are shown to be only a small proportion of the final retail price — about 22 per cent for a conventional cotton T-shirt. Therefore, an even greater increase in these extra organic costs need not necessarily cause significant rises in the retail price. In this example, distribution costs are creating a large differential between the retail price of organic and conventional garments.

Why *are* organic cotton clothes more expensive than conventional?

There are several reasons why production, processing, manufacturing, distribution and retail of organic clothing are more expensive than conventional, especially in the start-up phase (see Chapter 4).

Table 3: Egyptian conventional T-shirts: percentage retail price increases created in Western Europe (in US$ per T-shirt, 1996) by percentage increases in growing, manufacturing and processing costs of cotton fibre

	Conventional	20% extra growing costs	30% extra processing and manufacturing costs	20% + 30%
Growing	0.68	0.68	0.68	0.68
+20% on growing	–	0.14	–	0.14
Processing	1.30	1.30	1.30	1.30
Manufacturing	1.26	1.26	1.26	1.26
30% on processing and manufacturing	–	–	0.77	0.77
Per shirt ex-factory	*3.24*	*3.38*	*4.01*	*4.15*
Distribution	11.26	11.26	11.26	11.26
Retail price in W. Europe in US$	14.50	14.64	15.27	15.41
Price increase at retail level	*100.0%*	*100.9%*	*105.3%*	*106.2%*

Substantial investment may have to be made initially to set up and organize a project. In the Peruvian, Egyptian and Turkish cases discussed above, the initiative came from European enterprises which organized the chain from farmer to consumer. Even the costs of visiting all the participants in the chain may be significant, for example. Moreover, in the early years of a project, volumes may be small and processing may be more expensive without the advantage of economy of scale.

Overheads related to the need for expert organic advice and assistance in the early stages are also important. In the absence of suitable skills and experience in government extension systems, especially in African countries, for example, farm advisers from the industrialized countries have been involved. They work alongside local agronomists and extensionists on research, training and setting up documentation systems which are necessary to build the system. In the early stages of a project, when high input is required and output is still low, the cost of this service is relatively high. As experience is gained and projects mature, these costs will be reduced. When organic techniques are internalized into publicly funded structures, which exist to support agriculture generally, then sustainable cotton production will not have to support these extra costs.

A further important cost is certification (see Chapter 6). Certification is usually carried out by Northern organizations, sometimes with the involvement of local inspectors, and is an expensive process. Certification bodies are starting to be set up at national level in countries of the South which should reduce costs in the medium to long-term. Certification can be particularly expensive where a large number of smallholder farmers are involved as, for instance, in Uganda (see case study). As in other cost areas, economies of scale are important. Table 4 below gives some indication of the level of costs from some projects in several countries.

Table 4: Certification costs for organic cotton growing in selected countries

Country	Certification costs in relation to value of cotton fibre product
USA	1.3%
India	8.0%
Egypt	0.1%
Peru	0.5%
Uganda	4.3%

The problem of the costs of surviving the organic conversion period were discussed at the beginning of the chapter and can be a barrier to farmers wishing to convert unless some financial support is provided. In a number of countries, solutions have been found to the conversion period problem by adopting a field-by-field conversion strategy. In-conversion food crops or animal feed crops are grown for the first two years and then cotton in the third year. The cotton can then be marketed immediately as organic.

At the processing, manufacture and distribution level, there may also be extra costs such as investment in environmentally responsible dyeing plants. Some companies argue that there are extra costs at the design stage due to limitations on the range of types and colours of fabrics available (see Chapter 5). Lack of economies of scale are also important at the manufacturing level.

Table 2 demonstrates that for this particular garment, most of the cost is generated *after* the manufacturing stage in the country where the goods are sold. In this particular case there is a striking difference between the retail price of the conventional item and the organic — the organic version being 60 per cent more expensive. Limited retail outlets, higher risks, smaller volumes, the education of sales assistants and consumers are all significant in adding to the margins expected by the distributors and retailers.

Finally at the retail level, the price of a garment is not necessarily related to the costs of production. It can be determined by other factors such as whether it is well-designed, whether it is fashionable and, finally, what the market will bear. There is at present a market which is willing to pay prices for textiles which are not related to the costs of production. If organic is to become mainstream, however, retail prices for all products would have to be at or close to the retail price levels for conventional cotton goods. This in turn implies that the recovery of high initial costs would have to be spread over a longer time-frame than appears to have been used to date. The experience of Coop Switzerland shows that marketing organic cotton clothing can be very successful. In 1997 they sold over one million items at the same prices as conventional items. Coop insists that good marketing is a necessary part of the sales strategy and that clothes must be colourful and fashionable.

Internalizing environmental costs

The previous section indicates that, in cash terms, the cost of clothing and textiles made from organic cotton are more expensive than those made of conventional cotton. These extra costs are added at all levels — production, processing, manufacture, distribution and retailing. But earlier chapters (see Chapters 1 and 2) have drawn attention to the significant environmental and social costs involved in the current cotton production system. These costs are not taken into account in pricing conventional cotton but are borne externally in, for example, the negative environmental impacts and in the effects on the health of people involved in cotton pro-duction who are obliged to use hazardous pesticides. Little work has been done to quantify these costs, let alone to internalize them in conventional cotton production costs.

Recently some economists have started to look at environmental extern-alities in monetary terms using the Life Cycle Analysis (LCA) approach. Using a T-shirt as an example, researchers in the United States have exam-ined the various environmental costs associated with organic and conven-tional cotton production in California — one of the most input-intensive systems in the world. The research demonstrates that the environmental costs of soil erosion, water usage, pesticides and aerial spraying are less for organic cotton production than for conventional. Nutrient leaching and irrigation-related salinization were not measured but could be expected to show significant advantages for organic.

When it came to assessing the post-harvest impact, the research showed no difference between organic and conventional T-shirts. This is a surpris-ing result because, even for a white T-shirt, there are marked differences in conventional washing and bleaching in comparison with the alternative techniques for organic (Chapter 5). It appears therefore that the two T-shirts may have been treated in the same way at the processing stage. The findings also show that the environmental costs of the *processing* stage are minor compared with those at the *growing* stage. This is contrary to the widespread belief that the environmental impacts of both production and

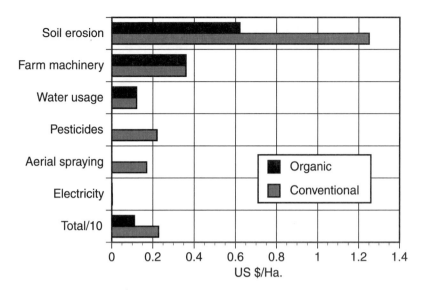

Figure 7: The comparative environmental cost of growing cotton fibre in US$ per kilogram, 1995

Source: Walsh and Brown (1995).

processing are both equally significant (see Chapter 6 for chemical use per kg of textile in Sweden). The authors also concluded that by far the greatest environmental impact in the life of a garment is in the repeated washing that takes place at the consumer stage (see Chapter 6).

Figure 8 reveals that the main environmental impact costs are incurred at the growing stage and at the transport stage in this particular situation. Extensive transportation of products at different stages in the chain is known to be a feature of the textile industry worldwide. If the figures were indicative of a more widespread state of affairs, then it would be an argument for the limitation of the transportation of cotton products at all stages in the life cycle. Manufacturing closer to the source of supply could reduce transport costs, including the environmental costs, and benefit developing countries. This strategy has been argued elsewhere in relation to food products.

In this example, if the environmental costs of production were incorporated into the retail prices of the two T-shirts, the one made from conventional cotton would cost US$1.11 more and the organic one would cost US$0.77 more. The extra environmental costs for the conventional T-shirt is US$0.34 or 15 per cent.

Earlier in this chapter it was argued that increased costs of production, processing and manufacture need not have a prohibitive effect on the final retail price of organic cotton products. If organic cotton products are to become mainstream items and we assume that economies of scale are met,

99

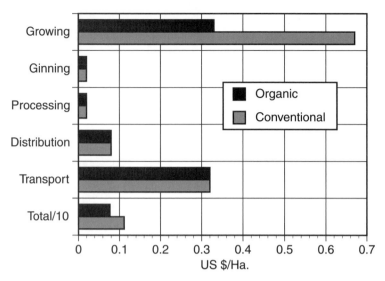

Figure 8:   The environmental cost of each stage *in the lifecycle of a cotton T-shirt in US$ per T-shirt, 1995*

Source: Walsh and Brown (1995).

they should be less than 10 per cent more expensive than their conventional counterparts. Taking a T-shirt as an example, this would mean then that the organic T-shirt would cost US$11.00 if the conventional T-shirt costs US$10.00. The environmental external costs of production and processing are so far not known and even broad assessments are unavailable but they would not have to be very great to account for an increase in value of 10 per cent at retail level. With an eye to the future, it is likely that as organic techniques improve and become more widespread, the costs of organic production and processing will decrease, yields are less likely to fall, and the ever-increasing costs of chemical inputs will all contribute to making organic cotton a seriously viable option.

This chapter represents a first attempt at an assessment of the economic viability of organic cotton. There is clearly an urgent need for data gathering, research and analysis on an array of aspects including the effects of taxes and subsidies, the incorporation of environmental and other externalities into pricing, the impact of the conversion period on farmers' incomes, price premiums, labour costs, the effects of economies of scale and others. As organic cotton projects mature, opportunities for generating data and answers to some of the many questions raised in this chapter will increase.

8
The market for organic cotton

PETER TON with contributions from NATHAN BOONE, DAN IMHOFF, KEVIN SWEENEY

Introduction

The crucial factor underlying the economic feasibility of organic cotton growing is the market for organic cotton products. Although organic cotton has been produced commercially since the 1980s it was the fashion industry in the early 1990s which created the demand and fostered the new relationships which turned organic cotton into a developing, albeit small, part of the textile industry.

In this chapter, Peter Ton reviews the recent trends in the worldwide organic cotton market. This introduction is followed by two shorter contributions which look specifically at how companies in Europe and the US have been developing organic cotton lines.

The development of the market for organic cotton

PETER TON

The early-1990s eco-trend in fashion

In the early-1990s, environmental issues had taken on important political significance. Consumers had also come to realize that they could influence production processes through their buying power, and companies started trying to produce consumer goods which would be perceived as more appealing to the environmentally motivated customer. Some trend-watchers working within the fashion industry realized that environmental considerations might become a new and important motivation for consumer choice. Anticipation of this market change was regarded as a strategic matter in some of the larger textile and clothing companies.

The fashion industry started to launch new textile products and clothing lines in the USA, Europe and South-East Asia, marketing them as 'green', 'natural', 'ecological' and 'eco-friendly' (see Chapter 6). These products may have been made from organic cotton or may have been produced in some other way considered to be more environmentally responsible. But there was little consistency of approach. These types of products were first launched in 1992, by fashion clothing companies such as Esprit (USA), Hennes and Mauritz (Sweden), Britta Steilmann (Germany), and Novotex (Denmark). They received considerable attention from the media, consumers and the industry and set a trend in fashion which lasted from around the autumn of 1992 to the autumn of 1994. This was judged by a Dutch designer, Lousmijn van der Akker, to have been 'the most important and influential fashion trend of the last 10 years'.

Fashion being what it is, the bubble soon burst. What were all these environmental claims of individual companies worth? Could using natural fibres like cotton be considered environmentally responsible? Is hand-picked cotton environmentally responsible? Should environmentally responsible products only be coloured with natural dyes or could synthetic dye-stuffs do as well? In fact, fashion houses and retailers world-wide proved to be uninformed about the environmental aspects of conventional textile and clothing production and unable to judge each other's environmental claims. Thus there was within the industry a confusion about the value of the differing environmental claims, which resulted in a proliferation of labels and trade-marks which appeared in the early-1990s. The main objective was to increase sales of the so-called eco-textiles.

Consumers, in their turn, had no idea of what was involved in conventional textile and clothing production, and were unable to judge the merits of the environmental claims being made. Labelling should have enabled consumers to make informed choices but it failed to spread the environmental message in a clear and comprehensible manner. Consumers and the fashion industry began to associate eco-textiles with un-dyed, natural colours—grey, yellow, light-brown and light-green. Interest eventually faded and the 'eco-trend' was replaced by a new trend which emphasized exactly the opposite: brightly coloured clothes made with synthetic fibres.

Reasons for the production and sale of eco-textiles

Even though the fashion industry turned its back on the 'eco-trend' in 1994, the underlying concept was not rejected. Discussions intensified on the environmental aspects of production and processing within the textile and clothing industry. In Europe, in particular, pragmatic commercial reasoning justified further integration of environmental issues into production and processing. In the US most environmentally responsible methods adopted by companies were more expensive and management intensive and required additional investment in technology and training.

The market was stimulated by three main factors. First of all, eco-textiles fulfil the demands of a small but significant group, an estimated 5–10 per cent of consumers who look explicitly for products produced in an environmentally responsible way and who are willing to pay a premium for them. According to the *Herald Tribune* (June 8, 1995), by 1994 the German market for environmentally responsible clothing already exceeded DM250 million (US$140 million).

Secondly, environmental legislation was pushing industries to investigate less-polluting production methods. The ban on azo-dyes in Germany (July 1995) and the Netherlands (May 1996), was expected to be followed by legislation on issues such as emissions, waste-water disposal, energy use, and the recycling responsibility of producers. Anticipation of this legislation was felt to be necessary, as it might give individual companies in Europe, the USA and Japan a competitive advantage over cheaper imported textiles from South-East Asia. Indeed, the competitiveness of most textile and clothing companies in high-salary countries had been eroded to such an extent that they were desperately looking for high-value 'niche'-markets, in order to survive. As Ernest Ehrismann, of the spinner Boller Winkler (Switzerland), put it: 'For us conventional spinning was not profitable anymore. The market for organic cotton yarns is small, but interesting and attractive'.

Finally, some companies hoped that the integration of environmental issues into management structures would lead to more rationalized production processes which would be cheaper than their conventional counterparts. For example, careful design could lead to less fabric wastage during production, the bleaching process could in some cases be left out, and dyestuffs could be recycled and re-used through waste-water treatment (see Chapter 5).

Eco-textiles encompass a whole range of products made from different fibres and blends and different processing techniques. As noted earlier, cotton-based products are a significant part of this larger group of eco-textiles. The discussion here is limited to cotton only, but within the context of the broader eco-trend which had a significant impact on the use and marketing of organic cotton fibre.

The US market

Organic cotton production in the US has its roots in the organic food movement that has steadily gained momentum in recent decades (see US case study, Chapter 9). Beginning in the late 1980s, the demands of 'environmentally conscious' consumers in the United States created niche markets for both organic and naturally pigmented cottons. In the early 1990s, the US was the dominant producer of organic cotton. By 1995, US organic cotton fibre production had reached an all-time high of 6750 tonnes. As the eco-fashion trend faded, however, markets for organic cotton evaporated. Farmers who had grown on speculation were devastated and many of those taking part in organic conversion programmes withdrew. In 1996, the US produced less than 40 per cent of the world's organic cotton. Organic farmers are now rebuilding their production capabilities to respond to a more co-ordinated industry effort to expand the use of organic cotton. The Organic Fiber Council, for example, has been formed as a

Organic cotton products are finding markets in Europe and the US
Credit: Hess Natur, Germany

Discussing the quality of organic cotton in the laboratories of Remei AG, Switzerland
Credit: Dorothy Myers, Pesticides Trust

working council of the Organic Trade Association, which aims to provide a forum to address topics of interest to all sectors within the organic cotton and agricultural fibre industries.

Companies have used a variety of approaches in engaging in the organic cotton market in the US. Esprit is a privately held company with approximately US$1 billion annual sales world-wide, catering primarily for young women, and distributing in 36 countries. Esprit was one of the first large companies to appreciate the market for environmentally responsible clothing and to market certified organic cotton products internationally. The launch of Esprit's Ecollection in Spring 1992, coincided with increased awareness of environmental issues. However by 1995, a combination of factors including internal company turmoil, high premiums for organic fibre and a market shift to synthetic fibres contributed to the phasing out the Ecollection line.

The Ecollection was first established as a small research and development model to demonstrate that ecological alternatives to conventional design choices could be found and applied throughout the industry. The range of items was limited to basic knitted garments as only one knitting mill was involved. Prices were high due to lack of competition, increased labour costs for the farmer and special handling by the mill.

In autumn 1993, the Ecollection team, along with other US companies, became involved in a series of Organic Cotton Conferences which brought together all sectors of the cotton industry to discuss the problems involved in bringing organic cotton to the marketplace. As a result of the conferences, more mills became involved in organic production and a greater variety of fabrics became available. In 1994, the Ecollection team made a direct pre-harvest commitment to farmers for a given quantity of organic fibre, based on the anticipated sales for the season. This new form of partnership resulted in a major shift in the company's business planning by purchasing fibre once a year at harvest instead of purchasing products six times a year.

The Ecollection forged new ground in many areas: low impact dyes, organic cotton denim and poplin, blends of organic cotton with flax and wool and natural dyes. Esprit was an example of an approach to ecologically responsible clothing, which other companies have learned from and built upon.

The outdoor clothing company Patagonia made a commitment in Spring 1996 that all the cotton they use will be certified organic or in-transition (conversion). Patagonia is a privately owned, medium-sized business founded in the late 1960s by a group of outdoor enthusiasts who wanted to develop a range of outdoor clothing. The company has outlets throughout Northern America, Europe, Japan, Korea and Australia (see box).

Ecosport is an example of a smaller privately owned company which turned to organic production as a means of realizing the company owners'

US company experience

As noted earlier, companies interested in organic cotton in the US have adopted a variety of market strategies. In this section, we look in more detail at those which have turned their cotton products over to organic cotton (Patagonia and Ecosport).

Patagonia: Approaches to marketing

Patagonia made the decision to stock only organic cotton products in 1994. Inquiries with existing fabric companies resulted in a number of refusals to undertake development of organic cotton products, which resulted in the company having to create new partnerships along the entire supply chain. The next two years were spent, therefore, sourcing organic fibre and working with companies throughout their supply chain to ensure that the ultimate product was of high quality. Fabrics which did not meet the company's quality criteria were rejected. As a result, short-term losses in sales were experienced in the spring of 1996 because the company was low on finished goods. The management felt, however, that the need to retain the company's reputation for producing quality products would, in the long term, reap benefits. In essence, Patagonia believes that although environmental innovation can enhance a product's image it cannot be the basis for a decision to purchase. Rather, it can tip the balance where two products of relatively similar cost and quality are marketed.

The use of organic cotton in Patagonia's products was made easier by some important decisions. Firstly, the company decided to use fully certified and in-conversion organic cotton, thus supporting those farmers which were in the process of conversion. Secondly, it was decided not to sell organic clothing, but clothing made with organic cotton. Patagonia thus still uses synthetic dyeing technologies and conventional or poly/cotton thread. Natural dyes did not meet their quality standards and potentially had environmental problems of their own, and thread is a mass-produced commodity that requires significant minimum quantities to begin being converted to organic. The company is working on eliminating formaldehyde, but it was decided that some styles using woven fabrics would still be treated with resin to minimize wrinkles.

Pricing the products made with organic cotton is a difficult issue. Increases in production costs varied by product but ranged from 15 to 40 per cent. Eventually it was decided to 'share' the increased costs between the company and the customers: Patagonia reduced their margins on most products to a maximum of 20 per cent.

In the US, cotton has an image of purity, of being 'natural'. To combat this image of purity, Patagonia introduced a campaign that was simple but educational. Catalogue essays and point-of-purchase materials explained the problems of conventional cotton farming, whilst making no assumptions that consumers would view organic cotton as necessarily a 'good' thing. Much of Patagonia's educational approach is based on the commitment to change attitudes towards agriculture and the purchasing power of consumers. There is also, however, a marketing link to be made. Companies that strive to teach consumers about an idea, and not just a product, are those which build strong relationships with their customers.

Patagonia sells its products through three channels: its mail order catalogue, retail stores in the US, Japan, France and Germany and through wholesale accounts worldwide. In the stores the company owns, and which now only stock organic cotton, aggressive presentations of the difference between organic and conventional cotton were made. For the wholesale accounts, which also sell conventional cotton, a less confrontational approach was promoted, with the emphasis being on the benefits of organic fibre. Staff education and development was also recognized as important and Patagonia employees were taken on tours of California's Central Valley, visiting conventional and organic farms.

Patagonia's production and marketing approach has been very successful. Demand for the products has been high and the attention the line has generated has added to the company's reputation and has in turn indirectly increased sales in other areas. It is clear that customers continue to gravitate towards quality, so a product that projects quality is more likely to be successful. If companies, however well-intentioned, teach consumers that they must choose between environmental improvement and product quality, they face the customer with a dilemma. Patagonia sees the challenge as trying to change the public's perception of quality, so that it includes the quality of life on Earth.

Ecosport: survival through diversity

In 1990, Daniel Sanders was the owner of a struggling clothing manufacturing business, and disillusioned with the lack of ethical and environmental standards in the fashion industry. Determined to change course, he began searching for market openings that were more compatible with his interest in protecting the environment. At about the same time, unbeknown to him, a handful of manufacturers, researchers and farmers were developing cleaner production methods. Chlorine bleach was being eliminated from cotton T-shirts and jeans, and new high-fixation dyes were successfully reducing energy and minimizing the release of chemicals in the effluent. At least one major California farmer had begun growing cotton in rotation with organic vegetables and had been certified by California Certified Organic Farming (CCOF). Plant breeder Sally Fox had improved her green and brown naturally pigmented varieties and was developing a seed farm on 40 acres in the southern San Joaquin valley.

Daniel Sanders' first step towards organic cotton production came after a Greenpeace merchandise manager informed him that cotton was being grown organically in Peru. A circuitous investigation led him ultimately to CalOrganics, a large Californian organic farm which was trying to sell its certified organic cottons at just a few cents above the price of conventional cotton. Suddenly, Sanders found himself in the market with 250 bales (approximately 55 000kg) of organic cotton—10 times more than he had planned for his trial runs. The challenge to turn this situation to an economic advantage kept Sanders up at night. About this time he and his business partner wife, Mary Lou, met up with Eddie Mandeau, an experienced manufacturer also eager for a change. Within six months, their new business, EcoSport, was converting organic cotton into fabrics for Greenpeace-Winterland, Seventh Generation and Esprit. The vitality of the operation was such that by 1993 they began to focus on producing clothes under their own label as well. As one of the first to contract directly with organic cotton farmers then convert fibre to yarns, yarns to fabrics and fabrics to finished products which could then be sold under other labels, Sanders and the company benefited significantly. For a short time, it seemed, all manufacturing roads led to EcoSport.

As the organic cotton industry grew, the company continued to diversify, branching out from manufacturing and subcontracting into designing and wholesale distribution. 'We call it "the octopus",' explains Sanders, 'because this many-tentacled strategy has kept us going through an unstable and ever-changing market.' EcoSport's own product range include fabric (primarily knits rather than wovens), T-shirts, children's clothes, and underwear. Yet Sanders is the first to admit that the business has been anything but predictable. 'If I told you what I'm selling today, I can also say it won't be the same in six months.' Hence the octopus approach.

Diversity can also be a liability, making a company top-heavy. EcoSport's stock is held in yarn, fabric and garments, so it is essential to read the markets right. 'You make your best projections about what's going to sell and how much and then you've got to live with those decisions. You see, a train doesn't stop as fast as a car does, and manufacturing is more like a train.'

Early problems for the company were the limited supply of certified organic cotton fibre available and the variations in quality—problems which have not changed very much. The difficulties of sourcing clean cotton without the use of defoliants is no nearer a solution. In addition, the complexities and quirks of manufacturing organic cotton differ from conventional cotton and are time consuming. EcoSport's major current concerns, however, have become those typical of any clothing company: the relentless competitive elements of a cut-throat industry, rising overheads, the continual need for new markets, and pricing.

Another major factor that needs to be addressed for the company's future is the dominance of manufacturing issues over marketing. Marketing may receive only 10 per cent of the company's energy, but it is the key to success.

'Despite all the media hoopla, it seems that Americans still don't understand the importance of what organic cotton means in terms of sustainable agriculture,' says Sanders. 'They think cotton is "natural". And companies and organizations help to heighten this confusion. I just read a catalogue advertising a ski sweater from Denmark and in one place it's described as "natural cotton" and on another page it says "organic". This is typical. The distinctions are not made clear and customers remain confused.'

Overseas competition is yet another key issue, not so much from foreign growers as from foreign mills. Trade barriers mean that, for example, Peru as a country with Most Favoured Nation status can export its goods into the European Community with no duty to pay, whereas the US incurs a 25 per cent duty when exporting to the EC. At the same time, importing cotton from Peru into the US attracts duty. This stifles the domestic industry, exacting a burden for both importers and exporters of organic goods.

Sanders believes that EcoSport will emerge from the 1990s as a significantly established brand name that could easily be turned into a successful conventional clothing company. But that is not the direction he and his wife want to take their company (their partner Eddie Mandeau died in late 1994). The couple sees their challenge as how to expand the market for organic cotton in an otherwise highly competitive industry. One answer may be to focus their product range better, narrowing selections and perhaps entering the home furnishings market. Increasing marketing efforts and having other companies make products for EcoSport may be another option.

'I'm not interested in short cuts,' says Sanders. 'EcoSport is here for the long term. Short cuts always come back to bite you in the end. I'm just really proud to be where we are today.'

'Patagonia' was by Kevin Sweeney, with additional material by Yvon Chouinard and Michael S. Brown, and 'Ecosport' was based on an interview with Daniel Sanders by Dan Imhoff.

ethical and environmental goals, and as a way to survive in a highly competitive market (see box on page 106).

Even more recently, three large public companies, The Gap, Levi's and Nike, have started to blend organic cotton with conventional cotton used in their mainline clothing products (see box on page 110). Though the percentage blend is small, these companies produce at such a large volume that the number of organic cotton bales purchased is significant for the suppliers. This should lead to greater areas in the US being converted from conventional to organic cotton.

The European market

In Europe, the production, processing and trade of organic cotton has always been in the hands of a large number of small and medium-sized companies. Those that were involved during the eco-trend (Hennes and Mauritz, and Esprit, for example) never came to dominate the market so that their subsequent withdrawal had little impact on the market for eco-textiles. The withdrawal of Esprit in particular did not affect the European market because most of its organic fibre was sourced in the USA.

Since most organic cotton production outside the USA and Australia finds its way to the European market, the European demand for organic cotton could be estimated to be roughly equal to organic cotton production outside those countries. Almost all US cotton is processed for the domestic market and organic cotton exports from the USA to Europe seem to

Blending organic cotton with conventional cotton

When larger textile and clothing companies contemplate using organic cotton, they are faced with a very limited supply situation compared to their total cotton usage. Levi-Strauss, for example, uses more than 90 million kilogrammes of cotton annually. How exactly do you integrate a very limited supply of organic cotton into this large-scale production scenario? In the United States, early attempts by larger clothing companies to develop 100 per cent organic cotton clothing lines or even single 100 per cent organic cotton products were not successful for a variety of real and imagined reasons. Costs were prohibitively high for mainstream consumers, and marketing was not linked with consumer education, for example. In a few short years, many 100 per cent organic cotton programmes were dropped as fast as they had been created.

In the United States, the age-old concept of blending various fibres to achieve desired characteristics has been applied to the organic cotton supply problem. Blending lower percentages of organic cotton into conventional fabric production offers a cost-effective strategy for using organic cotton while avoiding higher production costs. Blending avoids most additional organic processing costs and the increased cost is minimal, in many cases a few cents more per garment. Special labelling or marketing is not required if the company is not interested in emphasizing the environmental attributes of organic cotton. Ultimately, blending offers more flexibility and cost savings throughout the cotton production chain, while supporting organic cotton farmers and increasing organic cotton acreage.

Currently, Levi-Strauss, Gap and Nike are all purchasing organic cotton for blending programmes. In 1997, Levi-Strauss purchased more than 450 000kg of organic cotton from California growers. Nike has contracted 230 000kg and plans to expand organic cotton use dramatically over the next five years. These purchases have sent a strong message to the organic cotton industry by increasing the demand. They have also caused dramatic supply fluctuations, which has worried organic cotton mills, manufacturers and retailers that are involved in the 100 per cent organic cotton market. Forward contracts with farmers are rapidly becoming standard industry practice and soon the supply and demand situation will stabilize as contracts lead to a more rational expansion of organic acreage.

While 100 per cent organic purity may not be the goal of companies that choose blending, they claim to be committed to supporting organic cotton farmers, increasing organic cotton acreage and systematically reducing pesticide use in cotton. The next five years will tell if this incremental strategy for supporting the organic cotton industry will increase organic cotton acreage and stabilize the organic cotton market for everyone involved.

Benefits of blending (from a large clothing company perspective)
The benefits of blending organic cotton are numerous and address all segments of the cotton production chain. Clothing companies can significantly reduce synthetic pesticide and fertilizer use without developing a 100 per

110

Table 1: Organic cotton purchased for blending programmes 1997

Company	Organic cotton fibre purchased (kg)
Patagonia*	680 000
Levi-Strauss	520 000
Nike	230 000
Gap	75 000
TOTAL	1 507 000

Source: Organic Fibre Council, USA
*Patagonia uses only 100 per cent organic cotton. They are listed for comparison purposes only.

cent organic cotton programme. Also, the higher fibre costs of organic cotton are reduced by spreading the cost over all garments.

o small inefficient runs based on low-volume 100 per cent organic cotton lots are eliminated;
o extra clean-out costs are avoided, since blends are processed along with conventional cotton;
o limited organic fibre selection and grade availability are not a problem;
o separate handling for organic cotton is no longer necessary;
o companies can continue to use the same mills and manufacturers;
o speciality marketing and labelling are not required;
o blending increases demand for organic cotton and leads to contracts with farmers.

Problems with blending
o blending small percentages of organic cotton does not reduce pesticide and fertilizer use as rapidly as a 100 per cent organic approach.
o without a labelling system, it is not possible to identify and differentiate organic blended products in the marketplace;
o incrementally higher fibre costs of organic cotton would be incurred as a result of blending;
o blended products are not a viable alternative for the chemically sensitive consumer who needs chemical and pesticide-free products.

Nathan Boone

account for only a few hundred tons per year. US organic cotton is more expensive than other cottons, and thus imports are limited to speciality cottons, such as extra-long staple or naturally pigmented cottons. Australian organic cotton fibres are likely to find markets in Japan or the USA rather than in Europe, as do their conventional cotton fibres. Almost all other organic cotton projects world-wide are closely tied to European

111

companies. The European market for organic cotton was estimated at about 4500 tonnes of fibre in 1997. Over the years, organic cotton fibre destined for the European market has increased rapidly and in 1997 was more than 60 per cent of the global total.

An important feature of the organic cotton market in Europe is that most projects, importers and companies have their own specific marketing channels in which exclusive rights are being guaranteed and safe-guarded (see box on page 113). For example, Lichtschatz Projekte in Germany sells most of its fibres to the German clothing company Living Crafts, and Remei in Switzerland sells about 70 per cent of its organic cotton products to the Swiss market chain Coop-Schweiz.

These trade links are currently very close, so that new organic cotton importers entering the market generally need to establish new marketing outlets instead of taking over clients from other importers. Although there is no free and open market for organic cotton yet, the number of independent organic cotton projects is nevertheless on the increase and so are the companies. Consequently, the organic cotton market will steadily lose its opaque character, and come to function as a normal, open market in the future.

Germany is the primary market for organic cotton and eco-textiles in Europe, just as it is for health foods (Germany accounts for more than 50 per cent of health food sales in Europe). Environmental awareness amongst German consumers is relatively high, although it is concentrated mainly on the health aspects of textile and clothing production rather than on the whole life-cycle from fibre production to consumption.

All European companies name Germany as their primary market. The other European countries with well developed 'eco-textiles' markets are Switzerland, Austria, and to a lesser extent Sweden and the Netherlands. Other Scandinavian countries are believed to be promising. On the other hand, the 'eco-textiles' markets in countries such as the United Kingdom, France and Italy are reported to be 'underdeveloped' up to now.

The Japanese market[1]

The import of organic cotton from the USA, Peru and China, into Japan was started around 1990 by general trading companies and small-scale enterprises specializing in organic textiles (raw cotton, yarn, fabrics and finished products). As the trading companies do not publish the exact import figures and there is no institution which specifically collects trade statistics on organic cotton, there is very little information on the size of the market in Japan. The market demand appears, however, to be increasing, reflecting the growing ecological concern among people and enterprises who are seeking new business opportunities.

---

1. Information on the Japanese market was supplied by Mayumi Morizane-Saito.

European company experience

In Switzerland, Sweden and Germany three companies, Boller Winkler, Triconor and Hess Natur, respectively, are examples of the reorientation of European textile companies towards organic fibre. Although all the companies have different outlooks on the direction of the market and the best way of ensuring success in the organic marketplace, all three share a common goal to further the development of certified organic cotton products.

Boller Winkler

The Swiss company Boller Winkler has been producing cotton fabrics in its weaving mill for over 150 years. Despite such a long history the company decided in the 1990s that the only way to ensure future success was to develop new innovative programmes. During 1992 an investigation was made, with a view to finding an alternative to conventional cotton, into the kinds of environmentally responsible cotton available from the cotton brokers. Three alternatives were identified: hand-picked cotton, naturally pigmented cottons and organically cultivated cotton. A survey of the client base revealed an interest in environmentally responsible products, although the main concern was the maintenance of stable prices.

After introducing products made from hand-picked and naturally pigmented cotton between 1992 and 1994, the company began to look more seriously at cotton produced organically. As a result of the success of their organic yarns, the company decided that from the beginning of 1996 the mill would only use certified organic cotton.

Boller Winkler found that the customers of the conventional spinning mills did not know how to handle the certified organic cotton yarn or tended not to see the market potential for organic fabrics. Often companies which expressed an initial interest backed off when they realized the level of consumer information they would need to provide to their customers about the new organic products. Boller Winkler, therefore, needed to expand its client base as widely as possible. The importance of everyone in the chain needing to know the origin of the product and the subsequent development of that product became clear. Distributors and traders in organic products are a very small dedicated market and it is to their advantage to be able to inform present and prospective customers of the environmental strategy which guides their activities.

Boller Winkler believe that it is necessary to be aware of the latest fashion trends to sustain a growing market for their products. They feel it is essential to move away from the raw-white natural-coloured simple knitted garments which have characterized organic clothing to date in favour of a fashionable and colourful product. By collaborating with knitters, weavers, finishers and dyers, Boller Winkler hope to see the further development of more natural processes for dyeing and finishing which can then be woven into brightly coloured high-quality organic fabrics.

Triconor

The Swedish company Triconor, which specializes in underwear, employs 80 people and has a turnover of around US$9 million per annum. During the early 1990s, the declining market for its products and the sudden availability of reasonably priced machinery from a factory in the former East Germany, prompted the company to investigate using organic cotton in production.

When Triconor began to research the market for ecologically responsible textiles they soon realized a key problem was the plethora of eco-labels and marks which were applied to garments in the various countries in which the company operated. The company therefore decided to produce to the strictest standards available for organic products at the time—SSNC and KRAV (see Chapter 6). The company was certified by these two organizations in 1995 and 1996 respectively.

Product development has been challenging. The 'Organic Pure Cotton' project was split into three parts: production, products and markets. About 10 consultants were hired to advise and help solve the various problems arising from the decision to develop organic cotton products. It has taken four years from the initial idea to reach the stage of a marketable product, which has been time consuming and expensive.

The company has invested more than US$1 million in production machinery and equipment and the development of the new line. Although it will take some time to introduce the line into the 15 countries Triconor usually trades in, test sales of the product have been encouraging. In 1995, trials in Sweden made a turnover of US$0.1 million and was followed in 1996 by a more widespread introduction of the products. Turnover for 1997 was estimated at US$0.4 million and is expected to rise slowly over the next few years as the products are introduced more widely.

Triconor's experiences in developing its line of organic cotton underwear are an indication of the problems and the prospects for organic cotton products. Conventional companies expect the pay-off from new lines within a three- to five-year period. Triconor, however, expects to start profiting from its organic lines in seven to ten years. The main problem they identified in the production and marketing of their products is the massive ignorance of organic cotton throughout the production chain. Both the public and the market show immense interest in organic products, but they need more information to be able to understand the message. The provision of more consumer information, coupled with lower prices for raw material and greater efficiency in the production of organic cotton overall will, the company believes, lead to organic and naturally pigmented cotton having an enormous impact world-wide.

Hess Natur

The German mail order company, Hess Natur, has been promoting natural clothing products for over 20 years. The company has a turnover of over DM100 million per annum and employs nearly 300 people. The company began to investigate using organic cotton in the early 1990s.

Hess Natur was founded on the marketing policy of producing natural clothing items for the 'health and environment' conscious consumer. With the growing ecological awareness of consumers and increasing demands, the company experienced a rapid increase in sales as well as in the product range. Hess Natur set up a research department in 1995 in order to evaluate new, environmentally responsible processing techniques. With an expected turnover of about DM120 million in 1997 and some 600 000 customers getting the bi-annual catalogue, Hess Natur has achieved an economic stability enabling the company and co-operating manufactures to pursue environmentally responsible solutions.

According to the company, more than 95 per cent of the cotton used is from organic production sourced from a number of countries. The certification of the cotton is carried out by several institutions, including SKAL and IMO.

As sustainablity is one of the key tenets of company policy, it extends beyond the field of production and manufacture. Instead of following every new trend in fashion, the design department focuses on classic clothing design. One of the Hess Natur collections is called 'Long Life', which gives a three-year guarantee on fit and quality.

Contributions by Ernst Ehrismann, Bo Ottosson, Ute auf der Bruecken and Oliver Hanschke

One pioneer company, Avanti Inc, began the import of organic cotton fabrics from the USA in 1990. The Japan Texas Organic Cotton Association (JTOCA) was founded in 1993 on the initiative of Avanti Inc in order to inform Japanese consumers about organic cotton and to stimulate the market. JTOCA members produce organic cotton products such as bedding, especially for babies, cotton blankets, towels and so on. The members have their own cotton manufacturing line which follows TDA standards (see Chapter 6). Avanti has also established a subsidiary company certified by the TDA to distribute organic cotton products in Texas. JTOCA holds symposiums and runs campaigns to raise ecological concerns and to promote consumer understanding of organic cotton. According to a representative of JTOCA, 'The organic cotton market in Japan has been a very closed market; producing textiles especially for children suffering from skin diseases. But now there are more and more green consumers, so the market is definitely expanding'.

The other active organization developing the organic cotton market in Japan is the Nippon Organic Cotton Marketing Organization (NOC). Founded in 1994, the NOC aims to build up marketing systems for organic certified cotton, yarn and fabrics to keep prices low through stable supply and cost savings in direct co-operation with the producer. The 18 manufacturer members (14 domestic and 4 overseas companies) all use environmentally responsible processes. NOC co-operates with several overseas certification agencies including SKAL, OCIA (Organic Crop Improvement Association) and the TDA. A representative of NOC estimates that retail

115

sales of organic cotton products were around US$20 000 in 1996, 10 times higher than three years earlier, and (US$38 000) in 1997.

Although the market for organic cotton is expanding rapidly, problems remain both within the industry and with market demand. At present Japan has not developed national organic standards—for organic products or processing. One key problem is that the word 'organic' in Japanese, 'yuuki', is very ambiguous and does not have a generally accepted definition. For example, there are some manufacturing companies blending small percentages of organic cotton with conventional cotton and marketing the products as organic.

Product development

In the early-1990s, the number of eco-textile products made from organic cotton fibre was limited to T-shirts, socks and sanitary pads. The eco-textiles sector was still in its infancy, with a lack of expertise in textile and clothing production, and marketing, and a lack of available capital to invest in market research and product development.

The eco-textiles sector is evolving in its own way and at its own pace. By 1995, a much broader spectrum of products was available on the market, including: jeans, sweaters, jackets, high-quality sportswear, mattresses, bed sheets, towels, nappies, tampons, shopping bags, furnishing fabrics, curtains, childrenswear, etc. Many companies are now working on product diversification to extend sales and profits. Thus, in the next few years, the eco-textiles market will presumably include most of the textile products available to the conventional textile and clothing market.

Interviews with people involved in the industry indicate that the textile market sectors which are considered to be the most promising for the relatively expensive, organic cotton eco-textiles are:

○ products worn next to the skin (for example, underwear, socks, bedlinen and tampons)—developed in response to consumer fears, particularly in Germany, over allergies and skin diseases caused by toxic residues in fabrics;
○ baby and childrenswear products, which are particularly profitable as parents tend to safeguard their children's health before their own;
○ light-weight organic cotton products, for which raw material costs are less as a proportion of the total costs than for other products;
○ furnishing fabrics, for which consumers are more willing to pay higher prices because they are longer lasting purchases.

It should be noted, however, that other textile market segments including fashionable clothing are not necessarily thought to be less promising. Over-

116

all the picture is that markets simply need to be created and explored. Better designs, more large-scale operations resulting in lower consumer prices, awareness-raising and promotional activities, as well as government initiatives such as zero rating for value-added taxes on eco-textiles, would all contribute to this development.

Consumer market segments

Like the market for health foods, the market for eco-textiles consists of four main types of consumer:

○ committed consumers, who already buy environmentally responsible products out of strong environmental convictions;
○ health-conscious consumers, i.e. those caring for their children's and their own health, and fearing allergies and skin diseases;
○ sympathetic consumers, who occasionally buy environmentally responsible goods for environmental considerations; and
○ casual purchasers, who are motivated by considerations other than environmental.

For eco-textiles' sales to enter the mainstream textiles and clothing market, the last category, the casual purchasers, is seen as particularly important for developing the organic cotton market. For these consumers, factors such as design, colour, quality and price overrule the environmental considerations which they may, or may not, share with other consumers.

Recent developments

Eco-textile companies' efforts to enter mainstream textile markets are reflected in their participation in fairs and fashion shows, in the diversification of products and in product development, including better designs and colours.

The colour problem, as mentioned above, was a major reason for eco-textiles being seen as old-fashioned in the mid-1990s, when interest in 'natural' colours waned. However, since mid-1995 newly invented, more environmentally responsible dyes have come onto the market. Although these dyes are synthetic, many in the sector regard them as the best alternative to conventional dyes and eco-textiles are now available in a wide range of colours. Companies selling coloured eco-textiles report considerable increases in sales since their introduction. Alternatively, environmentally responsible dyeing methods may also include the use of natural, vegetable dyes. However, vegetable dyes are only available in limited quantity, as production and research on them has been phased-out in recent decades due to the predominance of cheaper synthetic dyes.

The question of quality is more confusing. Quality is measured in many different ways, and often technical quality is confused with an appreciation of design, colour and so on. However, when it comes to technical quality, it is agreed that organic cotton products and conventional products are of equal quality. Some even assume organic fibre quality to be higher, as the fibres have not been affected by chemicals, and some consumers perceive organic cotton products to have a softer feel than those conventionally produced.

The higher retail price of eco-textiles is still viewed as the main barrier to the growth of the organic cotton market. Many assume that customers are unwilling to pay more than a 5–10 per cent premium for eco-textiles. At present, it appears inevitable that prices are higher, as small-scale operations typical of the sector have yet to benefit from the advantages of economies of scale (see Chapter 7). Solutions to the price problem are being sought in:

○ economies of scale, such as increased fibre production per unit to reduce the costs of production or specialization by spinners in processing organic cotton fibres;
○ promotional activities to improve the image of eco-textiles;
○ concentration on specific textile and consumer market sectors in which price is of lesser importance;
○ temporary price subsidies by companies to increase markets;
○ governmental support through, for example, zero-rated value-added tax (VAT) for organic products;
○ blending, which could increase quantities used (see box).

Apart from the penetration of the mainstream consumer market for textiles and clothing, some companies are trying to enter the institutional textile markets. Particularly in Sweden, government and quasi-government organizations, like railway companies and postal services, are showing increased interest in purchasing eco-textiles for uniforms and the like. In the Netherlands, political pressure on institutional markets is leading to environmental considerations being integrated into purchasing behaviour, although as in Sweden this is directed at the broader categories of eco-textiles rather than just organic cotton products.

Conclusion

The growth in European demand for eco-textiles is reflected in increases in production of organic cotton destined for Europe, in the number and turnover of European companies and in the rising number of retail outlets. Although still only representing a fraction of total cotton production world-wide (see Table 1 in Chapter 1), the organic cotton market is growing steadily. Existing organic cotton projects will expand production and new projects are being launched. Designers and manufacturers are taking up the challenge of environmentally responsible design and investing in product development to overcome the 'alternative' image of eco-textiles.

At present, the market for organic cotton and eco-textiles is dominated by small companies. Larger companies are still hesitant about engaging in the eco-textiles trade, but there are signs that this is changing. Some of them view the eco-textiles market as promising and have committed themselves to organic cotton fibre use. The organic cotton market is evolving into an increasingly mature and normal market. Specialization by companies, presentations at conventional trade fairs, quality improvements in colour and design and increased efficiency are all indications of an increasingly mature organic cotton market.

Transparency and free competition are likely to increase with growing demand and with new organic cotton traders entering the market. Production costs will fall with economies of scale, and improved distribution and availability of organic cotton textiles will, in the end, lead to decreasing consumer prices.

Introduction to the case studies

As HAS BEEN NOTED in the earlier chapters of this book, organic cotton production and processing is a relatively recent development. Nevertheless, projects have become well-established in several countries: Peru, Egypt, Turkey, India and the United States. Elsewhere, mainly in Africa, experimental projects are under way. The selection of case study countries reflects this situation. Projects also exist in other countries which are not reported here but may have been referred to in earlier chapters (Nicaragua, Paraguay, Brazil, Mexico, Kenya, Pakistan, Australia and Israel).

The US, despite recent falls in production, remains the biggest single producer of organic cotton. The US case study includes a review of organic cotton in the country as well as more detailed accounts of organic growing in California and Texas.

Peru has a long history of cotton cultivation. Organic cotton is grown by small-scale farmers in systems which mix local traditional knowledge with modern technologies suitable for organic production. A detailed description of production in the Cañete Valley is included in the case study.

India likewise has a long history of cotton production and has the largest area of conventional cotton in the world. Although only a tiny amount of this is organic, successful projects are being carried out in several states. Descriptions of these projects are included in the case study.

Turkey has the longest record of organic cotton growing, going back to the late 1980s. As with the majority of organic cotton produced outside North America the impetus and continued development of the projects depend on the involvement and demand of a handful of European enterprises. However, the prospects of building an indigenous market are being investigated and state involvement in research is an encouraging sign of serious intent.

The development of organic agriculture in Africa has many benefits for small-scale producers. Organic cotton projects are emerging in several parts of the continent and interest is growing. In the final two case studies we look first at Egypt, a country where organic, and specifically biodynamic, agriculture has made impressive gains in recent years. We then take a look at several new organic cotton projects in Africa which are at present small but which show promise as an alternative production method which is viable for small farmers in certain situations.

9

USA

NATHAN BOONE, DAVID KATZ, SEAN SWEZEY, POLLY GOLDMAN, BRENT WISEMAN, LaRHEA PEPPER and LYNDA GROSE

US growers began to produce organic cotton in the late 1980s in California, New Mexico, Arizona and Texas. The Texas Department of Agriculture established the first organic cotton certification programme in 1991. Production gathered momentum in the early 1990s and peaked in 1993–4 at the height of the eco-fashion trend. At that time, US share of global production amounted to around 70 per cent. Discouraged by higher organic fibre processing costs and consumer resistance, several companies have, since then, withdrawn from the market and fibre production fell in the USA in 1995. Nevertheless, much has been learned by producers, mills and retailers and there are signs that the industry will gain strength. According to Bob Scowcroft, director of the Organic Farming Research Foundation, the market for organic cotton now seems to be poised for the next stage of evolutionary growth: 'Organic cotton looks to be about where organic vegetables were 15 years ago: the market was up and down and no one knew where it was headed. But after some difficult years vegetable growers learned what level of production the market could tolerate, and there has been steady growth ever since.'

Organic cotton production in the USA
NATHAN BOONE and DAVID KATZ

In 1997, the United States produced 21 per cent of the world's cotton, nearly 19 million bales, worth approximately US$6 billion. These impressive statistics, however, do not begin to calculate the ecological fallout caused by massive pesticide and fertilizer use in cotton production. More than 30 million kg of pesticides and 720 million kg of synthetic fertilizers are applied annually to US cotton fields.

Today's organic cotton production in the USA has its roots in the organic food movement that has been steadily gaining momentum over the past decades. US organic cotton production began in the late '80s in response to an emerging eco-fashion trend and a growing awareness that chemically sensitive individuals need pesticide-free products. In 1993–94, this eco-fashion market peaked, and by 1995 many large clothing companies experimenting with organic cotton had withdrawn from the market.

Table 1: US organic cotton production 1990–98: area in hectares and total fibre production (organic and transitional) in tonnes

Year	Area	Total fibre production
1990	367	262
1991	1343	972
1992	2574	1959
1993	5062	3885
1994	6472	4877
1995	10051	6750
1996	4399	3087
1997	3694	2600*
1998	4102	2900*

Source: Agricola Partners
*Estimates

The main organic fibre producing states are California and Texas with some production in New Mexico, South Carolina, Tennessee and Missouri.

The repercussions from this boom and bust cycle led to a 54 per cent reduction in US organic cotton production in 1996 over the previous year. The lack of a secure market or a specific buyer was identified as the main reason that US growers decreased organic cotton production in 1996. As a result, the US share of the world market in organic cotton has fallen from 70 per cent in the early 1990s to below 40 per cent in 1997.

Certification and labelling

Thirty states now have laws regulating organic standards including all the major cotton-producing states. At national level, organic standards and labelling recommendations were provided by the National Organic Standards Board (NOSB), which is in the process of finalizing organic certification standards. In the US, certification can be administered by a private or a state agency, each of which has its own criteria for organically grown cotton. The Texas Department of Agriculture (TDA) is the only body which has standards for handling and processing as well as production (see Chapter 6). Most organic cotton in the US is certified by the TDA, California Certified Organic Farmers (CCOF), the Organic Crop Improvement Association (OCIA) and the Quality Assurance International (QAI) (see Appendix 2 for contact addresses).

123

Economics

The average price for organic cotton lint from cotton merchants in the USA is 37 to 65 per cent higher than for conventional lint. These figures were derived by comparing the average prices of organic cotton fibre with conventional fibre in the six producing states for 1995/6.

The fibre also incurs extra costs in processing because the scale of supplies is small and hampers commercial-scale manufacturing. Processing of small amounts increases the costs at all stages: separate handling is required, labour costs are proportionately higher, lines must be closed down for cleaning to avoid contamination with conventional fibre. In addition there is a multiplier effect in costing which means that increases in costs are passed progressively on to the next stage. The following table shows the additional cost at each stage of processing for organic cotton compared with conventional (see also Chapter 7 for comparisons with other countries).

Table 2: Additional costs at each stage of processing for organic and conventional cotton fibre

Stage	Additional cost (organic over conventional)	Reasons
Organic fibre costs in the USA	37–65%	○ increased labour costs ○ mechanical weed control ○ increased fuel costs ○ lower initial yields ○ certification fees ○ higher interest rates for loans, as lenders are reluctant to give loans to organic farmers because of the perceived increased risks.
Ginning	1–2%	○ clean-out costs ○ separate handling required
Cleaning, carding, spinning and handling	20–50%	○ separate handling required ○ clean-out costs ○ smaller runs
Preparation and knitting	No additional cost reported	
Weaving	No additional cost reported	
Dyeing	Can be more expensive	○ organic dyeing can be more expensive depending on the type of dye used and its availability
Finishing	5–10%	○ additional shrinkage

Institutional developments

In 1994, the National Organic Cotton Association (NOCA) was formed by organic cotton growers, manufacturers, and retailers to respond to the diverse needs of the growing organic cotton industry. Around the same time, the California-based Sustainable Cotton Project (SCP) was formed to provide technical assistance to growers, educate the public about organic cotton and conduct on-farm research. The SCP and the Center for Agroecology and Sustainable Food Systems at the University of California have been conducting organic cotton research programmes in California, such as the Biological Agriculture System in Cotton (BASIC). The preliminary findings showed no significant differences between yields of organically and conventionally produced cotton. The research also includes analyses of economic factors, energy use, and soil factors in both systems.

In 1996, NOCA formally merged with the Organic Trade Association to create the Organic Fiber Council (OFC) (see Appendix 1).

Organic cotton in California: technical aspects of production

SEAN SWEZEY and POLLY GOLDMAN

Introduction

The California cotton production industry ranks second in cotton production in the nation with over 400 000ha of irrigated cropland. This comprises about 15 per cent of US cotton production, and about 4 per cent of the global total. Cotton is the fifth largest contributor to total farm income in the state, and regularly has a gross value of approximately $1 billion in seed and lint. The vast majority of California's cotton is produced in the San Joaquin Valley (SJV), with small areas in the Imperial, Palo Verde, and Sacramento Valleys.

Pesticide use reports indicate that California cotton is still highly dependent on synthetic pesticides, including herbicides, miticides, and insecticides. The environmental and human health impacts of cotton production are alarming. Over 8 million kg of pesticide active ingredient were sprayed in 1995 on over 400 000ha of cotton, making it the third most heavily sprayed crop in the state. Cotton ranks third among California crops for causing pesticide-related health problems. In 1996, more than 100 workers were exposed in a single incident when pesticides applied to a cotton field drifted onto farm workers in an adjacent vineyard. The aerial application of organophosphate defoliants has long been associated with increased flu-like symptoms in residents of cotton-growing communities in California. Numerous studies have documented the presence of commonly used cotton pesticides in ground and surface waters. The best documented and most visible environmental impact of pesticide use is in the toxic effect on wildlife, especially birds, fish, and other aquatic organisms.

Cotton is also a significant user of synthetic fertilizers, water, and energy, and its production leads to environmental impacts rarely considered by growers, policymakers, or the general public. However, rising costs of inputs, consumer interest, demand from the public, decreasing pesticide effectiveness due to greater resistance in target organisms, and impacts of environmental regulations, including pesticide regulatory pressures, have stimulated interest in cotton production systems which do not require conventional synthetic pesticides, fertilizers, or defoliants as inputs.

Research on reducing the chemical inputs for cotton production in California has a relatively long history compared to other crops. During the 1960s, the University of California launched a major programme of cotton research and outreach in the SJV which led to the development of the Integrated Pest Management (IPM) concept. Even though IPM concepts have led to cotton management techniques which have shown a high potential for success both ecologically and economically, these methods are not currently in wide use.

However, there has been a recent renewal of interest in the reduction of chemical use in cotton production. Although slower than the rest of the organic agricultural industry, in the past five years the production of certified organic cotton has increased, with a significant proportion of the total coming from the northern SJV. Although production dropped off nationwide in 1996, several SJV growers still devote a portion of their area to the production of organic cotton. SJV farms producing cotton are typically large, up to 1000ha, with growers committing all, or part, of their farm to organic production. Crops are also rotated in the organic system, making the area planted to organic cotton smaller than the total and usually ranging from 4 to 320ha each year. Crops rotated with organic cotton include alfalfa, dried beans, leguminous green manure crops (peas and vetch), processing tomatoes, oats, barley and wheat. In the northern SJV, grasses such as barley and wheat, and legumes such as cowpeas, garbanzos, winter peas, and vetch have been successfully managed and rotated as cover crops on a small-scale with cotton in the short winter between production seasons.

Land preparation and planting

Organic production practices typically begin by working the ground with initial tillage operations, after which a composted poultry manure is often spread and incorporated into the soil by two additional discings. This fertilizing material provides organic matter as well as nitrogen, phosphorus, potassium and other nutrients at varying levels. The volume of compost that is spread and the number of passes for each operation will vary and is dependent on soil fertility, surface residue and soil tilth. No other fertilizing materials are commonly applied prior to planting the crop, and nutrient depletion has not been detected in soils under organic management in the SJV Cotton Conversion Study. After the initial land preparation, fields are pre-irrigated once or twice in February or March depending on seasonal rainfall and water availability. In April, beds are ridged and then worked with a rolling cultivator to remove weeds and prepare for planting.

Organic cotton is direct seeded in April on single-row 1-metre (or less commonly 0.75 metre) beds (furrow to furrow). An approved Acala variety is planted. California state organic production laws and certification agency regulations stipulate the use of seed that has not been fungicide treated, if available. Organic cotton in the northern SJV is often planted less densely than conventionally grown cotton to minimize competition for sunlight, water and nutrients, to manage pests, and to encourage large per-plant boll loads.

Irrigation management

Crop irrigation is usually performed from May through to August. In a study conducted in the northern SJV by University of California researchers, total water use in 1994 was 763mm/yr for organic production, compared to 915mm/yr for conventional. The organic fields were irrigated using surface water from the local irrigation district and well water, delivered with gated aluminium or poly pipe. Alternate row irrigation was frequently employed for water conservation and pest management. Proper irrigation management is essential for cotton, and is used to balance vegetative growth with boll development, as well as to manage disease and insect populations. Excessive irrigation promotes vegetative growth over boll development. Not only is yield sacrificed but insect pests such as aphids (*Aphis gossypii*) and lygus bugs (*Lygus hesperus*) are more attracted to the lush vegetative growth that results. In contrast, too little water stresses cotton and also results in reduced boll development. Interestingly, for organic cotton, water management is commonly used as a crop preparation tool: by curtailing the supply of water earlier in the season than for conventionally grown cotton, plant desiccation for harvest is enhanced.

Pest management

Control of diseases, insects, mites, and weeds begins after planting and continues throughout the summer. Important arthropod pests found in organic cotton production systems in the Northern SJV include lygus bugs, cotton aphid and spider mites (*Tetranychus* spp.). These insects feed on plant foliage, the points at which flowers start to develop and flower buds. Although aphids are rarely an economic pest to early cotton, they excrete honeydew in the late season. Large amounts of honeydew can contaminate cotton lint, encouraging sooty mould growth. Aphid honeydew can also cause 'sticky cotton', a problem at harvest and during spinning as the sticky residue can gum up textile machinery.

The primary insect and mite pest management tools of Californian organic cotton growers are: regular and systematic monitoring of the population levels of pests, natural predators, parasites and parasitoids; and the release of biological control agents to augment those already existing in the field.

In-season monitoring of key arthropod population levels and damage to cotton fruiting parts is highly developed in California. Early insect leaf and sweep net sampling establishes the relationship between the plant development and potential pest pressure. The natural predators and parasitoids that are found in Northern SJV cotton fields include assassin bugs (Family *Reduviidae*), bigeyed bugs (*Geocoris* spp.), minute pirate bugs (*Orius* spp.) and various spiders and parasitic wasps. Green lacewing larvae (*Chrysoperla* spp.) are often released to help reduce populations of lygus bugs, mites and other soft-bodied insects such as aphids. Predatory mites and beneficial wasps of the genus *Trichogramma* have also been released to help reduce certain mite and caterpillar populations present in cotton fields. When necessary, sulphur dust is applied to fields or field edges as a natural acaricide to control mites. Other methods which can be used for lygus bug management include strip-cropping alfalfa, the preferred host of lygus bugs, and alternate-row watering practices to discourage both excessive cotton growth and lygus bugs.

Cotton growers may also maintain field strips of vegetation as beneficial insect habitats in which native predators are conserved and/or predators

*Researchers discussing organic cotton crop with the farmer, Linda
Sheppard, San Joaquin Valley, California, USA*
Credit: Dorothy Myers, Pesticide Trust

are released in the early spring. Natural enemy populations can also be
encouraged with companion crops such as strip-cut alfalfa. Released predators (e.g. lacewings, predacious mites) colonize early cotton plantings, and
predators have been observed in increased numbers in cotton plantings not
treated with insecticides when compared with conventional crops treated
with insecticides. Habitat strips can be established without sacrificing
production area by planting the strips in alleys, ditch banks, reservoir
banks, and road and stream margins.

Weed control during the cotton production year can be one of the biggest
challenges to organic production. Cotton grows slower than weeds and is
often a poor early competitor. Current methods of weed control for organically produced cotton in the SJV include a combination of mechanical
cultivation and hand hoeing. Beds are mechanically cultivated prior to planting to remove weeds. After planting, weeds are largely managed by tillage
with a cultivator that disturbs the weeds' root system and prevents re-growth.
The total number and exact timing of each cultivation is dependent on the
crop's planting date, the amount of soil moisture, the crop's stage of growth,
and the crop's ability to compete effectively with weeds. Options for weed
control in organic cotton production include using hooded rolling cultivators.
Hooded cultivators enable tillage implements to work extremely close to
small plants without covering them with soil. Other options allowed by

certification systems which have been tested include soil capping, flaming, mowing, close cultivation with wire sweeps, and alternate row irrigation. Following cotton emergence, in-row weed control can only be done by hand hoeing. Cotton is a successful competitor with weeds during the late-season growth, so weed control during this period is not so critical.

Boll maturation and harvest preparation

Prior to harvesting a conventionally grown cotton crop, synthetic growth regulators are applied to stimulate uniform boll maturation and defoliants to stimulate leaf drop. These practices increase the efficiency of mechanical harvesting and ginning. Plant leaves (trash) clog mechanical pickers, slow the harvesting, and stain cotton lint. If trash levels are high, ginning costs can increase because a greater amount of seed cotton is required to make a bale of cotton lint. In addition, stained lint reduces the grade of cotton. According to California State law, the growth regulators and defoliants used by conventional growers are not allowed for use by growers of organic cotton. Instead, organic cotton growers rely on nutrient manipulation, water management, mechanical topping, and organic acid-based foliar sprays to assist in boll maturation, boll opening, plant desiccation, and leaf drop. The nutrients most useful for these purposes are nitrogen and zinc sulphate.

While these techniques help with respect to boll maturation, plant desiccation, and leaf drop, they do not always achieve the same results as the synthetically formulated defoliants used by conventional growers. In cases where a low level of leaf drop is attained, harvests may be slowed and cotton grades reduced, with trash levels and ginning costs increased. In the 1994 harvest of the SJV Cotton Conversion Study mentioned above, some bales had elevated leaf ratings and some fibre staining. In subsequent years, organic grades and trash levels (leaf ratings) have improved considerably. Nevertheless, harvest preparation presents one of the greatest challenges for the production of organic cotton. This situation may be changing: in the 1996 production season, some organic fields attained almost complete leaf desiccation using a weak organic acid foliar spray.

Harvest and ginning

Organic cotton is mechanically harvested with spindle-type pickers by the grower, a custom operator, or a combination of the two. Harvesting takes place in October or November, depending on the seasonal conditions. Frequently organic growers perform a second harvest, as plant development, architecture and degree of plant desiccation and leaf drop may result in lower picking efficiency than for conventional production.

Harvested seed cotton is compressed near the field and transported to the cotton gin. While conventional cotton is usually harvested with a low moisture content (12 per cent or less), incomplete desiccation and leaf drop in organic fields may lead to wetter harvests. A low moisture content allows the cotton to be stored for a period of time prior to ginning without reducing quality or grade. Cotton that is harvested at a relatively high moisture content, and not ginned promptly, may result in lower grades being assigned due to lint staining by leaf trash. Low moisture content at harvest is therefore important for storage potential and is particularly important for organic production because state law and certification agency regulations require organic and conventional cotton to remain separated at the gin. Gins must clean out their machinery prior to processing organic cotton in order to meet these regulations. Consequently, a gin may not be able to gin the organic seed cotton immediately and so it must be stored.

Organic cotton growers have several ways of avoiding these problems, when faced with incomplete defoliation. First, organic cotton harvesting can begin later and finish earlier in the day than is typical for conventionally grown cotton. Second, organic growers frequently make arrangements for their cotton to be ginned immediately upon arrival. A third option—one that is currently only in the discussion stages—is to have a gin dedicated to processing organic cotton alone.

Yields and costs of production

Yields are, of course, influenced by many factors including production location, weather conditions, soil fertility, pest control, irrigation and grower management. Yields for organically produced cotton in the northern SJV range from 740 to 1420kg/ha for cotton lint, and 1250 to 1705kg/ha of cottonseed. This yield range was similar to yields from conventional cotton fields located in the same area, but is somewhat lower than the five-year range average for conventionally grown cotton in the SJV. In a sample taken in 1994, organic cotton fibre quality, in terms of fibre length, strength, and micronaire (cross-section of the cotton fibre), was consistently equivalent to that of conventional.

The total operating (or farm-gate) costs of organic cotton production in the northern SJV are about US$1725 per hectare. Operating costs do not include cash and non-cash overheads. Total costs of production, including overheads, have been calculated at US$2180 per hectare. These costs still do not include costs associated with the added risk of organic cotton production. Most of the extra operating cost of organic production can be attributed to higher labour costs, mainly for hand weeding, and to higher machinery costs, mainly due to multiple field passes at planting and harvest.

Analysis shows that the break-even point given a yield of 1.54 bales/acre is $1.15/lb (yield of 875 kg/ha; break-even $2.53/kg) for lint, and $0.154/lb ($0.34/kg) for cotton seed (after ginning costs have been deducted). In other words, using the production practices described in this chapter

131

organic growers rely on a price premium of about $0.35/lb ($0.77/kg) over conventional cotton prices in order to break even. This situation may change in the future as the production and marketing environments develop and improve.

A comparison of energy use in organic and conventional cotton production has shown a 16 per cent saving in total fossil energy use for organic cotton. Some of the value of organic production may lie in this energy saving. If prices of fossil fuels for agricultural inputs increase, conventional cotton production relative to organic production becomes more expensive.

Grower risk and marketing

Investment in organic production is risky for growers because it is never certain whether growers can sell at a price high enough to recover their costs in any one year.

Within this uncertain production and marketing environment, there are three major direct risks currently faced by organic cotton growers. First, sufficient plant desiccation and leaf drop can lead to slower harvests, multiple harvest runs through each field, decreased yields, and reduced overall cotton grades. A second, equally important production risk is that of securing a production loan on a year-to-year basis which is crucial to managing finances and bringing the crop to harvest. Market instability and the absence of established production practices can cause lenders to be hesitant about year-to-year production loans to organic growers. The third major risk is marketing or selling the crop after ginning has been completed. Commodities that are produced organically can often be sold for a premium price but supply, market competition and consumer demand all affect returns to growers. Sales contracts and price premiums are not guaranteed nor is all fibre necessarily sold at one set price. Growers are sometimes forced to sell their product on the conventional market when a market for organic cotton is not available.

In total, the risks associated with organic cotton at present are multiple and varied, and should not be underestimated. Many of these risks are associated with the new market. As the years of production, research and experience increase, leading to more effective and more standardized production methods, the market for organic cotton will stabilize and grow, which in turn will stimulate increased production of organic cotton.

Organic cotton in Texas

BRENT WISEMAN

Introduction

Active investigation into the production of organic cotton by the Texas Department of Agriculture (TDA) began in 1989 in response to inquiries from a mail-order retailer of environmentally responsible products. Many more inquiries were received during 1990 which marked the beginning of the 'eco-cotton' boom. Certified organic farmers in the 'High Plains' area of Texas indicated their interest in organic cotton production and TDA committed itself to the development of a certification programme for the 1991 season and developed the first textile processing standards in the USA (see Chapter 6).

The High Plains, Texas' major 'upland' cotton growing area, was selected for the initial pilot project because of its mild climate, lack of disease and insect pressures (especially the boll weevil), extensive use of integrated pest management techniques, close proximity to large quantities of animal manures, production and textile research facilities and water-efficient irrigation methods. (Under TDA's organic standards, there are currently limited pest management techniques which will effectively control the boll weevil to the extent that producers in boll weevil areas are actively discouraged from applying for organic certification). The TDA arranged contacts for farmers with potential buyers.

A further, and perhaps the more important, factor in the successful development of organic cotton production in Texas is easy defoliation. Early to mid-November frosts terminate cotton growth allowing natural defoliation, making machine harvesting easier. This gives Texas organic cotton a unique market advantage. Other states are experimenting with alternative defoliation technology including the use of magnesium chloride, sea salt, humic acids, weed oils or spindle-picking of green cotton with leaves on. All these methods however have serious drawbacks (see Californian case study).

The 1991 pilot programme resulted in over 200ha of cotton, producing almost 140 tonnes of certified organic cotton lint, which was used for futons, T-shirts and sportswear. About 15 tonnes was exported to Europe for cotton denim and other products. In 1992, the area was extended to 200ha of organic and 600ha in transition to organic; in 1993, 1200ha were organic and 4800 in transition including areas beyond the initial High Plains region; in 1994, 6000ha were organic and 4800 in transition. Poor weather in 1995 reduced the crop and only 3200ha of organic cotton was harvested. Further reductions occurred in 1996 because producers were planting other crops in rotation, such as peanuts, sesame, soybeans, maize, grain sorghum and wheat. In 1997, there was an increase in overall organic production with the cotton area remaining stable and other food crops expanding.

The Texas Organic Cotton Marketing Co-operative (TOCMC)

LaRHEA PEPPER and LYNDA GROSE

Several cotton growers in the High Plains area of Texas began converting to organic in the early 1990s. When a contract to sell their organic cotton fell through, one farming family, the Peppers, decided to deal directly with the spinning mill. In the United States, as in most other countries, a cotton farmer is normally not involved with the rest of the textile industry. American farmers typically sell their crops to a broker, who pays the farmer the US government loan price, and then sells the fibre to the mill agent at the highest possible price, thus making a good profit. The Peppers took a risk and decided to have their cotton processed into denim, which they then had to sell. Although they did find a market for the denim, they realized that to make their organic cotton successful they would have to create their own products and markets. They formed their own manufacturing company, 'Cotton Plus'.

The limited market for organic products meant that all the organic farmers in the area were in competition with each other in a new and volatile market. As a response to this problem and building on an existing growers' association which had been started to provide educational support, 40 farming families came together to form TOCMC in 1991. The Pepper's new company, Cotton Plus, was designated the marketing arm of the co-op. During the following years TOCMC and Cotton Plus built new relationships with mills and textile companies. As farmers became drawn into marketing decisions, they came to understand the need to create products, develop markets and promote their activities thus working in a more integrated way further up the chain. Trust amongst all the parties had to be built up by personal contact to develop good working relationships so that those involved were no longer adversaries but could work together to solve problems. A large amount of voluntary work has gone into the research, development and marketing of products made from organic cotton, in full co-operation with various mills.

Rather than each farmer selling the crop to a cotton broker, TOCMC pools all the fibre from the co-operative, pays the farmers on delivery the US Government loan price, and then markets the fibre at the highest price they can obtain. Extra profits above the US loan price are then distributed to co-op members at the end of the season. Each farmer is paid a percentage of the extra profits equivalent to the amount of fibre he or she contributed to the pool.

There are other benefits derived from working co-operatively. Through being more involved in the complete supply chain within the industry, TOCMC is discovering better ways of working, some of them based on information to which a farmer would not normally have access. The pooling system has provided a greater bulk supply of fibre to the mill. This has led to increased quality of the finished yarn in two ways: it has allowed more blending options and thus alleviated spinning problems associated with stickiness (caused by aphids) and it has also provided a greater consistency of fibre quality. Farmers are linked to each other financially through the pool and so they tend to share information with each other on successful organic farming methods. This has led to an overall increase in yields for the whole co-op, which has, in turn, increased income for the farmers and decreased costs to the industry. Normally, a mill takes the cotton fibre from the broker at time of purchase and holds it in storage until production spinning begins. A charge is incurred by the mill for warehouse storage. Working directly with the mill, TOCMC learned of this situation and now offers the service of holding the cotton until the mill is ready to spin. This offsets the carrying costs for the mill, whilst maintaining the actual value of the fibre with the farmer.

Having developed products which use the medium and better grades of cotton fibre, Cotton Plus has recently started to concentrate on developing products which use lower grade, shorter staple and left-over cotton not suitable for clothing. Organic Essentials, a joint venture between the farmers and TOCMC, has developed a line of personal and feminine care products, which uses shorter, lower grade cotton.

Overall, working together has allowed the members of TOCMC to sell more organic cotton at higher prices. However, because TOCMC was initially paying only US loan value to farmers for their cotton, some growers have been forced to drop out of the co-operative: they simply could not afford to wait several months before receiving full payment. TOCMC has some 27 families involved in producing over 550 tonnes of cotton per year. Initial hard work and dedication is now bringing results. The farmers' own line of 30 different woven fabrics and other items is marketed successfully through Cotton Plus which now also has relationships with two mills to produce knitted and woven fabrics. In addition, it represents and distributes organic cotton products for one mill and acts as a 'converter' (turning raw fibre into the final product for sale to wholesalers or retailers) for the other.

The farmers see themselves as more than just producers of raw material but as partners in an industry where risks and hard work can bring higher rewards. It is difficult for farmers who have been working for themselves all their lives to learn to work co-operatively, but people in TOCMC are deeply committed to the organic movement and are therefore highly motivated. The farmers have become business partners in the organic cotton chain rather than simply producers of raw materials.

10
Peru

LUIS GOMERO, PER JIBORN, ALFONSO LIZÁRRAGA,
CÉSAR MORÁN, ROBERTO UGÁS and
JAMES M. VREELAND Jnr

Introduction

Cotton production in Peru is extremely diverse and complex. It is grown in regions of highly contrasting climate and ecology with differing cultural and historical backgrounds. Coastal desert farms of plantation scale contrast with tiny holdings of indigenous farmers who practise slash-and-burn agriculture in the high tropical forest regions of the Amazon Basin in eastern Peru.

Peru has several major advantages which could contribute to expanded organic cotton production. The Andean region, and principally Peru, has generally been regarded as the centre of origin of the cotton species *Gossypium barbadense*, which includes the finest, longest-staple cotton produced commercially today (i.e. Pima, Egyptian and Sea Island). These varieties are available for adaptation to organic farming programmes and there is also a range of naturally pigmented cottons suitable for organic production (see Chapter 5). Cotton can be planted and harvested throughout the year in different regions, with the main harvests taking place between April and September, in advance of those of the northern hemisphere. Many farmers have substantial knowledge and experience of cotton production systems and indigenous and traditional peasant farming technologies survive that are often largely or wholly organic.

In 1997/8, it is estimated that organic cotton grown in Peru totalled 2–3000ha. with a total crop of organic cotton fibre around 1500 tonnes. However, as in other countries, accurate figures are hard to obtain as new projects are being developed which, to date, have given little indication of their capacity.

Organic cotton in the Cañete Valley of the Peruvian coast

CÉSAR MORÁN, ROBERTO UGÁS, ALFONSO LIZÁRRAGA and
LUIS GOMERO

The Cañete Valley has two advantages for commercial agriculture: it is on the Pan-American Highway and accessible to Peru's main port and airport,

El Callao, and there is a year-round water supply from the Cañete River. Soils are fertile, although highly variable, and a wide variety of crops are grown such as cotton, maize, potato, sweet potato and beans. In the 1950s it seemed likely that cotton production would no longer be ecologically or economically feasible in this area. Pest outbreaks in the monoculture system required increasingly heavy pesticide use resulting in growing resistance to major pesticides. Eventually a successful programme of IPM was introduced, demonstrating to farmers the value of basing pesticide use on pest scouting and threshold levels, and stressing the value of soil organic matter and biological pest control.

Cotton grown on the Peruvian Coast now receives lower quantities of pesticides than other major economic crops and less than in many other important cotton-growing regions in the world. Two or three sprays per season is normal compared with, for example, 40 to 50 per season in Nicaragua in the 1980s. It is not surprising, therefore, that Cañete and nearby cotton-growing valleys have been at the centre of organic cotton development in Peru.

Cotton is the most heavily regulated crop in the country, with precise rules for planting and harvesting dates, and seed requirements. Enforcement of these regulations has been greatly strengthened in recent years through penalties. Planting and harvesting dates are determined by law, climate and, in some areas, water availability. Local traditional knowledge and modern technologies (certified seed, chemical inputs, machinery) are combined in order to obtain high yields and good quality. One of the challenges for organic farmers is to overcome the legal requirement to lower pest pressures by burning the huge amounts of biomass left in the

The organic cotton harvest in Peru
Credit: Courtesy of Verner Frang AB. Photo by Stephan Bergman

field after harvest. Recycling nutrients—so necessary in the organic system—is impossible because all residues must be burnt, leaving little organic matter in the fields. The law also requires all ginning residues to be incinerated. Trials are needed for machinery to chop the cotton stems, and for ploughs better suited to organic soils.

The organic rotation

In the organic system, cotton is often intercropped with maize, some rows of which act as a reservoir of natural pest predators, and rotated with a limited, not always profitable, number of winter crops with a short-growing season, like green beans or fodder maize. In organic production it is essential to grow profitable crops throughout the rotation to recoup losses from the conversion period and retain profitability. There are, however, few alternative organic rotation crops as there is no significant local market for the produce. In the short-term, medicinal plants or some vegetables may be grown for processing. Crop rotation is also limited by the small areas which farmers have at their disposal, which restricts their opportunities to select different fields. In many cases monocultures (cotton–cotton rotations) with a clean field period, are the norm.

138

Cotton seed

The production of cotton seed is a well-established practice in Peru. All seed is locally produced and regulations state that seed has to be treated with 'protective-pesticides' prescribed by the national phytosanitary service (SENASA) against damping-off and cutworms. Farmers usually sow one hectare of cotton with around 45kg of seed, both for organic and conventional crops.

The availability of organic cotton seed is an issue for organic farmers who currently use untreated conventional seed. Ginneries are not permitted to return seed extracted from their seed cotton to organic farmers. Future certification programmes are likely to impose conditions, setting a time limit for full use of organic seed, yet most technicians and farmers seem unaware of this. Organic seed certification should be integrated into normal seed certification schemes. One solution would be to have seed production programmes organized by the farmers themselves, with adequate technical assistance.

Soil fertility

In the central coastal area, soil organic matter is frequently deficient and there are often salinity problems. Organic growers apply manure at considerably higher rates than conventional growers. The fields are fertilized with a mixture of one-third chicken manure and two-thirds 'guano' or sea bird droppings, a readily available local source of organic fertilizer. They may also use humus to complement the standard fertilization applied. Organic farmers may use some sources of natural fertilizers like rock phosphate or rock potash, sometimes mixed with various forms of organic matter.

Some technicians argue for on-site composting, but regulations specifically forbid composting cotton residues in the coastal region. There has as yet been no effective research on composting. Although green manuring is a promising technology being trialled in one project in Cañete, it is likely that farmers will be reluctant to grow green manure crops unless their cost is off-set by higher returns from organic cotton. Moreover, increased organic cotton yields following a green manure may not compensate for the loss of a rotation crop that could have been sold. Mixed arable farming/livestock systems may be a long-term solution but there is little tradition of mixed operations. Other alternatives for recycling organic matter, such as composting or vermiculture are likely to be too labour intensive.

Pest control

Preventive pest control measures are considered the norm rather than the exception in both organic and conventional cotton fields. These include a clean field period, setting specific planting and harvesting periods for each valley, using certified seed, adequate nutrient and irrigation management, and controlling seed cotton transport from one valley to another. Although not always fully implemented, these measures are a good basis for pest control. Organic cotton growers may need formulations of *Bacillus thuringiensis (Bt)*, rotenone, natural oils, pheromones, copper sulphate, sulphur, molasses, and may use parasitic wasps (*Trichogramma* spp). Rearing of *Trichogramma* is a common practice in the area. In addition, most organic and many conventional growers contract labour to hand-pick infested flower buds and bolls. Organic cotton producers in Cañete do not believe that pest and disease control is the major limiting factor. However, organic pest control is often merely seen as substituting inputs and the holistic vision of organic farming systems may not yet be fully understood.

In general, farmers producing organic cotton in the Cañete valley spend less money on fertilization and pest control than their conventional counterparts, as Table 1 shows. Other studies (see Chapter 7) indicate total production costs of organic cotton are higher.

Table 1: Cost comparison of fertilizer and pesticide use between organic and conventionally grown cotton in Cañete valley, Peru

	Organic cotton (US$) per ha	Conventional (US$) per ha
Pest management	65.42	100.00
Fertilization	154.42	249.00
TOTAL:	219.84	349.00

Source: Luis Gomero

Irrigation

All cotton on the coast is irrigated, either with water from rivers (very seasonal because it depends on rains in the Andes) or with groundwater from wells. The producers of organic cotton in Cañete clean their fields in June, incorporating into the soil or eliminating the crop residues of the former crop. Then they carry out a first, heavy irrigation of the field. They sow the area and establish an optimum water supply to the crop, irrigating in short time lapses and with small amounts of water. Farmers in the area tend to over-irrigate, which prolongs the growing season (from a minimum of 6.5 months up to 9 months), increases pest and disease problems, makes harvesting more difficult and affects fibre quality. New laws promoting private sector participation in irrigation water management are, however, bound to alter the price of water. Well-established organic fields with more soil organic matter, better water-holding capacity, and improved root growth may save money by reducing water use. Irrigating at the right time, and using the right quantity of water is a very important factor in the control and management of organic cotton fields.

Harvest and yields

Cotton is picked and put into cotton bags and transported to a collection point where primary selection is made, removing plant debris and insect-stained bolls. Then seed cotton is stuffed in a cotton canvas sack tied with cotton cord and transported to the ginnery. There is widespread awareness of the dangers of using jute or polypropylene bags to collect seed cotton. To avoid fibre contamination the buyer often provides the cotton picking bags and canvas.

Labour is needed for 100–130 days to produce a cotton crop, either organic or conventional, more than half of this for harvesting. Small farmers generally use family labour and may need to hire additional labour which can be difficult in the peak harvesting season.

Microclimate, soil fertility differences, farm size, investment capacity, and so on all affect cotton yields. According to official figures, the average national cotton fibre yield is 598kg/ha. In Cañete, however, minimum fibre yields fluctuate around 920kg/ha, with some intensive conventional fields producing 1840kg/ha or more. Organic cotton fibre yields are estimated by Verner Frang AB/TUSA to average 1100kg/ha. in the Cañete valley, which is approximately 10–15 per cent lower than conventional.

Lower yields are generally linked to problems with soil fertility. Pests and diseases are not considered to be the major limiting factor for the development of successful organic production in the Peruvian coast. With adequate soil fertility management, organic cotton could yield as much as conventional cotton under similar farming systems and levels of investment. This appears to be a major difference between this region and others in the world and underlines the potential for organic cotton production in Peru.

Purchasing and prices

Farmgate prices are variable, but not as much as with other crops, as cotton is a major crop and several agents intervene in price regulation. For example, in July 1996 the Ministry of Agriculture decided to fix a price and buy 'ecological' (in this case naturally pigmented) cotton produced on around 5000 hectares in the Huallaga area, as a way of promoting crops that could replace coca. In recent years, however, cotton prices fluctuated according to the market situation.

In the 1995/6 growing season, prices paid to farmers in Cañete for seed cotton were about US$0.65/kg, but in the previous season they went up to US$1.02/kg. The organic premium usually fluctuates between 10 and 20 per cent, but in years of higher price for conventional cotton, farmers may sell their cotton to the conventional market. This has happened in the past but, as ginneries or buyers become increasingly involved in other steps of the organic process such as giving technical assistance or facilitating the purchase of inputs, selling as conventional is less likely. In recent years with economic liberalization, the Peruvian cotton market has been flooded with competing poor-quality Korean and Chinese cotton fibre and textiles, which have affected the profitability of cotton growers and processors. However, prices for Peruvian cotton remain high on account of its high quality and, in 1997, a shortage of domestic cotton fibre.

Ginning and spinning

Relations between growers and buyers (ginneries and textile mills) in organic cotton projects are well-established. These companies not only buy the fibre but may also provide technical assistance and credit to finance the crop. This is especially important since the closure of the government Agricultural Bank and as private banks are reluctant to provide funds to small farmers.

Organic seed cotton must be stored separately and ginning equipment should be thoroughly cleaned before processing organic cotton. This process needs to be improved in some Peruvian ginneries where sometimes the first run of organic cotton is sold as conventional because of contamination from conventional cotton. When the ginnery itself buys seed cotton in the field, a normal practice, the farm-gate price of seed cotton is equal to the ginnery entry price. Special arrangements are made by the few ginneries and mills that process organic cotton. Ginning turnout is about 40 per cent fibre. The seed is sold for oil extraction, which provides most of the cooking oil used in the country. Presently there is no market for organic cotton seed nor for organic cotton seed oil, but it is possible that one could be found or created in Europe or the USA.

Spinning organic is similar to conventional cotton, except for the cleaning of equipment and the restrictions on the chemicals allowed. In Peru, around 90 per cent of the organic yarn produced is off-white, and only 10 per cent white (bleached). For white yarn the fibre is treated with peroxide. Upon request of the buyer, sodium chlorite could also be used. For the general public, organic cotton is associated with the off-white colour, which is why there is a low percentage of white cotton. If mercerizing is requested, caustic soda is used, plus a humidifying treatment. To wash out the soda, warm and cold water is used and an acid to neutralize the remaining traces.

Some cotton processors, such as FIJESA for example, are concerned with the environmental aspects of their activities. This mill has been inspected for organic certification and is now working on a funding scheme for small growers in Cañete, in co-operation with a local organization involved in rural development (Instituto Rurale Valle Grande). They are working with low-impact dyes, trying to treat all the mill effluents and taking into consideration the need for decent wages for workers. Moreover, they consider that sustainable cotton growing and processing should involve the whole cotton sector—a very positive approach.

The Peruvian firm, Textiles Unidas S.A. (TUSA) has processed cotton from a total of about 1000ha, from Cañete and the neighbouring Chincha Valleys, in the past three years. The cotton fibre is taken from TUSA to Trutex in Trujillo, 600km north of Lima, to be spun into yarn. It is certified by KRAV and exported to Verner Frang in Sweden for manufacture into socks, underwear and other items under the trade name 'White Cotton'. In 1998, Verner Frang AB, in co-operation with various Peruvian partners, produced organic cotton on close to 1100ha, the total crop was estimated to be in the region of 700 tonnes of organic cotton fibre.

Table 2: Organic cotton fibre: area and yields under the Verner Frang/TUSA Programme, Cañete Valley, Peru

Year	Area in ha	Production in tonnes
1993/4	330	310
1994/5	380	410
1995/6	380	410
1996/7	340	420

Source: Per Jiborn

As in other parts of the world, the impact of the chemical effluents produced by textile mills should be considered as the organic industry grows. This is something rarely taken into consideration by the regulations, or enforced by the authorities. At present, most effluents go directly into the urban sewage system. Little research is carried out in Peru on these issues. Solutions are most likely to be imported from Europe or other areas with more resources for industrial research.

Inspection and certification

At present, monitoring the growers' compliance with organic standards is done by the ginnery, which holds the organic certificate. This was a useful step at the start of the projects but does little to empower small farmers. Organic cotton in Peru has been certified by foreign certification programmes (OCIA, SKAL, KRAV, FVO). Recently, however, a local certifier (INKACERT) has been set up and is becoming involved in this process.

Although most certifiers are familiar with certification procedures they are not necessarily familiar with the dynamics of cotton production in Peru.

143

This applies in particular to foreign certifiers. As with any organic crop, organic cotton requires proper record-keeping and proper separation in production and storage. Those involved in the system in Peru do not consider these points to be particularly difficult. They do, however, consider that the monitoring and extension activities (ginneries controlling compliance of individual farmers, for example) place an enormous burden on them. This situation is a reflection of the lack of trust between farmers and buyers. Many farmers and processors take the view that 'organic' is simply another way to sell their cotton and they may switch back to conventional production if the price is right. This approach to organic production will not foster a change in agricultural systems in the longer term.

Export

A general decline in the Peruvian industrial sector is having a significant effect on the textile and manufacturing sectors, mainly because of the rapid increase in imports of cheap Asian textiles. In this context, the small market for organic cotton can do little to challenge or reverse the situation. Such competition is a worrying trend and raises broad issues about the competitiveness of environmentally responsible products in general on world markets. There are no official records of Peruvian certified organic cotton exports. Since the terms 'organic' or 'ecological' are frequently abused, naturally pigmented cotton fibre or poorly processed white fibre may be presented as organic in the domestic market and part of this may be exported as well. Without proper organic certification the integrity of the production and processing system cannot be guaranteed.

Peruvian organic cotton is exported as yarn, although, it is partly used to manufacture some knitted fabrics or garments. FIJESA has been spinning naturally pigmented cotton for Verner Frang AB and for Pakucho Pax. Pakucho Pax also exports yarns and garments made with naturally pigmented cotton, and is in the initial stages of work with organic Tangüis cotton in Arequipa, southern Peru.

The conversion issue

Organic cotton in Peru is a minor activity and no reliable comparison with the conventional sector can be made at present. A promising start has been made and further development will depend on the size of the export market and on the development of a local market. The only properly documented experience of research into conversion to organic cotton indicates that the production has not yet stabilized after four years. There is a perception that cotton is traditionally an 'organic' crop in Peru. This idea arises from the misconception that organic is simply a system which is free of synthetic chemical inputs. It is true that less chemicals are used on cotton, at least in the central coast, than most other crops of major economic importance but this does not in itself make it organic.

Major conversion to organic cotton throughout the Cañete valley would have a considerable effect on all Peruvian agriculture not only by reducing the amount of pesticides used on this important crop and limiting farmers' exposure to these substances, but also by improving knowledge of other aspects such as certification and local marketing of organic products. But this hypothetical conversion would probably reduce the total cotton output of the valley for several years. Up to now, some organic cotton fields in Cañete are showing that fertilizer use can be substantially reduced if not completely replaced in later stages by organic fertilizers and green manures, as well as by profitable crop rotations. An important question is whether enough manure would be available at affordable prices. At the same time, organic growers could contribute to the management of uncultivated areas, irrigation systems and even perhaps help establish more successful biological control at the watershed level. At this level, conversion to organic agriculture cannot be dependent on one major crop alone and should include several other crops of economic importance which at present rely heavily on synthetic inputs.

Training

Since 1994, the Red de Acción en Alternativas al uso de Agroquímicos (RAAA—the Pesticides Action Network (PAN) Regional Co-ordinator for Latin America), has been collaborating with TUSA and Verner Frang AB to carry out research, training and awareness-raising on the problems of chemically intensive cotton production and the need for, and viability of, organic alternatives in the Cañete valley. The project is supported by the Swedish Society for Nature Conservation and is part of the RAAA strategy to encourage the technical conversion in agriculture as the basis of sustainable agricultural systems.

The training element, carried out by RAAA with farmers and students, takes a broad approach and includes the basic principles of ecological agriculture, the importance of organic cotton for Cañete and the techniques which may be applied in crop production. Booklets for students and teachers have been produced as part of the project. One of the objectives is to evaluate the importance of cotton for the Cañete farmers and to explain to students the role this crop plays in the general development of the area. This collaboration between a local NGO and a commercial organic cotton project has produced good results in terms of raising awareness of the effects of chemically intensive agriculture and the need for alternatives, set in the context of local environmental action. Such collaboration can be mutually beneficial and lessons learned may be applicable in other situations.

145

Social impact

Although there are organizations and companies struggling to raise the standards of living of farmers and industrial workers, the organic movement is as yet too small to have much social impact. Labour conditions, child labour and gender issues are at present no different in organic and conventional cotton production systems. Social injustice cannot be resolved by organic agriculture but the issues can start to be addressed through, for example, the adoption of IFOAM guidelines containing social standards, or the establishment of fair trade principles. The organic projects are already showing that marketing these products, both in domestic and foreign markets, can benefit small farmers.

11
India

ALEXANDER DANIEL, BO VAN ELZAKKER and
TADEU CALDAS

Although India ranks first in the world in area under conventional cotton cultivation, estimated at about 8.8 million hectares in 1997, it only ranks third in production, due to low yields. In 1997, the average yield in India was 294kg/ha lint compared to 1000kg/ha in China, the largest producer, and 762kg/ha in the USA. Total Indian production is around 2.2 million tonnes per year. Cotton is grown in almost all states, with Punjab, Gujarat, Haryana and Maharashtra accounting for about 64 per cent of the total area under cotton. Punjab has the largest area under cotton cultivation. Productivity is higher in the states of Punjab, Haryana and Rajasthan, due to irrigation and better cropping practices. In Maharashtra, by comparison, almost all the cotton is rainfed.

The Indian textile industry is the country's second largest sector next to agriculture, providing direct and indirect employment to more than 50 million people and accounting for over 20 per cent of the total industrial output. As a proportion of exports, 38 per cent of the total value is contributed by textiles, of which about 65 per cent is cotton.

Historical background

India is considered by many people not only to be the birthplace of cotton cultivation but also of the textile industry, with a history going back to 4000 BC. Cotton was traditionally grown as a rainfed crop in India, intercropped with lentils and other food crops.

The early cotton varieties, derived from the Roji plant, are known as 'desi' cotton and belong to the *Gossypium arboreum* and *G. herbaceum* species. In India, at present, *desi* varieties such as 'Eknath', 'Namdeo', 'Savita', 'O-18', 'LRK-516' and 'NH-452' are grown. There are many varieties of *desi* cotton which are well adapted to the agroclimatic conditions of the country, including varieties suitable for heavy rainfall areas like Assam and the North East, as well as drought-prone areas. *Desi* varieties also include naturally pigmented varieties such as the creamy yellow cotton of the North East and the pink *yerra pethi* of east Godavari. The *desi* varieties differ from the Western varieties, *G. hirsutum*, *G. barbadense* and *G. peruvianum*, in their chromosome structure.

The British arrival in India heralded the decline of the traditional textile industry. The colonization of India and the industrial revolution in Europe in the eighteenth century crushed the traditional processing industry. The invention of the spinning jenny, the spinning mule and the powerloom increased the efficiency of the industry and the demand for cotton lint from India, leading to a shortage for the domestic industry.

The handloom textile sector was however revived by the Swadeshi movements popularized by Gandhi in the 1940s, which aimed for rural self-sufficiency in textiles. The decentralized sector grew rapidly after independence in 1947 and especially after 1980. The sector, which had a 21 per cent share of the total production in 1951, now controls 94 per cent of production. Decentralized, small-scale operations are thus much more important than the centralized, large-scale factories.

The American cotton varieties, widely introduced into India during the late nineteenth and early twentieth century were heralded for their high-yield potential, but had many disadvantages. The traditional *desi* varieties can withstand long periods without rainfall unlike the American varieties, which are thus more prone to crop failure. The American varieties became popular in pockets of good, irrigated land, giving rise to monoculture. Monoculturing and frequent irrigation led to increases in pest infestation and the consequent widespread use of synthetic pesticides. Pesticide use is heavy on the cotton crop, with 55 per cent of the total pesticides used being applied to crops occupying only 5 per cent of the land. Cotton cultivation thus became the enterprise of the rich who could afford the cost of irrigation and pesticides. All over India, the practice of inter-cropping with other food crops declined and poor and marginal farmers slowly abandoned the traditional methods of cotton cultivation.

During 1992–93, about 40 per cent of the production was extra-long staple, 10 per cent long staple, 45 per cent medium and superior medium staple and 5 per cent short staple. Government policy has squeezed out many small farmers growing short-staple varieties in small and marginal holdings, leading to a decline in area under short-staple varieties.

Currently, the cotton sector in India operates in a very haphazard way and reforms are needed for any long-term growth to occur. Production is stagnant at around 2.2 million tonnes per annum and domestic consumption is outpacing domestic production. In spite of the steady rise in prices over the last two years, export restrictions are held responsible for the low prices of raw cotton in comparison with world prices.

The potential to improve production in the rainfed areas is enormous, and doubling of the current yield could make the country the largest cotton producer in the world. As much as 70 per cent of the total cotton area is rainfed and massive improvements could be achieved by focusing on the cotton growers who cannot afford expensive inputs. These farmers should have access to good-quality seed material and fertilization and appropriate pest management strategies. Low yields are also linked to the high incidence of pests, mainly due to the monoculture of cotton in the irrigated areas.

Organic cotton being transported to the gin, the Maikaal project, India
Credit: Christine Baerlocher, WWF Switzerland

Organic production

In India, the production of certified organic cotton and organic manufactured products at present constitutes only a minute proportion of total cotton and textile production. The production of certified organic raw cotton in India was estimated to be 272 tonnes in 1994–95, mainly produced in the states of Madhya Pradesh and Maharashtra. Latest indications are that the level of certified organic cotton fibre production is in the region of 1000 tonnes.

In Madhya Pradesh, the Maikaal project, based near Indore, covers an area of 2200 hectares with 800 farmers involved in the programme. The farmers receive a 20–25 per cent premium for their organic cotton crops and a social fund is maintained for meeting crop failures and community needs.

In Maharashtra, since 1995, 135 farmers are involved in the Vidharba Organic Farmers Association (VOFA), with 1200 hectares in the Vidharba region under organic cotton. A new project (Ginni Project) has also recently been established in the region.

These projects show the potential for organic cotton projects in India, both in terms of production and profitability. In Vidharba, for example, although yields are 25 per cent lower, costs per hectare are considerably reduced to a level of approximately 80 per cent of conventional costs which includes the cost of inspection and certification. In an experimental project in Gujarat (which has been discontinued) production costs for organic cotton were 60 per cent of those in conventional production. Similarly in the Maikaal project, production costs are 37 per cent lower than in the conventional system.

Table 1: Summary of Organic Cotton production in India

	Year	Farmers	Area (in ha)	Output of fibre (tonnes)	Av. yield of fibre (kg/ha) fibre	Premium paid
Maikaal	1997	800	2200	900	400	>20%
VOFA	1995	135	1200	105	200	25–50%

Organic farming in Madhya Pradesh: the Maikaal project

An initial feasibility study for an organic cotton project in Madhya Pradesh was carried out in 1992. In 1992/3 a 4ha trial was carried out. In the second year 240ha were turned over to organic production. In 1997, organic production was carried out by 800 farmers, working 2200ha of land and producing 900 tonnes of fibre, with 1200ha of organic food produced for the local market. Crops included wheat, mung, groundnut, pigeonpea, cowpea, maize, sorghum, millet, chilli pepper, soybeans, banana and sugar cane (see Chapter 7 for a discussion of economic aspects of the project).

The project covers 85 villages in a 50km diameter area. A team of 10 extension workers are being trained to facilitate the process at the farmer level and to adopt a more participatory approach to technical developments. Dialogue amongst the farmers continues throughout the season, up to the final evaluation of the year and the discussion on the necessary improvements regarding prices, grading system, transport and supply of inputs, farming techniques, cost-benefit analysis, experimentation, etc. The system is therefore adjusted to farmers' needs and their experiences and comments are fed into the chain. Extra resources can be made available and premium prices can be evaluated against fluctuations in yields and production costs.

As the project has progressed, many technical hurdles have been overcome. Farmers have become aware of the soil-fertility resources available for short- and long-term nutrient needs (bio-fertilizers for seed dressing, Azotobacter, Azospirillum and Phosphorus Solubilizing Bacteria (PSB)) and liquid fertilizers for foliar sprays, oilcakes, compost and locally made biodynamic preparations. As a consequence yields have increased and with them the average income.

Certain sucking pests such as aphids and whitefly are no longer a problem, since plant nutrition is more balanced, and the population of natural predators, such as the green lacewing and ladybird beetles, have increased many times. In fact the biological regeneration of the area has become a very clear indicator of the organic quality of the fields, as well as being a gift from organic farmers to their conventional neighbours. Numbers of fruit- and fibre-damaging species have been kept relatively low due to a combination of proper population monitoring, trapping of male moths with sexual pheromones, the use of local botanical repellents and local or manufactured botanical pesticides. Releases of artificially reared entomoparasites such as *Trichogramma* wasps and *Chrysoperla carnea* have been stopped. Species-specific entomopathogens, such as Nuclear Polyhedrosis Virus (NPV), or those which are more wide-ranging, such as *Bacillus thuringiensis,* have been released whenever the presence of bollworms goes beyond economic threshold levels. Every year evaluations are made to assess the cost-effectiveness of each measure.

Remei AG: The India–Switzerland connection
The Swiss yarn and textile company Remei was instrumental in setting up the Maikaal project in India. Initially the organic cotton, certified by the Swiss Institute for Market Ecology (IMO), was only sold as yarn, but since 1995 the firm has begun to market its own clothing collection 'bioRe'. In 1993 a spinning mill, Maikaal Fibres, was established to assure farmers guaranteed sales.

Certification by IMO is gradually being extended along the production and processing line. The cotton gin and spinning mill are subject to certification, and successive processing phases are also being integrated into the system.

Remei markets the Maikaal cotton products in Europe. The first garments made with organic cotton from the project were available in Switzerland in 1995. In 1997, outlets were further expanded when the German mail-order company, Otto-Versand, began to include clothes from the bioRe range.

The method of production has been made transparent at the point of sale. The Coop-Schweiz, a consumer co-operative and the second largest retailer in Switzerland, has, for example, provided information on the source of the cotton for its customers, so allowing the 'face' of the producer to be visible and enabling the consumer to make an informed choice.

Remei calculates that production costs of textiles made from organic cotton are approximately 25 per cent higher than comparable products from conventional cotton. This is due to the raw material being more expensive, the yields may be less and certification needs to be financed. Environmentally responsible dyes also cost more than conventional ones. However, costs are lowered through the supplier–customer chain, because each partner in the chain waives short-term maximization of profits in favour of long-term co-operation. Therefore, bioRe clothing is only slightly more expensive than comparable products produced conventionally and are thus affordable by a broad section of consumers (see Chapter 7).

Organic farming in Maharashtra: Vidharba Organic Farmers Association (VOFA)

Prakruti, a voluntary organization promoting organic farming in the Vidharba cotton-growing area of Maharashtra, and the Environmental Protection Encouragement Agency (EPEA) based in Hamburg have been concerned about the intensive use of pesticides in cotton cultivation for some years. In 1994, with the help of Prakruti, the organic farmers in the region formed themselves into an association, VOFA, and decided to embark on an organic cotton project. Farmers from five districts (Nagpur, Wardha, Yavatmal, Amravati and Akola) took part in the first project meeting, resulting in 135 farmers committing 1200ha to the project — an average of almost 9ha per farmer. Cultivation began in May 1995, and the first 105 tonnes of certified cotton fibre was produced in 1995/6.

In most of the Vidharba region, cotton production, which is mainly of the long-stapled variety, is rainfed. There are extremes of temperature and a long dry season precludes sowing between January and May. The organic cotton crop is sown by dibbling, at spaces of 90cm × 90cm. Strip cropping — alternating 1–2 lines of pigeonpea with 6–12 lines of cotton — is practised on most of the VOFA farms. Sesame and sorghum and other crops are intercropped. To thin the seed coating and promote germination, seeds are soaked in water, wrapped in cloth and left overnight. Seeds are then dried in the sun before sowing. The roots of the cotton plant grow deep into the soil which must be loose and aerated by harrowing 2–3 times per season.

The application of compost is crucial to the success of the organic crop. Crop residues are collected, composted and applied at rates of 16 tonnes per hectare, before the last harrowing. Where sunhemp, sesame, bulrush millet and cowpea are intercropped, they are ploughed in after 30–40 days. The biomass, at about 12 to 14 tonnes/ha, decomposes in about 15 days during the monsoon, generating an estimated 2500kg dry weight of humus per hectare. Biofertilizers, containing phosphate-solubilizing micro-organisms (phosphatica), are applied at the rate of 5kg per hectare. Other micro-organisms, including the nitrogen-fixing bacteria Azotobacter and Azospirillum, are applied at the rate of 5kg/ha. Vermicompost, produced by earthworms which turn organic wastes into compost, is applied to tracts that have sufficient irrigation facilities in quantities of about 5 tonnes/ha. Otherwise, manuring is done by applying locally available cow, goat and chicken manure. If supplies of compost and manure are insufficient, farmers buy in extra, and animal herds are rented from nomads from Rajastan which stay overnight in the fields to provide their manure after the cotton harvest.

In the irrigated areas, 3–4 light irrigations are usually applied. The first irrigation is carried out 10–12 days after sowing. The subsequent irrigations are completed at intervals of 15–20 days. The first manual weeding takes place 25–30 days after sowing. After this, 2 or 3 subsequent weedings are carried out using a traditional wooden hoe at intervals of 30–40 days. Hoeing is essential as it controls the growth of weeds, improves soil aeration and moisture conservation.

On the conventional farms, synthetic pesticides are the main method of pest control management, apart from the management of bollworm, which is generally controlled by the parasitic wasp *Trichogramma* spp. Pests such as aphids, jassids, bollworms and whiteflies, however, still account for about 20 per cent of losses in conventional cotton crops. Crop protection on the organic farms is mainly against bollworms. As well as using *Trichogramma* spp., farmers release cultured *Baculovirus* (NPV) which is a viral pathogen, and green lacewing (*Chrysoperla carnea*) which is a predator. Bollworm larvae are collected from the intercropped plantings such as pigeonpea and repellent solutions for spraying are made from garlic, chilli and neem. Some pest-repellent plants such as marigold are planted around the cotton crop and sometimes pheromone traps are used. Farms which are fully organic generally have a lower incidence of pest attacks than their conventional counterparts.

Harvesting is carried out manually in three or four pickings as the cotton bolls open and mature. The yield for conventional cotton in the area is in the range of 1500kg to 2000kg/ha, which is well above the national average, while the yield for organic is around 250 to 1500kg/ha seed cotton during the first year of organic farming, with an average of 600kg/ha (200kg/ha cotton fibre).

The organic cotton produced by the farmers in the Association is certified by Agreco, an approved German control body. The team from Agreco visited the organic farms for the first time during November 1995. Farmers were interviewed, farms were inspected and various tests were conducted on the soil and plants. On the basis of these results and the period under organic cultivation, the certification was done according to three different evaluation categories — 'A', 'O' and 'U'. The 'A' category included farms with fully organic cotton from fields which had been under organic cultivation for more than two years before sowing. Farms which produced cotton organically for at least one year were in category 'U', with permission to label cotton as a product in conversion to organic agriculture. Farms which were at the beginning of the conversion period were in the category 'O' and did not have permission for organic labelling.

On request of VOFA, the Cotton Federation, which runs the Monopoly Procurement Scheme in the state of Maharashtra, provides separate ginning and processing facilities for the organic farmers to avoid their products being mixed with the conventional cotton. According to VOFA, organic farmers receive a premium of between 25 to 50 per cent on their crops.

The future of organic cotton in India

Although organic cotton production in India only accounts at present for a tiny percentage of total production, the projects currently in operation do provide an optimistic outlook for the future. Although it has been stressed earlier in this book that traditional production does not automatically represent an organic crop in waiting, there is no doubt that in areas where the worse aspects of industrialized agriculture have been avoided, the potential for conversion to organic production is great.

In general, synthetic chemicals are not used by small farmers who farm the 5 million hectares of dryland in India. If these areas were converted to organic production, India would be by far the largest organic cotton producer in the world. There seems to be a tremendous potential for improving rainfed cotton growing using organic systems and simple, cheap, locally available resources. Organic residues can be composted into a valuable fertilizer and mass-reared *Trichogramma* parasitic wasps, for example, offer a better and cheaper alternative to synthetic sprays for the control of boll-worms.

Although organic practices vary, the Indian examples show that organic cultivation has a lower cost price per hectare than conventional production, thanks to savings in the purchase of synthetic fertilizers and pesticides (see Chapter 7). Yields are, however, also lower, but if a 20 per cent premium is paid for certified organic cotton, it can provide the same gross margin per unit of land as conventional.

In cotton processing, the clear division between high labour/low capital-investment industries and high capital investment/less labour demanding industries is observed. Small-scale industries using natural dyes could benefit from the interest of the western consumer of natural textiles — but this has not yet happened probably due to the lack of market access. However, both the use of natural dyes and modern reactive dyes requires modern technology and mills which are lacking in much of India. The textile industry does not appear to keep up with international developments. The bigger factories are not geared to handle smaller orders which are required at present in the organic sector. For these reasons, most processing, and certainly the manufacture, of organic textiles is done outside India (but see earlier exceptions).

The handloom sector of India, which produces about 20 per cent of the total textile production, could play a major role with regard to organic textiles, as this is a sector in which handmade and custom-made designs of fabrics can easily be handled. The change over from conventional to organic textiles need not be a big problem in this sector given the availability

154

of traditional know-how and means of processing. Furthermore, targeting the handloom sector for organic cotton processing would strengthen employment in the rural communities.

At present organic production is aimed at the export market because so far consumers and farmers in India lack information about and awareness of the dangers of pesticides. The creation of a domestic market for organic textiles and cotton could only happen on a large scale with the general improvement of environmental health and safety education in the country.

12
Turkey

CELIK ARUOBA

Introduction

Turkey is the sixth most important cotton producer in the world after China, USA, India, Pakistan and Uzbekistan. It is expected that production will increase substantially in the near future due to increased domestic demand and the opening up of new cotton cropping areas in south-eastern Turkey. Cotton is an important cash and export crop, grown intensively in the more fertile, irrigated plains and valleys of western and southern Turkey. Production, which has been encouraged by market demand and government subsidies, has increased from 581 000 tonnes of cotton fibre in the 1992/3 season to 760 000 in the 1997/98 season.

Cotton production has been characterized by high levels of inputs, especially fertilizers. Large quantities of water are used and the leaching of fertilizer nutrients into the sea, surface water and groundwater is common. Concentration levels of nitrogen, phosphorus and potassium are not monitored in the cotton-growing areas, but the environmental effects are very noticeable in the form of algal blooms, eutrophication and chemical contamination of water and soils. The irrigated areas are good habitats for cotton pests and high levels of pesticides are used. More than 11 kinds of cotton pest are regarded as harmful, including the red spider mite (*Tetranychus* spp), the cotton bollworm (*Helicoverpa armigera*), the pink bollworm (*Pectinophora gossypiella*), aphid species and whitefly (*Bemisia tabaci*). A 'covering and coating' insecticide application strategy is used involving aerial spraying.

In the 1993/4 season, Turkish cotton prices fell behind world prices. Together with increased processing capacity, this generated higher domestic demand and Turkey has recently become a net importer of about 200 000 tonnes per year. Prices are now generally in line with international prices which, at the beginning of the 1995/6 season, were US$1.86 to US$1.94/kg.

Organic agriculture in Turkey

Organic farming in Turkey began in the 1985/6 season, initiated by the demand of a European company for organic figs. Since then, demand has grown steadily both in the variety of products and in the quantities produced. By 1996, the different products numbered about 37 with more than

4000 farmers involved in farming over 16 000ha producing over 40 000 tonnes of certified produce. Organic cotton growing started a few years later—in the late 1980s—as an extension of the existing organic farming activities and has expanded rapidly since. It is produced in two main areas: Kahramanmaras in south-east Anatolia and several areas in the Aegean region, including Salihli, Soke and Dalyan. Both European and Turkish companies are involved. Production has so far been export driven, but further expansion is expected with the creation of a domestic market. The public and the private sector are both involved and a range of institutions have been created to deal with regulation, trade promotion, the provision of advice, certification and a range of other functions related to organic agriculture.

In the so-called 'first phase' of Turkish organic agriculture up to December 1994, inspection and certification was undertaken by European agencies according to the IFOAM guidelines. SKAL and IMO were the most active certification bodies. After 18 December 1994, the EU Regulations were adopted as standard in Turkey. A certification system has been established under the Turkish Ministry of Agriculture and all foreign inspection and certification bodies must set up an office in Turkey and employ local inspectors. Five foreign certification organizations have established themselves in Turkey: IMO, SKAL, INAC, Ecocert and Bio Control Systems (BCS). One local organization, ETKO, a former partner of SKAL, has been granted a licence by the Ministry of Agriculture.

Organic cotton in Turkey

Organic cotton production was started in Turkey in the late 1980s. Groups of farmers were contracted by foreign companies in the south-eastern area of Kahramanmaras and in Soke, western Turkey. Other foreign companies followed suit, extending the production areas to the Aegean. In the early 1990s, some textile and garment manufacturers in Denizli, Istanbul, Izmir and Adana which exported conventionally produced products to Germany, the Netherlands and Sweden began to invest in organic production in the western and south-eastern parts of Turkey.

Kahramanmaras, already an established cotton-growing area, has some features which favour organic production. Cultural practices can easily replace herbicides for weed control; beneficial insect populations are high and easy to maintain. Insect attacks have been lower than in other areas of the country, and consequently insecticide use has been lower, leading to less disruption of the beneficial insect population. Seasonal labour is cheap.

The Aegean area is generally regarded as the most promising for the expansion of organic production, due to low and reducing insecticide use, good soils, educated and well-informed farmers, an abundance of research and extension institutions, proximity to marketing channels and high-quality fibre production. The south-eastern irrigated area is also regarded as promising for organic production by many authorities.

Table 1 shows organic seed cotton production for 1992, 1994, and 1996.

Table 1: Organic seed cotton production in Turkey, 1992–96

	1992	1994	1996
Farmers	24	41	34
Total area in ha	380	280	466
Average farm size in ha	15.8	6.8	13.7
Production in tonnes	900	390	1304
Average yield kg/ha	2368	1389	2800

Cotton yields vary enormously between regions and between individual farms within a region due to a range of factors including soils, technology, farmers' education, efficiency of extension services, farm size, finance, etc. Table 2 shows that in two areas average differences between conventional and organic yields are not that significant. Differences are apparently more significant if maximum conventional yields are compared with maximum organic yields.

Table 2: Comparison of conventional and organic cotton yields in Turkey based on average figures for 1992–95

	Conventional average yields (kg/ha)	Organic average yields (kg/ha)
Soke	3700	3500
Kahramanmaras	2700	2500

Organic farming practices and costs

In areas where natural balances have not been seriously disrupted, farming practices do not differ greatly between conventional and organic farming. Table 3 makes some comparisons between conventional and organic farming practices.

The main differences between conventional and organic farming are in the use of external inputs. Purchasing non-conventional inputs and finding suitable information about application can be problematic for independent organic farmers. To encourage the uptake of organic farming, a good level of extension support is needed, as well as the provision of inputs not readily available in the marketplace.

Table 3: Comparison of conventional and organic farming practices in Turkey

	Conventional	Organic
Tilling	Twice with tractor plough and disc harrow and alternately chisel plough	Twice with tractor plough
Fertilizing	500–900 kg/ha base fertilizer and urea or 26% nitrate. Alternatively 20:20:0 or 15:15:15 compound fertilizers.	3–5 tonnes/ha farmyard manure or green manure applied; also plant waste composts and other ecological nutrients.
Seed	40–70 kg/ha normal seed.	40–70 kg/ha normal seed.
Mechanical hoeing	3–5 times each planting period with tractor hoe.	3–5 times each planting period with tractor hoe.
Hand hoeing	2–3 times each planting period.	4–5 times each planting period.
Irrigation	5–8 times each planting period.	3–5 times each planting period.
Pesticides	4–7 times each planting period with contact or systemic pesticides.	2–3 times each planting period with ecological prescriptions and/or predators are used. Cultural measures are fundamental.

Source: Mehmet Tozan of Bo Weevil Organic Cotton and Good Food Foundation, Izmir, Turkey, February 1996.

Reduced yields and the lack of an organic premium during the three-year conversion period are the main factors limiting the uptake of organic farming in Turkey. Costs during this period should be differentiated between those carried by the farmer and those carried by the contractor. In the case of contract farmers, companies can help accommodate these losses, but often market conditions limit the extent of this form of support. Help may be needed for those independent farmers wishing to convert, if organic farming is to be encouraged. A three-year conversion period is required by Turkish and EC regulations. But there is at present in Turkey no support given by the Ministry of Agriculture and Rural Affairs for conversion to organic systems. On the contrary, all the policies are geared towards subsidizing fertilizers and, to a lesser extent, pesticides.

Once the conversion period has been achieved, however, a comparison of costs of the various steps in cotton production for the Aegean (Soke) region indicate that the cost of organic cotton growing is probably less than that of conventional production. Even when taking into account the yields and looking at the product cost per unit, the figures seem to favour organic production. Opinions are divided, however, and some organic cotton experts in Turkey suggest that it may be slightly more expensive to grow organic cotton due to lower yields. If premiums are paid it may, nevertheless, be more profitable. One contract company (Bo Weevil) has stated that they will pay a premium of approximately 20 per cent to their contracting farmers in the Kahramanmaras region.

The free market makes it difficult to obtain information about prices of organic cotton fibre. Seed cotton prices vary greatly, even in one area, on account of differences in quality. For example, in October 1995, the minimum price for seed cotton in Odemis in the Aegean area was US$0.35 and the maximum was US$1.11 for the best quality, whereas in Adana in the same month they were respectively US$0.28 and US$0.82. (In October 1995, US$1 = 50 985 Turkish Lira).

Certification

Inspection charges are calculated on a per visit basis and all the six certifiers charge similar fees which are standard for all products. The number of visits per season for organic cotton can vary between one and four and is determined by the certifying body. Farms already certified, or those which are part of a contracting scheme need fewer inspections. The ratio of inspection and certification costs to total costs varies according to the size of the farm and the number of visits required.

The organic textile industry in Turkey

The textile and clothing industry in Turkey is large and well established. The industry features up-to-date technology and is very sound financially as well as being market conscious and competitive. Almost all companies, and especially the exporters established within the past 10 years, are producing according to international, country or company health, environmental and quality standards. Many companies are 'total quality companies' certified under the appropriate internationally recognized standard. As a consequence Turkey is a very important provider of high-quality textile goods into the EU market.

Many companies are already exporting textiles and clothing under various eco-labels. They do not believe that technical obstacles related to organic production are significant. It seems that most production, whether of conventionally produced or organic cotton, is carried out under environmentally responsible conditions. The industry believes that the main cost differential is in the purchase of the organic fibre.

Firms generally produce organic textiles and clothing on contract for European importers such as Hess Natur, Living Crafts and Boller Winkler. The market is limited but prices are good, and manufacturers find the profits satisfactory even though the production costs of organic textiles are high.

The German company, Lichtschatz-Projekte runs the Woven Wind Organic Project in Izmir, Turkey. The project produces cotton fibre, naturally pigmented cotton fibre and oils from naturally pigmented, hand-picked organic cottons. Production in 1997 was 74 tonnes from approximately 150ha; a further 150 tonnes were bought in from another project. In 1998, production is scheduled to be between 120 and 150 tonnes, with an added 250–300 tonnes of purchased cotton.

The Turkish industry argues that it has a strong competitive advantage in producing eco-textiles and clothing. Several Turkish companies are in the process of encouraging organic and naturally pigmented cotton growing through investment. They are also importing organic yarns and fabrics from the USA and India and investing in machinery and equipment which will enable them to meet the required standards. Many companies are trying to obtain an eco-label, most commonly the 'Oko-tex 100' label (which has its limitations: see Chapter 6). Many companies established since 1980 have had the opportunity to take environmental standards into account when setting up. In addition, many longer-established companies have up-graded the quality of their technology and products.

Turkey has the capacity to produce a wider range of organic products more cheaply than any other Mediterranean country, on account of the abundance of land and water resources and the prevalence of small family farms and cheap labour. However, these advantages may not be sufficient to keep Turkish production competitive if governments of other countries are providing support to their producers.

It seems that most Turkish companies accept the standards called for by their trading partners in Europe as an integral part of their continued relationship. Owners and managers of the Turkish companies are well-informed about the constantly changing environmental standards and the general level of awareness of these issues is increasing. Many European companies visit the factories in Turkey to ensure compliance with their standards before awarding contracts and are very often concerned about identifying all the links in the production chain. Requirements can in some cases extend to social and welfare criteria including, for example, better factory working conditions.

Organic textile manufacture

Companies produce according to a diverse array of requirements set by various certifying bodies, eco-labelling schemes or importing companies. There is a limited supply of the production inputs, however, such as natural soap, environmentally responsible dyes and, of course, organic cotton. The need for investment and the costs of some of the inputs make producing this type of textile and clothing more expensive than the conventional counterpart. Companies producing for the European or American organic cotton

161

markets do not use bleaching processes which employ chlorine or chlorine compounds, but use hydrogen peroxide instead. All washing is done with pure water and natural soap. Strict requirements for the types and processes involved in dyeing are observed by most of the exporting companies. Dyes which are in accordance with European environmental standards are usually obtained from European companies. The use of formaldehyde is prohibited in the finishing of eco-textiles under most sets of criteria and so most Turkish exporting companies do not use it (see Chapter 6). Also shrinking by chemical processes is not allowed, and special machinery has to be used to shrink fabrics and garments mechanically.

The future of organic cotton in Turkey

The future of organic cotton growing in Turkey depends on developments in the organic farming sector on the one hand and on the cotton and textiles sector on the other. The growth and development of organic farming is reliant on an increase in demand by foreign companies because at present almost all production is geared to the needs of several European enterprises. There are, however, signs that a domestic market for organic food products is growing. For example, one very large supermarket chain, Migros, is implementing a scheme to retail organic products. At present, about 90 per cent of organic foods are dried fruits such as figs, raisins and apricots. The prospects for cotton fibre exports, are similar to those of other organic products, that is, dependent on demand from foreign companies. Some organic cotton clothing manufacturers believe, however, that, if properly marketed and advertised, these products could also have a market in Turkey. It seems that a certain supply level is necessary before successful domestic marketing can be undertaken.

Organic cotton growers in Turkey tend to be relatively well educated, innovative and financially secure than the average cotton farmer. Organic cotton producers also benefit from a high level of interaction with technicians, representatives of contractor companies, extensionists and certification inspectors, all of whom provide ongoing guidance and support. For those organic cotton farmers producing in geographically favourable areas, considerable savings can be made in organic agriculture with little loss in yields, resulting in higher revenues.

Considerable effort is being put into research and development concentrated in University agricultural faculties and in the Ministry of Agriculture. A growing number of research reports are being produced and there is a large amount of applied research on faculty farms and designated private and public holdings. The universities of the Aegean and Cukurova are located in two of the most important cotton-growing regions and both have projects focusing on organic cotton product. Both universities have a special interest in naturally pigmented cotton and have established research projects.

Technical and cost conditions in the agriculture sector favour organic cotton production in Turkey. For organic farming in Turkey to expand beyond the realms of contractual farming, financial and technical support, especially in the initial conversion period, is crucial in order to gain the interest of independent farmers.

13

Egypt

AHMED EL-ARABY and KLAUS MERCKENS

Introduction

Cotton has been grown in Egypt since about 300 BC. Production for export started around 1830 and was improved with the introduction of foreign varieties around 1860. At that time, production in the southern USA had come to a standstill because of the American Civil War and Egypt was able to establish itself as an important cotton exporter. Egyptian cotton is known the world over for its long to extra-long staple. In the 1970s, 75 per cent of the world's long-staple cotton came from Egypt, which at that time produced about 5 per cent of the total global production. Textile manufacturing is the single largest industry in the country and textiles are the most important export commodity.

The cotton industry in Egypt has hitherto been highly regulated by the government but this situation is now changing. Until recently, the state controlled inputs including seed, provided credit for fertilizers and pesticides, set the farm-gate price and purchased all the cotton from the farmers. It also marketed the cotton abroad, often in barter deals. Liberalization of the cotton sector started a few years ago but the government still supplies seed and sets minimum prices. The domestic cotton industry continues to be protected by an import prohibition on clothing. This situation is likely to change with further trade liberalization.

The building of the Aswan high dam had a major effect on agricultural production in Egypt. In restricting the fertile flooding of the Nile, the dam initiated more intensive use of agrochemicals. In only 20 years the total amount of pesticide active ingredient used in cotton cultivation increased to 1800 tonnes, while the average yield of seed cotton remained at round 3000kg/ha.

In 1980, the Egyptian Government started a programme of integrated pest management (IPM) for cotton in order to reduce pesticide applications. The emphasis was on biological control using pheromone traps for monitoring and spot spraying. This programme was very successful, especially in Fayum Governorate, and expanded to about 20 000ha. This approach to pest control has provided useful technical information for the developing biodynamic and organic cotton sectors.

Climatic conditions in Egypt are excellent for cotton production, the crop needing a minimum temperature of 18°C for germination and optimum temperatures of 27–35°C during the growing period. For the seven months, between sowing in February–March until the harvest in around September–October, Egypt has an average temperature of 26°C. Cotton is the most favoured summer crop in Egypt. It is grown on approximately 400 000ha or 13 per cent of the total arable land in the delta and the Nile Valley.

Organic and biodynamic production in Egypt

The founding of the Sekem farm by Dr Ibrahim Abouleish in 1977 prompted the growth of the biodynamic movement in Egypt (see Preface for note on terminology). Based on anthroposophic principles, the organization aims to integrate rural development with biodynamic farming. Across the country there are now more than 150 farms with a total area of approximately 2000ha producing on biodynamic principles. About 100 farmers, members of the Egyptian Bio-Dynamic Association (EBDA), are contracted to grow vegetables, herbs and other products for Sekem. Their production is processed, packed and exported by Sekem companies which also ensure quality control, organize organic certification and undertake to buy at a fixed price.

The EBDA provides farmers with training, advice, and certain specific farming inputs. A biodynamic agricultural adviser regularly visits the contracted farmers and the cost of these services is covered from the profits made from exporting the final product.

On the basis of positive experience in the biodynamic cultivation of herbs, cereals and vegetables, Sekem started to apply biodynamic methods to cotton, in close co-operation with scientists, farmers, consultants and consumers. Despite initial scepticism, the system was successful.

The Sekem producers grow their cotton crops according to the international biodynamic standards of the Demeterbund, based in Germany. The Demeter standards are in compliance with, and exceed, the IFOAM Basic Standards for Organic Agriculture. They also exceed the standards of the EU organic regulation on organic agricultural products. For processing, the standards of the German Arbeitskreis Naturtextil e.V. (AKN) are used (see Chapter 6).

Since 1995, the Union of Growers and Exporters of Organic and Bio-dynamic Agriculture (UGEOBA) has also been active in the promotion of organic agriculture in Egypt. UGEOBA members are drawn from all over Egypt and include farmers, traders, processors and exporters interested in organic and biodynamic agriculture. Producer members of UGEOBA are free to export through and to any company they wish to deal with. The producer members of UGEOBA must abide by the IFOAM Basic Standards, EU Regulation 2092/91 and its amendments, Naturland standards and guidelines as well as those of the Soil Association of UK. More than 75 farms with an area of 800ha are included and seven companies with processing, packing and trading for local and export markets are also involved. Cotton produced by the UGEOBA is exported as yarn rather than as finished goods.

Members grow a wide array of produce in addition to cotton and are provided with services including extension, marketing and promotional services. The Egyptian Centre for Organic Agriculture (ECOA) is an independent inspection and certification body which was established in parallel to UGEOBA to carry out these services for its members and others. ECOA is reviewed annually by IMO and co-operates closely with Naturland in Germany and the Soil Association in the UK as well as OCIA in the United States. External inspection bodies increasingly use local inspectors and there are moves to set up an Egyptian organic certification body which would certify according to IFOAM and EU standards. ECOA is co-operating with the Egyptian Government to develop an Egyptian law on organic agriculture.

In both UGEOBA and the EBDA, agricultural consultants work with the farmers during the conversion period and support farmers during all cultivation processes. In UGEOBA, farmers pay a small membership fee which entitles them to participate in regular lectures about aspects of organic farming. Most of the transfer of organic know-how however is done in the field, during group visits and inspection.

Organic cotton in Egypt

Organic cotton production started in Egypt in 1991 on a small area of 20ha in the Gharbia governorate in the Nile Delta. It was a successful trial and in the following year more than 120 hectares were under organic cotton. By 1996, there were more than 400 hectares of organic cotton in Fayoum and Kaliubea in the southern Nile Delta area and in Abou Matameer in the north.

In Egypt, the main incentive for farmers to convert to organic production is the promise of higher prices for their products. Farmers in Egypt generally need the full three-year conversion period to establish a well-developed organic farm system, but this varies from farmer to farmer. There are always those who are slow in picking up the ideas and farmers who do not have enough funds to invest in a complete conversion, just as there are some farmers who like to experiment and whose farms are producing close to the standards of organic production even before contact with the organic movement.

In Egypt, cotton is generally grown by small-scale farmers. On larger fields, tractors are often used for manure spreading, ploughing and seed-bed preparation, whereas manual labour would be used on small fields. In all situations, cotton requires considerable labour which in Egypt is not in short supply. Farm work, village life and school terms are adapted to the work that needs to be done in the cotton fields to ensure that enough labour is available.

Rotations and soil fertility

Cotton is generally grown in rotation with other crops and organic farmers tend to diversify their farm system more than conventional growers. Seed-beds are ploughed, harrowed and ridged. Fertilization is based on the application of compost, with deficiencies corrected through mineral soil amendments. Nitrogen is fixed in the soil by growing leguminous crops in the rotation. Compost is made from animal manure, crop residues and any other organic materials.

It is recommended that cotton growers keep animals because of the importance of animal manure in compost making. When fodder crops are grown in the cotton rotation, and the manure returned to the field as a fertilizer, the system can be truly said to be 'organic'. However, as most farms in Egypt are small, farmers have tended to specialize and animal husbandry is abandoned, leaving the farmer dependent on external inputs.

Seed

Cotton seed (two varieties of extra-long staple and long-season types) are provided by the government. As germinating cotton seeds and cotton seed-lings are prone to attack by a complex of soil-borne pathogens, it is a legal requirement for cotton seed to be treated with synthetic fungicides (for example Ridomil or Captan). The Egyptian Ministry of Agriculture allows an exception to be made for organic production and an alternative technique using *Trichoderma* isolates has been developed.

Irrigation

Irrigation in Egypt is carried out by the furrow system for both conventional and organic systems. In organic farming, because of the more intensive attention by agronomists, more emphasis may be put on proper levelling and shorter basin length, but otherwise practices are the same in both types of farm operation. Between 6 and 7 applications of water take place, with the last one 30–40 days before harvesting. In Egypt, water is free.

Pest control

In general, pest pressure in Egypt can be classed as average. The major pests are the leaf worm (*Spodoptera littoralis*), the pink bollworm (*Pectinophora gossypiella*) and the spiny bollworm (*Earias insulana*). Organic cotton production has benefited from Integrated Pest Management (IPM) systems and its biological control component, which are relatively well developed in Egypt. At the same time, organic cotton fields provide an excellent opportunity for testing new technologies because of the absence of toxic sprays.

Harvesting and processing

Cotton is harvested manually in Egypt, employing thousands of women, men and children in two or three picking rounds. In general, organization and supervision is more intensive in the organic system.

In Egypt, ginneries are able to handle small quantities of seed cotton so there are no extra overheads for keeping the organic cotton separate, or cleaning the gins between runs. The minimum quantity for ginning should be approximately 20 tonnes. The sale of cotton seed can provide extra income to the farmers.

After spinning and weaving, the cloth is washed, bleached and dyed. Significant differences occur here in treatments between conventional cotton and organic. Under the AKN standards, a large number of substances are prohibited in the washing process and standards for dyes are very detailed, leading to a significant cost differential between conventional and organic cotton (see Chapter 7).

Garment manufacturing is carried out in Egypt. Partners in the production chain include: El Mahalla and Misr Iran for ginning and spinning; Shalty and Delta for dyeing and knitting and Delta and Hosny for pre-treatment, washing and finishing.

Financing

Whereas conventional cotton farmers can obtain credit from the state agricultural bank for the purchase of fertilizers or pesticides, organic farmers cannot ask for credits for compost making or application. Although this could be seen as a drawback for many organic farmers, Egyptian farmers are often reluctant to take up loans as the practice of charging interest is inconsistent with the Muslim faith. Farmers have, therefore, adopted the practice of requesting a pre-payment from the buyer to help with the extra expenses that are incurred at the beginning of the season. This can also act as a guarantee against what many perceive to be the extra risk in organic farming. The cost of this pre-payment is reflected in the somewhat higher price for the final product.

Economics

In conventional cotton growing the average production of seed cotton is 2800kg/ha. At a farm-gate price of US$1.01/kg, the gross return per hectare would be US$2815/ha. With a total cost of production of US$1839/ha, the profit in conventional growing is on average US$976/ha (see also Chapter 7).

In the first few years of organic cotton growing, production can be significantly lower—around 2400kg/ha—whereas in well-established organic cotton farms the production comes very close to the conventional yield. Average yield can be around 2600kg/ha of organic seed cotton. The farm-gate price for organic cotton is US$1.16/kg and the gross return is then US$3016/ha. With a total cost of production of US$1864/ha, the profit in organic growing is US$1152/ha or 18 per cent higher than conventional.

Since their introduction, the fertilizers and pesticides required in conventional cotton production have been subsidized by the government, which also promoted their use by providing them on credit. Subsidies and credit are now being abandoned, and the expected price increases in both fertilizers and pesticides will have an impact on the economy of the conventional system and should favour organic production.

The biodynamic approach to cotton production in Egypt

The biodynamic approach to production varies in some respects from organic. The biodynamic system for cotton, now well established on the Sekem farms, is described in detail below and is an important example of this approach.

Pre-crops

Large areas are planted with *Trifolium alexandrinum*, the best pre-crop for cotton, during the winter season. The crop is ploughed in during February. Potatoes, which are harvested in February, are also used as a pre-crop. Because of problems connected with cotton cultivation, it is best to use a long-term crop rotation so that cotton is only grown on the same field every two, or even better, every three years.

Soil and soil preparation

For thousands of years, the Nile valley and Delta were covered by fertile mud during the annual Nile flooding. The soil is very deep and provides excellent conditions for cotton cultivation provided its structure is maintained. If cotton is grown in desert areas, increasingly common in Egypt, the soil should be under cultivation for 10 years at least. If not, the soil probably cannot meet the high demands of the cotton plants.

After harvesting the pre-crop, the field is ploughed thoroughly crosswise, composted manure is worked in and then the field is divided by dams in an east-west direction forming the ditches for later irrigation.

Fertilization

Soil analysis is carried out primarily for physical structure, salinity and macro elements in the soil. Fertilization is done by applying $30–40m^3$ of composted cow manure per ha. On biodynamic farms, six biodynamic medicinal plant preparations are added to the compost. For later additional fertilization, about $6m^3$ composted chicken manure per hectare is used. If the soil analysis shows a phosphate shortage, approximately 400–700kg/ha of 13 per cent Egyptian rock phosphate may be added to the compost. If the soil needs potassium, approximately 600kg of Sinai Potassium Feldspat

(9.5% K_2O) may be added to the compost, or wood ash at 250kg/ha is applied directly to the field before ploughing.

Due to the arid climate and the need for irrigation, soils can become over-salinized in the top layers, but this does not generally occur in organic farms except in cases of mismanagement or drainage problems. Techniques are available if salinity reaches unacceptable levels.

Sowing

In Egypt the government prescribes the seed varieties to be used by the farmers of each cotton cultivation region. The seeds are treated the day before with a suspension of *Trichoderma harzianum* and *Bacillus subtilis* as an alternative to the chemical fungicide treatment required by government regulations. This suspension is sprayed over the seeds. After that they are mixed and covered for about 24 hours to encourage fermentation. The fungal diseases of seedlings during the germination period are produced by *Rhizoctinia solani*, *Sclerotium rolfsii*, *Macrophomina phaseolina*, *Phymatotrichum omnivorum*, *Phytium* spp., *Aspergillus* spp. and *Fusarium* spp. *Trichoderma* can be effective against these diseases within a few days.

Directly before sowing, the biodynamic preparation '500' or 'horn manure', (about 40litres/ha) is sprayed in droplets on the soil in the late afternoon and sowing starts next morning. All cultivation steps from now on are done by hand, although soil tillage and fertilization are normally carried out by tractors. Small hollows, about 60–70cm apart are prepared on the south side of the ridges into which about 8 seeds are placed. The seeds are often covered with a handful of pure quartz sand, which is brought from the nearby desert. The sand maintains warmth and prevents attack from the larvae of *Agrotis ypsilon* (cutworm) which attacks the germinating seedling. The treatments described above repel the different pests and mean that pesticides are not necessary. Plant density reaches 90 000–100 000 plants/hectare, which produces a high yield.

Dangers during the first three weeks

The field must be irrigated thoroughly directly after sowing. During the first three weeks after germination, the young plants are very vulnerable to attack. Climatic changes in Egypt may result in the temperature decreasing and plant development may be interrupted by fungal attack. From the time of the appearance of the seedling leaves, the plant needs care and protection against various small insects such as white flies (*Bemisia tabacii*), spider mites (*Tetranychus* spp), aphids (*Aphis gossypii*), thrips (*Thrips* spp.) and cotton jassids (*Empoasca* spp.).

These small insects can be trapped with yellow sticky sheet traps (30x20cm) placed against the wind direction so that their lower edge is at the height of the plant tops and parallel to the soil. Up to 30 yellow sticky traps per hectare are normally sufficient. Small insects can be active until harvest—especially aphids and spider mites—and the traps should remain in place until that time. These small insects can also be controlled during the first 3–4 weeks by a diluted potassium soap produced from cotton-seed oil or by neem extract applied in the parts of the field affected.

There is an added danger from the combination of temperature decrease and fungal attack by the fungi described earlier which can affect the stem and roots of the seedlings. If rot appears in plant seedling bunches, the next irrigation must not take place in order to regulate the moisture content in the soil and to stop the fungal attack. Most of the outer plants in the bunch remain healthy and resistant which is the reason why more than one seed is planted. Later the most healthy and strongest seedlings are selected, until only one or two remain.

Irrigation

In northern Egypt, the rainfall may be only 100mm per year so that agriculture depends on regular irrigation. The water sources are either from the Nile canalization system or from farm wells. The irrigation frequency is normally every 14 days but in very fertile soils farmers could wait four weeks for the second irrigation after sowing. Correct water management at this stage improves the root development of the young plants. When cotton is cultivated between onions, one of the usual irrigations has to be dropped to facilitate the ripening of the onion plants. Directly after onion harvesting, irrigation with a small amount of water has the effect of optimizing the soil structure to enable good root development and nutritional quality in the upper soil.

Traditionally, Egyptian farmers are artists in the management of irrigation systems. However, sometimes too much water is applied, which leads to poor air concentration between the soil particles. Experiments are done to increase the irrigation during the flowering stage of cotton then later decreasing the amount of water to enhance plant ripening. This gives homogeneous flowering and bud development and advantages for plant protection. In cold autumns, some capsules could be prevented from ripening and the capsules could be lost. The bad ripening can be improved by stopping the irrigation for 30–40 days (according to observation) before harvesting. The soil dries out and deep hand-wide cracks appear in the soil because of the shrinkage. The vegetative growing impulse then stops at the at the end of August and the required ripening process can take place.

Flushing is necessary if the irrigation water analysis shows a high salinity or if the soils are too saline due to mineral fertilization in former years. To achieve optimum results, the whole field has to be flooded quickly to the level of the top of the planting dams. After some hours the salt is dissolved in the water and then the whole field has to be drained as quickly as possible.

Protection at the vegetative stage

From the middle of May, the main leaf developing phase, the larvae of the cotton leaf worm (*Spodoptora littoralis*) attacks, producing between 4000–10000 egg masses per hectare, each one with about 250 eggs. In Egypt, *Spodoptora* may produce seven generations in one year, of which four generations coincide with the growth period of cotton plants. This means that every four weeks a new generation has to be dealt with.

Laboratory-based research on sex pheromones was applied on a large-scale on 11 hectares of Sekem fields during the first phase of biodynamic cotton production. With 2 traps per hectare counted every third day, up to 800 insects were caught. Traditionally at this time of the year, the cotton leaves with the egg masses are collected and burned on the edges of the fields. This method was also applied in the biodynamic cultivation system and has played an important role in *Spodoptora* control. On the plot treated with pheromones, only 50 to 100 egg masses per hectare were found and most of those eggs were infertile.

The second screening of the cotton plants for *Spodoptera* eggs follows 20 days after the larvae of the first generation hatch. Neighbouring fields cultivated by conventional methods and using pesticides displayed three times more foliage damage than the biodynamic plants. If any late damage does appear in certain areas, it can be sprayed with *Bacillus thuringiensis*. These methods have the advantage of working without pesticides and useful insects such as *Cochineal, Scymnus, Trichogramma* and *Chrysoperla* are not harmed. Undamaged leaves create optimum conditions for high yields.

To encourage the plant metabolism through the well-developed leaves, the biodynamic '501' or 'Silica' preparation is sprayed directly the first flowers appear. The first spraying has to take place in the morning immediately after sunrise.

During the vegetative stage, weeding should take place once or twice. Usually on the second weeding, chicken manure compost is spread on the planting side of the ridges and soil from the neighbouring ridge is used to cover the distributed compost.

Controlling bollworms

During the reproductive phase, the night active moths begin to attack the capsules. The pink bollworm (*Pectinophora gossypiella)* and the American bollworm *(Helicoverpa armigera)* are the most dangerous. At the beginning of the reproductive stage, 2–3 delta traps per hectare are placed in the fields to monitor levels of pink bollworm activity. Container traps are also used in monitoring. In these traps, an attracting substance is used and insects are caught in the soapy water in the bottom of the container.

To control harmful insects, especially the pink bollworm, the mating disruption technique is applied. When the monitoring in the delta trap shows that the flying time has begun, the small long plastic tubes or pink bollworm (PB) ropes, containing pheromone, are placed on several plants dispersed about the field on the upper part of the cotton plant stem. The pheromone migrates through the plastic tube over a period of four weeks and hinders the reproduction of the insects. The method proved to be so effective that the Ministry of Agriculture produced an illustrated pamphlet for farmers in which the methods were clearly illustrated and described.

Since 1994, a new cotton pest has emerged all over Egypt, the spiny bollworm (*Earias insulana*). Pheromones have not been effective here in combating this problem so a trap ring around the cotton fields, mainly on the borders, against the main wind direction, was used. Enough adults are caught to limit the damage.

Predators
The widespread adoption of pheromone treatment (now around 300 000ha) and consequent reduction in pesticide use, has had a favourable effect on the appearance of beneficial insects and other fauna such as bats, rodents and birds. As many as 64 different species have been observed. The most common is *Orius* spp. followed by spiders, ladybirds and *Chrysoperla*. The density of predators in the pheromone-treated fields has been shown to be twice that in the conventional fields.

Harvesting and processing
Irrigation is stopped about 30 to 40 days before the expected harvest in order to enhance the ripening process. One additional application of '501' or 'Silica' in the afternoon can support the ripening as well. Biodynamic fields have green leaves growing well up to the point of ripening, whilst leaves in conventional fields are often grey and discoloured or have died off because of the use of pesticides and exposure to the hot sun. Dead leaves lead to impurities in the cotton which one seldom finds with biodynamic cotton. The picking is done by hand. One picker can harvest up to 100kg seed cotton per day. In the first picking which yields the best quality, 70–75 per cent of the total yield is harvested. The harvest is sorted on simple wooden tables into two qualities, before being packed into clearly identified bags of about 160kg.

Processing and marketing
Directly after harvesting, the bags are taken to existing state-accredited mills where it is ginned, yielding about 60 per cent seeds and 40 per cent fibre. This process is also inspected by the Centre for Organic Agriculture in Egypt (COAE). The fibre is baled, marked and sent to be processed into yarn at an Egyptian spinning mill. Biodynamic cotton shows better fibre elasticity and other fibre quality parameters than conventional cotton. In special processing steps, developed with Egyptian experts, the biodynamic

cotton is spun, knitted or woven, dyed and finished without synthetic chemicals.

The yarn is partly exported and partly used in Egypt for knitted and woven fabrics which are manufactured in Sekem's own Conytex company into clothing for mostly European clients. High-quality children's and baby wear are produced and marketed under the trade name 'Cotton People Organic' in co-operation with a sales partner Alnatura in Germany. Distribution is arranged through two routes: first, through Alnatura which supplies wholesalers in Germany, Switzerland and Austria and secondly through local marketing in Egypt in the three Sekem shops and a retail chain of 10 shops in Cairo and Alexandria.

The Sekem initiative has about 400 hectares now using the biodynamic system of production. Even in the first year, the biodynamic farmers harvested 25 per cent more raw cotton than the conventionally cultivated government fields in the surrounding area which is largely attributed to the metabolic activities of the '501' or 'Silica' preparation. In succeeding years, harvests yielded 8–12 per cent more seed cotton than the conventionally cultivated fields.

Conclusion

The success of the Egyptian biodynamic and organic cotton sector has been achieved, in part, through the collaboration between Sekem, its trading arm Cotton People Organic, and the German group Alnatura. These companies believe that good ecological quality products, especially textiles, can only be produced if all the steps are taken with the close co-operation of all involved which leads to better understanding and efficiency. There is more direct contact in this system between the farmers and the buyers, and most farmers know in which markets their cotton will be sold and where and how it will be used. This knowledge improves their self-esteem. Due to the high level of advisory and inspection visits they receive, organic and biodynamic farmers get a better training in farm management than other farmers and they are thus able to improve the performance of their farms.

Although few research institutes are directly involved in research into organic production, new and alternative techniques are being developed. Farmers in Egypt have clearly benefited from the state-supported biological pest control system and is used by both Sekem farms and the farmer members of the UGEOBA. Both organic and biodynamic systems of cotton cultivation have achieved convincing results through a combination of modern scientific knowledge and generations of experience. Yields are impressive. In most established organic and biodynamic farms, cotton yields are equal to conventional with much better quality yarn and cotton seed oil (which is edible in Egypt), and in addition there are many environmental and health benefits.

From an environmental point of view, organic and biodynamic growing has clear advantages in Egypt. In areas under these systems field workers and villagers are no longer exposed to insecticides and fungicides. Toxic residues no longer threaten children playing and swimming in the irrigation canals in which backpack sprayers used to be cleaned. Drainage water and surface water run-off are no longer contaminated. There is less leaching of nutrients in the surface run-off and groundwater drainage, which means less eutrophication of surface waters and less nitrates in drinking water. In processing and manufacturing, materials which are harmful to factory workers, the environment and the consumers of textiles are no longer used. The reactive dyeing technology makes it possible to use very low quantities of dyes which are easily recycled or treated so that the impact on the environment is minimal.

14
New developments in Africa

GERD RATTER, FORTUNATE NYAKANDA,
GUNNAR RUNDGREN, BO VAN ELZAKKER,
NORBERTO MAHALAMBE, IQBAL JAVAID, ABOU THIAM,
NGONE WAR TOURE and SIMPLICE DAVO VODOUHE

Introduction

Africa's share of global cotton production is small (about 10 per cent) and, according to the World Bank, has declined since the mid-1980s due to reductions in areas and yields. Efforts in many countries are being made to restore the confidence of growers in the crop and good progress has been made in Francophone West Africa, Zimbabwe and South Africa. Production is expected to increase in the future, but at a rate slower than in the period 1970 to 1990. At the same time consumption is expected to increase at a faster rate in the period up to 2005. State control of the cotton sector has been a major feature of African cotton production; however, it is now being re-examined. Markets are being liberalized and consequently there is an increased involvement of the private sector and NGOs in agriculture generally, and in cotton production in particular.

Smallholder organic cotton projects have proliferated in Africa. In just a few years, cotton projects in Tanzania, Uganda and Mozambique, for example, have produced marketable amounts of organic cotton fibre. Experimental projects have been developed in Senegal, Benin and Zimbabwe, and other projects are about to start in Kenya, Madagascar, Ghana and Mali. Although no detailed research has been carried out to date on farmers' motivation for conversion, indications are that the spiralling costs of synthetic chemical inputs (described in several case studies) have been a prime factor in persuading farmers to seek alternatives. Other factors have also played a part in stimulating moves away from conventional cotton production, such as the relaxation of government controls over the cotton crop, a growing market for organic cotton in Europe, the availability of support packages, and a growing awareness amongst farming communities of the dangers of pesticides to health and the environment. Reasons for conversion vary from country to country and are generally described in each case study.

A key element in the conversion pattern to date has been the support of outside agencies such as bilateral agencies (German GTZ and Swedish Sida), NGOs such as the Pesticides Trust, or European companies. Incentives in the form of a premium payment to farmers for their seed cotton have often been provided against the higher prices that can be obtained for organic cotton fibre sold in Europe. A better level of extension support than would normally be provided for conventional production has also been a feature of the projects, as has the provision of consultancy advice in the early stages of the projects.

Small-scale farming is very much a feature of African production in most countries, except for parts of South Africa, Zimbabwe, Egypt and Sudan. In some areas food security has been undermined by large-scale cotton production dominating the most viable agricultural land and thus reducing the area under production and yields of food crops. The use of rotations is key in organic agriculture and the husbandry of animals is encouraged which, although it will lead to a reduction in cotton yields, increases the variety and range of crops produced. To this extent, cotton-focused organic systems can contribute substantially to food security.

Making links

A recent initiative (1998) by PAN-Africa brought together participants in organic cotton projects from many countries of Africa to share experience and identify areas of common concern and interest. Issues identified included the need to develop local organic certification systems and explore domestic as well as export markets. The need for further analysis of results from the organic projects was also identified, as was the need to take issues of gender into account in all aspects of the work. Initial efforts in the latter area can be seen in reports from Senegal and Zimbabwe.

The projects detailed here illustrate the diverse nature of organic cotton production and together represent progress in a promising new direction.

Organic cotton in Tanzania
GERD RATTER

Introduction

Located in eastern Africa, Tanzania has borders with Kenya, Rwanda, Burundi, Zambia and Mozambique, and a long Indian Ocean coastline to the east. Cotton is the second most important source of foreign exchange for the country after coffee. The crop is produced mostly by smallholders who use few agricultural inputs. Tanzania's cotton area is divided into two main territories, namely the Western Cotton Growing Area (WCGA) and the Eastern Cotton Growing Area (ECGA).

Until 1994, Tanzanian law allowed only co-operative unions to purchase seed cotton from farmers and carry out ginning. This local monopoly in the seed cotton market led to a series of problems only too familiar in the cotton sector in Africa, such as mismanagement in the co-operative unions, agricultural inputs not being available at the appropriate time, and farmers waiting a long time for payment for their seed cotton or, sometimes, not being paid at all. Consequently, many farmers lost interest in cotton production, and the area of cotton cultivation decreased. Starting in the 1993/94 season, however, the Tanzanian Government liberalized the seed cotton market, allowing private entrepreneurs to purchase seed cotton from farmers and to run their own ginneries.

A favourable setting for organic production

The liberalization of the cotton industry in Tanzania allowed the possibility of developing private company-based organic projects. The demand for certified organic cotton in Europe from its Swiss customer, Remei AG, led the Tanzanian textile company, CIC Limited to investigate organic cotton production in the country. At the request of CIC Limited, the GTZ-Protrade programme financed a feasibility study for an organic cotton programme in 1994.

A village in Meatu District, Shinyanga Region was identified by the Protrade consultants as the most suitable production area for the project. The district is situated in the north-west of the country and is part of the WCGA. The topography is generally flat or gently undulating with altitudes in the range 900–1400 metres. Annual rainfall ranges from 500–1200mm per year with two rainy seasons in the seven months between the end of September and the beginning of May. The growing season is about 150 days long and extends in normal years from November until May. The area of Meatu District is close to 9000km^2 and is three-quarters arable. The farmers in the area mainly keep cattle, but also grow maize, sorghum, ground-nuts and sweet potatoes for home consumption. Less important crops are beans, cow-peas, chick-peas, rice, sesame and water-melon. The only cash crop is cotton. Farmers are not, however, heavily reliant on monetary income from crops, as they produce their own food and have cattle to sell for cash. The risks of going into organic cotton cultivation were therefore lower than in other areas. All the farmers are smallholders and although the farms are quite big (average 14.3ha), most of their land is fallow or is used as grazing land or for firewood production.

Agricultural statistics for the area from 1990/91 indicate that only about 10 per cent of the arable area had been under cultivation. Soils are light sandy to heavy loam and are quite fertile. Most of the farmers see no need to apply fertilizers.

Meatu District offered the best conditions for implementing an organic cotton project for a number of reasons:

○ The farmers were very interested in participating in an organic cotton programme, and as cotton production is carried out by smallholders at a low-yield level, there was less risk of yield reduction during conversion.

- The dry climate in the district makes cotton the only cash crop worth growing.
- Farms are quite big but farmers grow cotton on only 20 to 25 per cent of their farm land, thus allowing areas of fallow land to act as a refuge for natural enemies of insect pests, and therefore insect pests are not a major problem.
- The area was settled only 40 years ago and much of the land has only recently come under cultivation.
- About 75 per cent of farmers use pesticides on cotton and, if used, spray up to 4 times, whereas the official recommendation is 6 sprayings per season.
- Farmers have a large number of cattle (average 25 head per farmer) which allows for fertilization with animal manure.
- Oxen are commonly used for land preparation and the use of ox-driven weeders was identified as important for the improvement of cotton production.
- Socio-economic data on the area was available from local development projects (e.g. GTZ-Integrated Pest Management (IPM) Project, Dutch Rural Development Project); the GTZ-IPM project offered support in the training of extension staff and research into alternative plant protection methods, which is particularly important as poor extension services were identified as a factor in low yields.
- Two private ginneries were under construction in the area and one new ginnery was already operating.

Implementation of the project

Following the fact-finding mission by the Protrade consultants, a development plan was drawn up for the project and agreed with CIC Limited. Extension staff were recruited and a Protrade consultant undertook the training of one Extension Manager and two field extensionists in November 1994.

Organic cotton production began in the 1994/95 season with 45 farmers who were contracted by the textile company. The terms of the contract promised the farmers the support of the company through extension services, including the supply of inputs and a guaranteed market for the organic cotton at a premium price with payment in cash. In return, the farmers agreed to practise the recommended methods for organic agriculture on their whole farm, especially preventive measures for pest control such as crop rotation and the cultivation of trap crops. Practising crop rotation was one of the preconditions for joining the programme.

For the second season a third extensionist was recruited by the company and the number of contract farmers increased to 110. These farmers cultivated cotton on 645ha and harvested about 450 tonnes of seed cotton.

Unfortunately internal problems and changes in the textile company's management delayed the start of purchase, so that much of the organic cotton was sold to other companies as conventional cotton. The 1996/97 season involved 134 registered farmers who grew 778ha of organic cotton. From this, 516 tons of fully certified organic cotton was harvested, but only 60 per cent of this quantity was purchased by Tansales Ltd (CIC Ltd went out of business and Tansales took over the project). Due to cash-flow problems in the company and illegal competition on the seed cotton market, the rest was purchased by other companies.

One of the main difficulties during the first two years of the programme was recruiting an efficient extension manager for the agricultural programme. In November 1996 a fourth person was appointed to the post, and even his performance is not, as yet, seen as satisfactory. As the efficiency of the extension manager has a major impact on the work of the field extensionists, the effectiveness of staff in this post is crucial.

In general, the experience in Tanzania shows that for a textile company to enter into an agricultural programme is a considerable challenge. Working closely with farmers and agricultural extension staff is a new experience, and organizing activities within a fixed time schedule is critical. The support of the local GTZ-IPM project in Shinyanga, which provides training courses for the extension staff, and regular visits to the company from a Protrade consultant who is an expert in international organic agriculture are important factors in the project's success.

The future plan of the company Tansales Ltd. is to create a joint-venture company with its Swiss customer Remei AG and to extend the organic cotton production in Meatu. Tansales would also like to extend into another area with different climatic and socio-economic conditions closer to the company's own ginnery. This new area has the potential for better lint quality because of higher rainfall.

Research and cultivation

Research work, financed by GTZ, on alternative plant protection methods, including the effects of botanical insecticides and trap plants, is being carried out by the Ukiriguru Research Institute in Mwanza, the leading research institute for cotton cultivation in Tanzania.

Trials for botanical insecticides have been carried out with extracts of pyrethrum, neem (*Azadirachta indica*), *Derris elliptica*, *Tephrosia vogelii* and *Jatropha curcas*. All products were shown to be effective against the key pests, such as the American bollworm (*Helicoverpa armigera*) and aphids. In the field, the extracts were applied with a newly developed ULVA + sprayer which allows water solutions to be sprayed in a quantity of about 20 litres/acre. This new sprayer has an important advantage over the normal ULV-sprayers and also over the knapsack-sprayers because the required quantity of water and working time is considerably reduced. The company bought these expensive sprayers for all field extensionists so that they are available for their contract farmers.

Besides crop rotation, the cultivation of trap crops like sunflower and pigeon pea are important pest control measures. The positive effects of sunflowers have been shown in the results of a study on beneficial ants carried out by a Kenyan entomologist on behalf of the GTZ-IPM project in Shinyanga. She found that on organic cotton plots with sunflowers, there were up to ten times more beneficial ants than on cotton plots without sunflowers. It is known that these ants reduce the eggs and larvae of the American bollworm. Most of the contract farmers reported the positive effects of sunflower as a trap crop on their cotton yield.

The variation in farm size, cotton area and yield per hectare (see Table 1) indicates that the structure of the farms and the management efficiency of the farmers are very variable. It became evident that farmers who managed early sowing and weeding achieved much better yields per hectare than their colleagues who were later. The common sowing practice in the region is simply to broadcast the cotton seeds before ploughing. Consequently the seed bed preparation is poor and weeding is a labour-intensive activity. The weeding can only be done by hand hoe because the cotton is not sown in rows, which means that labour for weeding is the single most important limiting factor for successful cotton production. Family members are important at these times and women sometimes neglect food crops and children sometimes miss school to carry out the work. When money is available, weeding can be organized with paid labour, but this then represents an important cost factor in production, especially when big plots are cultivated and the yield per hectare is low. An alternative crop management practice would be the introduction of sowing in rows and weeding with an ox-driven weeder. The textile company is promoting this method through training courses, demonstration plots and by offering an ox-weeder for hire, but up to now most of the farmers sow only the trap plants in rows.

One reason for the reluctance to change practices is that after the long dry season the lack of cattle fodder means that the oxen are weak. The farmers feel under time pressure to plough and sow the fields for food crops like maize and sorghum and then the cotton cash crop. In this situation, farmers are afraid to take the time to carry out seed bed preparation and sowing in rows. For most of the farmers it would be better to invest more time and effort in cultivating smaller plots of cotton and getting higher yields per hectare. At the end of the season the same quantity of cotton could be harvested, but would involve less work ploughing and weeding. Fodder for the oxen at the beginning of the cultivation period could be increased by using sunflower oil cake and by the cultivation of the legume Crotalaria. The company has made a manual oil press available so that farmers can produce their own oil for cooking and oil cake for the

Table 1: Results for the first three seasons (1994/95, 95/96 and 96/97) from the Tanzania organic cotton project

	1994/95	1995/96	1996/97
No. of contract farmers	45	110	134
AREA OF FARMS (ha)			
Total	1056	3102	3652
Average	23	28	27
Maximum	160	160	160
Minimum	3.2	1.6	1.6
ACREAGE OF ORGANIC COTTON			
Total (ha)	141	645	778
% of farm land	13	21	21
Average (ha)	3.1	5.9	5.8
Maximum (ha)	10	60	40
Minimum (ha)	0.4	0.4	0.4
YIELD (SEED COTTON)			
Total (kg)	105 161	443 300	516 042
Average (kg/ha)	746	687	663
Maximum (kg/ha)	1495	1238	1389
Minimum (kg/ha)	228	218	236

Note: The decrease in average yield per hectare was caused by different climatic conditions over the three seasons and was not an effect of the conversion to organic farming methods. The conventional cotton producers faced the same problems and produced similar yields.

cattle from sunflowers, groundnuts and sesame. Crotalaria seeds have also been distributed to interested farmers so that fodder for the oxen could be grown and soil fertility improved.

Certification

In May 1995, an inspector from the Swiss certification body IMO completed the first inspection of the organic cotton programme. As a result, about 30 tonnes of cotton yarn certified as 'organic in conversion' were exported to Switzerland. During the first two seasons only four farmers dropped out of the programme, either because they decided to use pesticides or they felt they did not have enough suitable land for cotton production and the required crop rotation. In 1997 the annual inspection

Reviewing the organic cotton crop in Tanzania
Credit: Gerd Ratter

by IMO attested to the good progress in the programme and the production was certified as fully organic.

Conclusion

Organic cotton production is an attractive alternative to conventional cotton production for smallholder farmers in Western Tanzania. The low yield level and low intensification of conventional cotton production allow a similar average yield of organic and conventional cotton production in the area.

The conditions for successful organic cotton production include a guaranteed market with a premium payment for the organic seed cotton and an intensive extension service provided by the purchasing company. Many farmers are interested in joining the organic cotton project, but the number of contract farmers is limited according to the market demand and capacity of the extension service to provide the required assistance to the farmers.

Three years of practical experience of organic cotton production by smallholder farmers has produced good results with an average yield similar to that of their conventional neighbours. The big yield variation of the participating farmers is however a clear indication that good crop management is the most important factor for high yields and this must be given attention in the coming years.

Zimbabwe: organic cotton pilot project

FORTUNATE NYAKANDA

Background

Lower Guruve is a low-lying area 300–600m above sea level in the mid-Zambezi Valley. The climate is hot and dry with maximum daytime temperatures reaching 43°C in October/November. Mean daily temperatures range between 25–30°C in September to April and 20–23°C during May to August. There is a short rainy season from the end of November to early March. Mean annual rainfall is 650–800mm, but approximately 200mm of this is lost in evaporation. During the rainy season there may be severe dry spells and seasonal periodic droughts. Thus the area is characterized by a fragile ecosystem due to both physical and climatic conditions. The soils are fertile, made up of alluvial clay and silt.

Cotton has been cultivated in the Lowere Guruve as a cash crop for the last 20 years and dominates the local economy. There is also limited cultivation of maize, sorghum and millet as staple food crops, which the people have to supplement by buying grain from grain surplus areas on the Zimbabwean plateau.

Scattered human settlements cluster around the relatively fertile scarp foot and along rivers where farmers practice streambank cultivation of food crops. However, government village organization programmes and internal migration are leading to the settlement of the higher ground away from the valleys. Average landholdings are restricted to about 4.8ha where the 'villagization' programme has been implemented, but elsewhere this varies according to the availability of tillage services.

Pilot organic project

The pilot project for growing organic cotton was launched after an environmental awareness workshop was held with community leaders, political leaders and some influential people from local communities. The workshop was organized by the Lower Guruve Development Association (LGDA), a local NGO, in October 1993 with the purpose of identifying possible environmental activities.

When cotton production began in the early 1970s, it was possible to grow the crop successfully without using pesticides. This remained true even as the area increased in the mid-1970s. However, it emerged during discussions at the workshop that recent increased pesticide use on cotton had led to numerous environmental problems. It was noted, for instance, that:

○ Pests were becoming resistant to pesticides, leading to increased chemical usage.

184

o Changes in pesticide use were resulting in higher purchasing costs and a reduction in farmers' gross margins.

o Pesticides were harming beneficial plants and animals. For instance, mice, used as a dietary supplement, were being poisoned in the fields and honey which had been widely collected, was becoming rare as bees were poisoned when collecting nectar from sprayed cotton plants.

o Water sources were contaminated during chemical disposal, either when equipment was washed after spraying, or, when carried out away from water points, through run-off and seepage reaching the water table. Contamination extended to the rivers and streams as pesticide residues entered water courses during the rainy season.

o Fish, an important food source, were either killed or the chemicals accumulated in their tissues which were then eaten by the local people.

o Wildlife and domestic livestock were drinking contaminated water.

o Partly from ignorance, or because people are poor, chemicals have not been used or stored safely; for instance chemicals are often stored in the same rooms as food, leading to further opportunities for chemical poisoning.

o Farmers cannot afford to use protective clothing, thus increasing the likelihood of breathing or absorbing chemicals.

o Easy access to chemicals means that they have also become a means of committing suicide, a common occurance when harvests are poor.

In view of these findings people were forced to consider possible alternative methods of cotton production which would reduce or eliminate the use of pesticides.

Getting started

LGDA had heard of the possibility of growing cotton without chemicals from one of their overseas donors. An experimental organic cotton plot was started in the 1993/94 season, demonstrating the possibilities of controlling pests without using chemicals.

At the beginning of the 1995/96 season, meetings were held in different parts of the Guruve area to encourage conversion to organic cotton production. Five meetings were convened by the LGDA, facilitated by an agronomist with experience of organic cotton conversion and supported by Novib and The Pesticides Trust. Ten farmers from each ward became involved in the pilot project, which was a small percentage of those who had expressed interest. Each farmer grew a rotation of 0.2ha cotton and 0.2ha groundnuts (*Arachis hypogaea*), a legume planted to fix nitrogen. The experimental plots were set 10 metres away from the conventional crop to prevent contamination by chemical sprays.

Farmers were asked to use any natural remedies they knew for combating pests and diseases. Spraying was not allowed until six weeks after germination to give predators a chance to reduce pests. The plan was to advise destruction of the crop if farmers were unable to control the pest populations. However, no farmer experienced this problem. There was variability in the level of knowledge of natural methods of pest control, so local 'look and learn' visits were organized. In addition, a one-day workshop was held for farmers to share ideas and experiences during the season. The result of the workshop was the drawing up of a list of natural pesticides, which at present remains confidential as there was anxiety that farmers' knowledge would be abused and also a feeling among farmers that experts place little value on their local knowledge.

Women account for about 42 per cent of the project membership. They are often the ones who are most affected by the use of pesticides in cotton production through their roles as providers of clean water and food for the family. If the food and water is contaminated and the family are affected, it is the women who bear the responsibility. Women are very interested in organic production but low literacy levels and domestic responsibilities make attending training sessions difficult. Access to land can also be a problem. Even when land is allocated to women by their husbands it is often too small an area to be able to carry out the rotations required in organic production.

To publicize the project, some judging of the crop was carried out by a government agent, and four field days were held on the best fields. One of the women farmers, Emelda Wingwiri, had the best field. She works on her own, with help from her children during weekends and holidays, as her husband is permanently employed in Harare. The presentation of her field and her work programme provide a convincing example of organic cotton production as a workable alternative method (see box on page 187).

The future

The first season saw an average harvest of 400kg/ha seed cotton as well as about 500kg groundnuts, which helped increase families' nutrient intake. In 1996/7, an excessively wet year, farmers gained confidence and decided to use almost a hectare for their organic cotton crop, resulting in a yield of over 600kg/ha. Many conventional cotton fields did not yield so well and were affected by sooty mould caused by honeydew from aphids. The organic cotton was not affected and stayed very white. During the 1997/8 season, 300 farmers will plant organic cotton with assistance from 30 farmer field-workers, many of them women, drawn from communities who have been trained in organic production methods and natural pest control. Links are now being created which will allow for processing and marketing of the organic cotton crop.

Emelda Wingwiri, Zimbabwe

We started organic farming in 1995–6, after a meeting held by the organizers of Lower Guruve Development Association (LGDA). It was suggested that we spray our cotton using products of some trees. We knew trees that we thought would be helpful. A few weeks after the meeting we were provided with groundnuts, cotton seed, Leucaena and some knapsacks sprayers which were to be used only in the spraying of organic cotton. Field officers from LGDA were appointed to supervise our work.

The area I started farming organically is about half a hectare. We were supposed to sow our seeds on 26 November. I did it on 1 December because the rains had not fallen enough before 26th. I waited for the soil to be soaked. I planted both the cotton and groundnuts. I ploughed the field using an ox-drawn plough, marking the distance between the rows, which was 1 metre. The seed was planted 30cm apart.

On sowing groundnuts I walked behind the ox-drawn plough dropping seeds, and then passed back over with the plough to cover the seeds to make a uniform soil cover. The plot was divided in two. I grew half with cotton and half with groundnuts (about 0.25ha each). At the end of my organic plot, I planted some Leucaena trees. This was a windbreak.

Pests included aphids, African bollworms, pink bollworms and leaf eaters. I used tree leaves, roots and buds to spray. I mashed these and put them in a container with water and covered them for 24 hours or more, then strained and sprayed my cotton for 7 weeks, 1 day a week.

Differences between cotton grown with pesticides and organically

Organic growing is not laborious or dangerous. Pesticides are poisonous to human beings and also to bees and animals. The organic manure gives fertility to the soil but fertilizers disturb the soil. The yield was 150kg of cotton and 450kg groundnuts and marketing was a problem. Rainfall was 450mm.

In the second year (1996/7), we were given instructions by the LGDA to grow our cotton in new lands, in fields that had not been used for three years. We were given notebooks for keeping records. The area of my organic cotton was two acres or nearly a hectare. I ploughed in winter and planted earlier because by then I had felt confident and needed less supervision. I knew what I was doing. I had planted by 28 November and made my rain gauge. I used it every day to measure the amount of rain though I was not sure I was doing the right thing. I had to go to a nearby mission to verify and their measurements were similar to mine. I was impressed. Pests seen in the field were only a few bollworms. I was doing spot spraying. I had no problems in the 1996–7 season. Predators seen in the field were wasps, spiders, ladybird and the Assasin bug (*Phonocutonus* spp.). At harvest I got 3 bales or 600kg.

The research plot, 1996–97

On 16 April 1996, Dr Sam Page of ZIP Research asked me for about an acre in my field to be used as a research plot. On 6 December, she and Mrs Nyakanda brought some trees to be planted on the plot. The area is almost half a hectare. At the end the area was 16 lines of cotton and 16 lines of cowpeas with Tephrosia and pigeon pea in the middle. The plot measured 34 × 140 metres. Around the plot I planted on two corners *Jatropha* trees as a living fence, which is not eaten by goats, and in another corner *Acacia albida*, and in one corner *Leucaena* as a wind break. I also inter-cropped with cow pea. Tephrosia, planted along the centre of the plot, attracts predators and was used as a spray. Interspersed were pumpkins (as a live mulch and to encourage insects), and sweet potatoes and some other strong-smelling bushes among the cotton lines. I also planted *Azanza galziena*, which looks like cotton, to harbour predators on the perimeter. As time went by I saw some wasps, spiders, frogs, ladybirds and Assasin bugs. I did not spray, but I was scouting every week. For my interest, I took two bollworms (American and pink bollworms), one which fed on flowers and the other which fed on bolls. The one which fed on flowers stayed as pupae for 14 days and then became a moth. The one that fed on bolls stayed for 21 days and became a moth. The experiments gave me knowledge about the worms and about what they fed on during their life span, and what they turn into.

After harvesting I got 100kg cotton, 140kg cowpeas, 60kg sweet potatoes, 40kg cowpea.

Farmer meetings have provided a good opportunity for the exchange of information and knowledge. In the coming years the theme of the meetings will be to encourage farmers to spread cow dung on their fields and to make compost for use on the crops. It will also be necessary to convince farmers of the benefits of intercropping cotton with other crops to reduce pest infestations.

Organic cotton from Uganda

BO VAN ELZAKKER and GUNNAR RUNDGREN

Introduction

In modern times, the economy of Uganda has always been based on the export of two crops, coffee and cotton. In the 1930s cotton provided 80 per cent of the country's export earnings. In 1950 it was surpassed by coffee. In the past, cotton was also important as it was linked to local processing, which was an important segment of the country's manufacturing sector. Most of this capacity has degenerated due to civil strife and mismanagement, but following the recent liberalization, spinning mills and manufacturing industry is slowly being built up again.

Over 90 per cent of the population of Uganda lives in rural areas and 83 per cent of the working population is employed in agriculture. Cotton is produced in the northern and eastern regions. For many years it was the only cash crop in these regions. Cotton is grown predominantly by 2.2 million smallholders using very few inputs. The typical smallholder has about two hectares, although in the north farms may be larger. A third of this area may be planted with cotton, the rest being devoted to food crops. Millet is the second most important crop, followed by root crops like cassava and sweet potatoes, and a variety of pulses (groundnuts, beans, cowpeas) and oil seeds (sesame). In the past, cotton was interplanted with food crops, but today it is more likely to be grown on its own.

Organic cotton in Uganda

The potential for exporting certified organic cotton and other products from Uganda was investigated in 1994 when a series of studies and field trips were undertaken by Agro Eco Consultancy on behalf of the Swedish International Development Agency (Sida) and the districts of Lira and Apach were chosen for a pilot organic project.

These areas seemed to be favourable for organic cotton production because: the local Lango Co-operative Union (LCU) was an interested partner; the area has a tradition of cotton cultivation and has potential to expand; most farms are small, soils are fertile, and rainfall is fairly reliable; farmers rotate crops regularly and intercropping is common; there was almost no use of agrochemicals; and farmers use small black ants of the Acantholepsis family which feed on aphids and other larvae.

The Sida Export Promotion of Organic Products from Africa (EPOPA) programme provided assistance to the project for organization and management, research and extension, initial inspection and certification, and marketing, to the value of US$45 000 per year.

Farming practices

In Uganda, the farmers are organized by village, with several villages constituting a 'primary society', and in this instance, several primary societies making up the Lango Co-operative Union which operates a ginnery. Farmers grow cash crops such as cotton and sesame for export, and sunflower, soyabeans, beans, pigeon peas, sorghum, millet, cassava, sweet potatoes, plantains and other crops for domestic consumption and the home market. With such a wide range of crops they practise extensive crop rotations and frequently intercrop. Traditionally, farmers raised cattle and used oxen for cultivation. Farmers have not, however, been able to restock herds rustled during the 1985 civil war, so many fields now lie fallow and work is carried out manually. One aim of the project is to reintroduce animal husbandry in the area.

Certification

The project's first certified organic cotton was produced in 1994. Normally there is a 'conversion period' of 12–24 months before certification can take place, but in this case the Swedish-based certification agency, KRAV, decided that local conditions allowed this period to be waived. This judgment was backed by recommendations from the inspector, reports from Agro Eco and by local consultants acting on behalf of Sida, verifying that the production system had followed organic standards passively for many years. Residue analyses of samples of crops were also taken, but it should be recognized that this plays a minor role in the process of achieving certification.

Although the produce was awarded certification, a number of operating conditions and a time schedule for their implementation were set.

○ The whole village should be organic. Normally a farm is the 'organic unit', but in this case it was appropriate to use a 'village' unit because of the complexity of village relationships (one farmer can have different wives with different children all farming scattered plots) and the lack of maps confirming farm boundaries. Therefore, if one farmer uses pesticides all of his neighbours will lose their certification, so this creates the need for a high level of common responsibility, or social control.
○ Farmers must achieve the relevant standards for organic production and be contracted.
○ The use of treated seed should be discouraged, and trials of non-treated seeds should be begun (seed distribution was controlled by the governmental Cotton Development Organization that insisted on treatment with a copper-based fungicide).
○ An internal control system must be established.

The internal control system has been developed through a dialogue between the Lango Organic Project, Agro Eco and KRAV. It has been further refined in the light of experience and has also been adapted to the criteria for smallholder certification set by IFOAM's International Organic Accreditation Services Inc. which were published in 1996.

The project employs a number of field officers and a field supervisor. A special documentation officer has been employed to ensure proper management of the 6500 records. The field officers, all of whom have some basic agricultural education, are each responsible for around nine villages. They visit all the farmers, organize village meetings, document crops, investigate practices and provide assistance and advice. They also keep records of all sales. The field officers share responsibility for running the internal quality control system, which also verifies handling in the stores and oversees the cotton ginnery, where delivery data are checked against farm records.

190

One of the key features of organic certification is the provision of information by both the certification agency and the farmer in a two-way process. From the certification agency's point of view, farmers must understand the organic standards and the inspection process. From the farmer's point of view, it is important to understand the details of the contract with the certification agency and about the information that must be provided. Apart from verbal communications, the project distributed posters in the villages.

The Lango Organic Project has devised a set of forms and procedures for reporting necessary information, which could provide a model for other village certification schemes. The forms include:

○ *The farmer's entrance form*: for new farmers registering with the scheme, the form asks for a three-year history of the fields being converted to organic production.
○ *The contract*: in which the farmer pledges to follow the standards laid down, to provide accurate information and accept the inspection process. The Lango Project contracts are in Luo, the local language of Lira district. Where older farmers may not be able to read, their children usually can.
○ *Standards*: important points of the KRAV standards have been added to the contract. This is backed up by posters and advice from the field officer.
○ *Farm questionnaire and inspection report*: gives information on current production, yield estimates, and inspection activities and is filled in by the field officers.
○ *Growers' list*: a list compiled for each village with data on cash crops, acreage, yield estimates, and harvest. The list provides the necessary information for KRAV to certify each farm (village) and its produce.
○ *Catchment area registration form*: a summary of all villages in the 'catchment area', plus the area from which the cotton is supplied to the project's stores.
○ *Maps*: a map of each village has been drawn up using participatory mapping techniques. Each village map shows the location of each farm household and the main features of the village.
○ *Regular reports on all levels*: field officers report to the field supervisor, who reports to the project, and the field supervisor and document officer both report to the certification agency.

The focus of the inspection made by the certification agency is to evaluate the internal control system, by visiting a sample of the producers and inspecting their farms, and by assessing and comparing internal control documents with the findings of the inspectors. A sample of 5–10 per cent of the farms will be visited by external inspectors. The education of field officers, their work, the overall documentation and the accuracy of the reporting is also

191

assessed. The ginnery is inspected. Between October 1994 and November 1997, 10 inspections were made. Civil unrest interrupted the visits in 1996 but they have since been resumed. Most of the inspections have been carried out by Ugandan inspectors assigned by the external certification agency.

Marketing

Three years after the project started, 5500 farming families are involved in organic cotton production. The co-operative employs 3 organic project staff and 12 field workers who also act as internal quality control inspectors. In 1996, 400 tonnes of organic cotton lint were produced, representing 2 per cent of the total Uganda cotton harvest. Due to a lack of crop finance on the part of the marketing agents, only 70 tonnes were exported.

In 1996 the project also started marketing sesame seed, of which 100 tonnes have been exported. The potential for marketing other crops produced in the area is also being explored. This may include local processing, for example of oilseeds. Farmers will continue to grow their staple foods of corn, millet and cassava, and surplus production may also be sold. One of the main benefits of this project is that as the whole area is organic, more than 30 000 people now have a diet which is almost 100 per cent organic.

In the 1997 marketing season, organic production in the project area totaled approximately 800 tonnes of cotton fibre and about 300 tonnes organic sesame. Again, due to a lack of crop finance, only part of it was actually purchased and exported as organic. Over the years the organic farmers in the project received on average a 20 per cent better farm-gate price compared with other farmers. In the 1997 marketing season, farmers received a 40 per cent higher farm-gate price for their cotton and sesame, as world prices for conventional cotton and sesame were low, whereas those for organic produce remained steady.

In 1998, a second cotton project will be started in Uganda, aiming at harvesting 100 tonnes of lint in 1998 and 350 tonnes by the year 2000.

Challenges

Converting whole villages to organic production techniques has not been easy and several serious problems have emerged during the project. It is, for example, a difficult decision to decertify a whole village when the majority in the village has been unable to keep one or two farmers from giving in to pressure from pesticide salesmen to try a product for free. In many countries, including Uganda, governments are still aggressively following a policy of encouraging higher levels of input into farming. Four villages and more than 100 farmers were excluded for a period from the project following the government's Cotton Development Organization delivering pesticides into the area, despite knowing that there was an active organic project in place.

Pesticide contamination is one of the most serious problems facing organic growers world-wide. In the Lango project, this problem arose when cotton was kept in a former pesticide store, even though no pesticides had been kept there for over 10 years.

There are also problems in setting up and running such a large and ambitious project. To farm organically is one thing; to be certified is another. Certification involves a lot of paperwork, and it has not always been easy to ensure that everybody understands the meaning and use of the various forms and reports. To extend the internal control system from information collection to actual verification has been a major concern for the certification agency. Deciding which procedures are applicable is difficult. Transport poses a constant challenge for field officers, field supervisors and inspectors: vehicles are not readily available and often get damaged on the roads. Finally, there is the question of money. The cost of inspection and certification in the first year was almost equal to the value of the organic goods sold. In 1996/97, however, the cost decreased to around 3 per cent of the value of the organic sales. Sida provided a loan for 75 per cent of the certification costs in 1996/97, but now the project should be able to generate enough income to pay for certification itself.

Obtaining crop finance in the form of commercial loans at current rates, is a key element in the development of many projects. A major problem encountered in Uganda was the refusal by banks to provide crop finance to the exporters. Eventually a crop financing system was set up and administered through a joint venture of the African Fair Trade Association (AFTA) and the Dutch development agency, DGIS. The risks of the loan are underwritten by the Hivos/Triodos Fund, also based in the Netherlands, which provides funds for environmental and social development projects in developing countries. All the partners list their costs and claim a fixed margin based on open books. AFTA then looks for the best possible market price. Any excess funds are paid out to the farmers as a second payment over and above the premium they already received at delivery of the product. Alternatively, the excess funds are used as a development fund to benefit the farmers which ensures that they gain maximum benefit from the organic premium. The method of allocating a fair price along the supply chain results in producers, traders, and retailers all receiving a reasonable margin of profit in dealing with organic produce. However, despite the money being available in Kampala, local banks are not always able to deliver the money, in cash, in sufficient quantities to enable a smooth buying operation, and some of the crops are still being sold to conventional buyers who provide cash in hand.

A further problem, typical of some parts of Africa, has been the recent unrest in the north of Uganda. Rebel attacks on villages are very destabilizing, making it difficult for villagers to pay attention to new developments such as the demands created by converting to organic production. Inspection work is also hampered as inspectors cannot always reach the area.

Conclusion

The project has generated much interest in organic growing in the area, among farmers and the district authorities. Despite this interest, further projects have not been organized because such large projects are not easy to set-up. In many villages farmers' societies do not function well. An organic project needs a good and reliable farmers' organization which is able to take on tasks like extension, the provision of untreated (organic) seed, on-farm research, quality control, an internal inspection system and marketing assistance. Farmers' organizations capable of doing all these tasks are quite sparse. Another problem is that the success of the project has attracted other donors, who are courting the Lango Co-operative Union with promises of more and better aid, confusing the members of the Union and delaying further project development.

Organic cotton in Mozambique
NORBERTO MAHALAMBE and IQBAL JAVAID

Introduction

Mozambique has tremendous potential for cotton production. In 1973, the total seed cotton production reached 144 000 tonnes but dropped dramatically due to war and other reasons to a mere 5000 tonnes in 1985. In order to reinstate the earnings from this major export crop, the government initiated a programme to increase cotton production. The Projecto de Relancamento de Algodao (PRA), was launched by the Cotton Institute of Mozambique (IAM) in collaboration with joint venture companies and by 1997 production had recovered to a level of 72 000 tonnes. Most cotton is grown in the northern provinces, and 75–80 per cent of cotton is produced by small-scale farmers.

Converting to organic

Structural adjustment programmes in Mozambique have led to the removal of subsidies on cotton pesticides which, as in many other African countries, has led to a dramatic increase in pesticides costs for small producers. In the 1995/6 growing season, costs increased by 450 per cent and in the 1996/7 season there was an increase of 100 per cent. In addition, the negative effects of pesticides are well-known and small-scale farmers do not have training in the proper application of pesticides. It was therefore decided to investigate growing cotton without the use of synthetic agrochemicals. The intention to take a new approach coincided with a visit in February 1995 of an official from Sida to IAM to discuss organic cotton production. A feasibility study was conducted in May 1995 by Agro Eco Consultancy. The results of the study were favourable and a seminar on the production and marketing of organic cotton was held in Maputo in May 1995, which in turn recommended further investigation into technical aspects, and training. Organic conversion was initiated in Mozambique by IAM with the support of Sida-EPOPA. Certification has been carried out by KRAV and is funded by EPOPA.

Getting started

The organic cotton project (PAB) started in the 1995/96 agricultural season in Inhambane Province. Farmers used to grow cotton before independence and so were familiar with the crop but production stopped during the civil war. When the situation improved, people displaced during the war began to return home to their farms and were in need of income from cash crops such as cotton. Organic cotton requires little in the way of inputs and cotton seed was being supplied free. The strategy was also seen as a way of encouraging people to return to the rural areas rather than migrate to the towns in search of work. Organic cotton is potentially important for the economy of the country as a source of much-needed foreign exchange and also for the domestic market.

The PAB is a 'hand of action' of IAM distributing organic information through rural extension. The extension is managed by the National Directorate for Rural Development (DNDR). As the PAB covers rainfed, small-scale farms where farmers have no previous experience of organic systems, a fairly major extension programme has been needed to provide the necessary information. A detailed study on the impact of this project on peasant farmers and extension workers is currently being planned. PAB activities include:

○ the promotion of organic techniques at peasant level and training of extension workers;
○ the organization of inspection documents for certification;
○ the organization of ginning;
○ the co-ordination and funding of organic systems research by the National Institute of Agricultural Research (INIA);
○ the marketing of fibre;
○ the promotion of a Mozambican inspection and certification agency.

At present, the project is centred in the cotton-growing areas where synthetic chemical fertilizers and pesticides have not been used since independence in 1975, or since the civil war in the 1980s. This has enabled a fairly smooth transition to organic production and to the certification of the crop. The system is based on resistant varieties, crop rotation, agro-technical and cultural practices including the incorporation of organic matter (green manure and vegetable residues), and biodiversity preservation and management (equilibrium between pests and their natural enemies). Small-scale farmers in Inhambane Province mostly grow cereal crops and legumes. Cotton is a deep-rooted crop and if grown in rotation with a shallow-rooted crop such as maize, soil fertility can improve. It is also more drought resistant than maize and could still yield even when the rains finish early. An effort is being made to use natural resources to increase organic cotton production. For example, in Mozambique, there are about 800 000 tonnes of bat manure (guano) in various areas, including 300 000 in the mines in Inhambane Province. The effects of the use of guano at different dosage levels will be evaluated in the organic cotton systems in the 1997/8 season. Varieties planted include Deltapine-90 and Albar-637–24 which has resistance to jassids *(Jacobiella fascialis)*.

Pest management

The most important insect pests include the American bollworm *(Helicoverpa armigera)*, the red bollworm *(Diparopsis castanea)*, the pink bollworm *(Pectinophora gossypiella)*, jassids *(Jacobiella fascialis)*, aphid *(Aphis gossypii)* and cotton stainers *(Dysdercus* spp). Leaf eaters *(Spodoptera littoralis)* and leaf rollers *(Sylepta derogata)* and sucking insects also cause damage. A large number of predators were observed in the 1996/7 season in the farmers' fields, including coccinellid beatles, lacewings, spiders, syrphid flies, ants, *Phonoctonus* spp., and various parasites including *Apanteles* spp. which showed a very high rate of parasitism on the cotton leaf roller *(Sylepta derogata)*. Organic fields are small and isolated and there are a large number of uncultivated plants and weeds around the fields which are alternative hosts for various insects and natural enemies. Biological diversity is desirable from the pest management point of view. The use of natural pesticides such as neem *(Azadarichta indica)*, seringa *(Melia azadirach)*, tobacco *(Nicotiana tabacum)* and others is encouraged. In the season 1997/8, it is hoped to introduce the use of pheromone traps and Baculoviruses. Weeds were controlled by hand weeding using hoes.

Research and demonstration

The challenge in the research programme is to obtain effective, environmentally responsible and economically viable production and control methods. A series of pest management trials were carried out in Inhambane Province in the 1996/7 season conducted by the National Institute of Agronomic Research (INIA) in collaboration with IAM. Field trials included an evaluation of *Bacillus thuringiensis* (Bt), baculoviruses and botanicals. Various parasitoids such as *Trichogramma* and *Braconids* are also being imported for evaluation. The effects of intercropping currently practised by small farmers is also being evaluated in field trials. Preliminary results of the field trials showed that *Bacillus thuringiensis* and leaf extracts of the seringa tree were promising, whereas tobacco and *Baculoviridae* were not very effective.

Another very important issue is water conservation. Many of the organic growers live in very dry areas far from water sources and cannot obtain enough water to treat at the rate of 250–400 litres/treatment/hectare required for normal sprays. Research is being carried out to try to reduce the water volume required for sprays to 10 litres/treatment/hectare.

On-farm demonstrations were organized in farmers' fields in the 1996/7 season to show the importance of non-chemical pest management practices including early sowing, early thinning, early and proper weeding, timely harvesting and the destruction of plant debris immediately after harvest. Observance of the 'close season' of two months is also very important, as are the rotation systems. Research results show that an increase of 250–300 per cent can be obtained by timely sowing, thinning and weeding (see Table 2).

Supply of inputs and extension

IAM is responsible for the supply of inputs including seeds, tobacco powder and packing materials. It also provides extension services to the farmers and training for extension workers who are expected to pass on their knowledge to the farmers. But training so far has been limited. A new strategy is being developed in which farmers will play a more important role in their own training using the 'farmer field-school' approach.

Table 2: Preliminary dates from Contact Farmers' Demonstration Fields

Variants		Yield of seed cotton in kg/ha	% Increase
	Sowing time		
V3	24-02-1997	150	0
V2	14-02-1997	460	206
V1	05-02-1997	600	300
	Weeding time		
V3	09–12/04/97	400	0
V2	12–15/03/97	550	37.5
V1	21–27/02/97	1000	250
	Thinning time		
V3	03–05-1997	260	0
V2	04–04-1997	210	−20
V1	05–03-1997	1200	361

197

Results

In the 1995/6 season, 500 small-scale farmers were involved and organic cotton was grown on about 500ha in Inhambane Province. The crop was successfully inspected and certified by KRAV. Organic cotton was also introduced into other provinces including Zambezia, Gaza, Tete and Maputo. In Inhambane Province the total area was not increased as much in 1996/97 as expected, due to drought which discouraged the farmers. However, the total organic cotton production in 1996/97 was 200 tonnes from 600ha including the output of organic cotton from the new provinces. A big increase is expected in 1997/8 to about 9000ha in all five provinces.

There was a wide range of yields of organic cotton in 1995/6 and again in 1996/7. The maximum was about 800kg/ha, where agricultural practices are good, and the average yield was 350kg/ha compared with an average of 400kg/ha for conventional.

The response from farmers in Inhambane Province in the first year, 1995/6, was encouraging. Farmers were paid a premium of 17 per cent over the conventional prices and benefited from free seeds and other inputs. In 1996/7 the premium was 23 per cent. Table 3 gives an indication of the level of profit farmers can expect for organic over conventional cotton production in Inhambane Province.

Table 3: Cost–benefit study for organic and conventional cotton production

Cotton production system	Yield of seed cotton in kg/ha	Plant protection costs (US$/ha)	Price for seed cotton (US$/kg)	Gross benefit (US$/ha)	Net benefit (US$/ha)
Conventional	400	30	0.28	112.34	82.34
Organic without premium	350	10	0.28	98	88
Organic with premium (20%)	350	10	0.34	119.15	109.15

IAM collects the seed cotton at the end of the season and farmers are paid promptly for their output, including the premium. A range of incentives is provided to the organic farmers in addition to the organic premium, free supply of seeds and tobacco powder. These include incentives to the more successful farmers of oxen, clothes, radios, bicycles and construction materials. IAM also collaborates with other government departments to provide community services such as drinking water facilities, schools and health centres in the target areas.

IAM collects the seed cotton from the farmers and supervises the ginning. IAM is also responsible for the sale of the cotton fibre. In order to export, a minimum of 300 tonnes of fibre is required, and this has not yet been produced and certified. Production so far has been sold in the conventional market at conventional prices. National and regional textile companies are reluctant to engage in processing without an assured market.

Problems

Several areas have been identified in the project which could be improved. For example, farmers are sometimes not able to follow the recommendations called for in an organic system. Inspection and certification is very costly when certifiers from overseas are involved. In discussions with representatives of other projects, this issue is seen as a major problem for new projects in Africa.

The organic markets in Europe, Asia and the United States are difficult to access and gain knowledge about, since large volumes of organic cotton to trade are required. Further assistance is required to facilitate making connections between the projects and possible markets in Europe and elsewhere. South–south contacts and partnerships are still in the early stages but such activity could be very beneficial for the new African projects.

As of early 1998, the collaboration with Sida-EPOPA has come to an end, but IAM continues to support organic cotton production without certification and marketing as organic.

Organic cotton production in Senegal

ABOU THIAM and NGONE WAR TOURE

Introduction

Cotton cultivation in Senegal is carried out in the eastern and southern parts of the country entirely under rainfed conditions. It is the second most important export crop after peanuts. Cotton plays an important role in the economy of Senegal. After a record season in 1991/2 in which 50 576 tonnes of seed cotton was produced, output has fallen each season to 47 552 in 1992/3 and 28 663 in 1994/5. The number of farmers choosing to grow cotton has fallen from 77 768 in 1992 to 58 300 in 1995. This decline is linked to the cost of chemical inputs increasing dramatically after the devaluation of the CFA in 1994 and reductions in extension services, which mean farmers no longer receive the level of support they are used to. Prices are not sufficiently attractive to offset these factors which have contributed to the increasing reluctance of farmers to engage in cotton production.

Until recently, Senegalese law allowed only Sodefitex, the State Cotton Board, to engage in cotton production. Structural adjustment programmes put in place by the international financial institutions (World Bank, IMF) brought about the liberalization of the cotton sector and conditions were created in which it became possible for other organizations to become involved in cotton production. This provided the opportunity to start an organic cotton project with a group of volunteer farmers.

Koussanar, the location of the pilot project, is situated 430km east of Dakar in the Tambacounda region. The administrative area has 94 villages and 11 000 people composed of 56 per cent Peulhs, 37 per cent Manding, 4 per cent Bambara and 2 per cent Wolof. It is a very flat, low-lying area with scattered depressions often occupied by lakes and seasonal water courses. Lateritic outcrops appear in certain places. Soils are generally red 'ferralitiques' and often of sandy texture. The Sudano-sahelian climate is characterized by a long dry season from November to May and a rainy season from June to October. Rainfall is very irregular both in timing and location, and varies from 600 to 800mm per year. Temperatures are high, reaching 40°C during the warmer months of the year.

Agriculture is the dominant activity of the people of the area and cattle rearing is a very important part of it. Fertilization of the soils with organic material is the basis of organic agricultural systems. The large number of animals in the area is an asset, provided the organic material can be collected and applied in a suitable form to the fields.

Project initiation
In 1993, ENDA-Pronat, a West African NGO based in Dakar, concerned with sustainable agriculture participated in an international workshop on *Digitaria exilis* organized by UGAPS, a small farmers' organization from Kongheul, a village near Koussanar. As a result of this meeting, a group of farmers from Koussanar asked ENDA-Pronat for help in converting to more sustainable agricultural systems. At the same time, the Pesticides Trust was looking to support organic cotton conversion. Discussions took place between ENDA-Pronat and the Pesticides Trust on the one hand and Pronat and the Koussanar farmers on the other hand, which resulted in the establishment of an experimental organic cotton project, initially of three years' duration.

The project objectives are:

○ to reduce or eliminate the use of synthetic chemicals in cotton production in the area;
○ to reduce the impact of synthetic chemicals on the health of people, stock and the environment;
○ to ensure improved income and reduce indebtedness for the farmers; and
○ to use the pilot project, if successful, for demonstration and replication.

During the 1994 season, two volunteer farmers made the first attempts at organic cotton cultivation based on recommendations of a consultant agronomist provided by the Pesticides Trust. In November of the same year, two members of the ENDA-Pronat team participated in a study visit to several European countries (Germany, Italy, Switzerland, Netherlands and UK) to familiarize themselves with developments in the eco-textile area and to meet the various actors involved in processing and manufacturing organic cotton.

In the dry season of 1995, ENDA-Pronat and the Pesticides Trust organized a workshop at Koussanar for farmers in the area who were interested in alternative cotton production methods as well as local officials of Sodefitex and the Senegalese Agricultural Research Institute (ISRA). The ISRA research centre is based in Tambacounda, near Koussanar and is mainly involved in cotton research. The workshop was an occasion to explain to those present the main objectives, methodology and means of putting the project into practice and in addition to lay the foundations for collaborative activities with all those involved in cotton production in the region. It was also an opportunity for farmers to discuss and present their problems with the present mode of production. The consultant agronomist from Ecotropic was able to explain criteria for the selection of farmers and the basis of the technical operation of the project.

In order to provide effective and rapid support to the farmers, it was decided to put in place in Koussanar a permanent team consisting of an agronomist and an extensionist. Working with the recommendations of the consultant, they were charged with the selection of the farmer volunteers following a census among the local farmers, the preparation of the cotton production system in 1995 which included the provision of seeds, purchase of agricultural implements, contacts with ISRA for experimental design and much more. The team was reinforced by a second extensionist in the 1996 season. In parallel with these activities, contacts were established at a high level with Sodefitex and ISRA in order to benefit from their experience in the area and to establish a good level of collaboration which would benefit all concerned.

Progress and first results

In the first season in 1995, 53 farmers from 10 villages in the immediate vicinity of Koussanar took part in the project. The farmers were self-selected but certain criteria were applied, such as the type of preceding crop in the proposed cotton field and the availability to the farmer of farmyard manure, which is essential in improving the fertility of the soil. Most farmers planted cotton on 0.25–0.5ha. Technical recommendations to the farmers included ploughing before sowing and sowing as early as possible. Three varieties of seed were supplied by ISRA (Stam F, Stam 42 and IRMA 772) which were

Demby Sy, Koussanar Farmer

I grow many crops: rice, cotton, millet and other things. In the past we had many problems planting cotton. In the beginning, inputs were provided free and the price paid for the cotton was CFAFr 100. We could afford to buy animals and build our houses. But in recent years, we have had to start paying for inputs and there were other problems. But we did not understand the system and felt that we were cheated because of the two grades of cotton. We thought that all the cotton was paid at the lower grade. There were many things we did not understand and could not find out where the grades are indicated. And then Sodefitex decided how much we owed for inputs and there is nothing we can do about it because we can't show how much we have used. If one farmer cannot pay then the whole group suffers. We are always in debt and often we cannot even pay for our children's education. Sodefitex trained the farmers in literacy which farmers appreciate, but they place too many constraints on us and so I decided to try organic. Before we could not pay our debts and we were often forced to resell the materials provided by Sodefitex. But now with the new system (with ENDA-Pronat), I have no debts and even though my yields are lower all the money I get will be mine.

I went to the nearby village, Koussanar, where I heard that people were trying new ideas. I visited the farmers and saw what the farmers who were working with ENDA had achieved. We went on a tour to visit other farmers' organizations and then we started organizing ourselves. We have visited many villages and have set up eight farmers' organizations with a co-ordinating office in Koussanar.

ENDA has been very helpful. They gave us seeds for CFAFr 40 per kg which we have to repay after selling the cotton. We have also had loans to buy tools and will also repay the amount when we sell our cotton. When farmers see our progress they want to join us, but we have certain requirements. Farmers also want to grow organic peanuts and sesame. There has been a lot of deforestation and many farmers know about the need to preserve the environment. The project has shown us what to do and how to organize to take control when they have to withdraw. Contact farmers who can help train other farmers have been identified and equipped with bicycles. They work with extension workers.

I have been collaborating with ENDA-Pronat to do some experiments on my land with different types of fertilization. I used 0.25ha divided into four parts. I left one part untreated, I put 500kg manure on the next and cow urine on the next (using 20 litres/625 square metres) and I put 50kg of wood ash on the next. I compared the results and found that the one with 500kg manure had good results. I compared wood ash with manure and found that with manure the cotton grows fast but has few capsules. There are more pests with manure than with wood ash. I invited farmers to visit my land to see what I was doing. I invited other farmers to see the experiments and that way I can spread the experience.

delinted using Baobab *(Adamsonia digitata)* fruit juice and used at a rate of 30kg/ha with recommended spacing of 80 × 25 cm. Cultivation practices include weeding about 20 days after seedling appearance and 'earthing up' 20 days after germination. Pheromone traps were used to monitor the more important pest populations. Neem *(Azadirachta indica)* seed powder was the main means of pest control. The seeds were ground into powder which was left in water for a day and the liquor used as spray. Cow urine was also used as foliar feed and to tackle pests. The seed cotton is hand-picked. A total of 15.5ha was harvested with a total production of 4.6 tonnes of seed cotton and an average yield of 296kg/ha. Ecocert carried out a baseline inspection and indicated that in the following season the crop could be certified as 'in conversion' according to EU regulations.

In the second season (1996), the total area increased to 71ha with 152 farmers involved, who produced close to 19 tonnes of seed cotton. Many more farmers wished to join the programme but numbers had to be limited to the capacity of the support team. The average yield increased from 296kg/ha in 1995 to 317kg/ha in 1996. Although the average yield figure is still low, some farmers have achieved yields very much higher at around 900kg/ha. In 1997, 523 farmers were involved with an area of 232.75ha and a total of 23 tonnes of seed cotton was harvested with a much lower average yield than in former years. The reasons for this drop in yield are poor rainfall, late sowing and management problems. In the 1998 season, the same farmers will be involved in the project.

Marketing links are being established both locally within Senegal and beyond. A local spinning mill is interested in buying the organic cotton fibre and selling on to a local knitting and manufacturing company which in turn can export into the European market. Other possibilities include direct sale of fibre to a company based in Germany.

Gender dimension

Much of the emphasis to date in this, as in other projects, has been on the technical and economic aspects. Social aspects are now receiving more attention and in particular the gender (defined as the differential roles and responsibilities of women and men in a given situation) implications of the conversion work. Although a gender approach was implied from the outset in the project, the implementation of the approach started to develop during 1997. In the first year, 3 women were involved, in the second year 17, and a further increase in the 1998 season is expected. Two highly successful women's 'grouppement de neem' have played a key role in gathering, preparing and selling neem powder, a key element in pest control, to the male and female farmers participating in the project. Women are represented in the structures of the new farmers' organization at the village level and also at the executive level.

Bakary Fofana, farmer

I was in the army for 32 years and when I came back to the rural area six years ago I noticed many changes in the time I was away. I did not like the changes, although some were negative and some were positive. When I was young, we had honey but now there was none. It provided us with vitamins. I decided to go back to farming. Before I went away, cotton farming was rare in my area, though we grew it for family needs. In the past there were a small number of pests but they did not endanger the harvest. The current methods were new to me, so at first I planted cereals but my children badgered me to grow some cash crops. I have been growing cotton for only three years. They say we need money, so I have to follow what they say.

I knew there were advantages and disadvantages. For example there are problems of pesticides which need great care. The first year my children dealt with cotton production and it was a good year. There was a pest infestation but they used pesticides and had good yields. The following year, encouraged by the first year, and because of a shortage of peanut seeds, we grew more cotton. That year we had bad luck and there were no results at all. There was a worm infestation and the pesticide was almost useless. In the previous year, the pesticide was really efficient, but last year, using the same product, the effect was totally different. Farmers using pesticides left over from the previous year had a better result. Both the supplier and the farmers that used this are now suing the company that sold the products. This is my second year, and I keep hoping that the result of last year will not repeat itself. This harvest season when I was expecting to sow seeds for conventional farming I met a friend who told me that, although organic cotton production is not well introduced in my region, some farmers are involved. That's how I came into organic cotton production. Maybe I didn't know that I was organic, but I have always loved insects and always tried to protect them. So I was not difficult to convince. The results are here to see. But since I have tried both kinds of farming, I prefer organic.

During an external evaluation of the project in June 1997, some information gathering was carried out using PRA methodologies. It was established that there are already in the Koussanar area a number of women growing cotton. Many are interested in organic cotton, as are the men, for its economic benefits. Organic cotton is of special interest to women because it does not require chemical inputs which are costly and spraying is traditionally not an area of activity in which women are involved because the work is 'too dangerous'. Women are also well aware of the dangers to health of using pesticides. It is very difficult for women to obtain credit and the necessary supplies for conventional cotton growing, which provides further encouragement for women to try the organic approach.

More emphasis on gender differentiation and encouragement to women to join the project can be expected in the future.

Conclusions

The farmers themselves report in the evaluation sessions that organic agriculture can be profitable and at the same time can protect their health, that of their animals and the environment. Whilst envisioning consolidation and then further expansion of the project, it is important that the project eventually becomes self-sustaining under the management of the farmers themselves with the technicians and consultants intervening as advisers. The emphasis should be placed increasingly on the further development of the farmers' organizations which can handle the interaction between the farmers and the various project partners at local, national and international level.

The outcome of the two seasons in Koussanar demonstrates that organic cotton can be grown in this region. The project is still in its early phase of development. There is much scope for further analysis and improvement based on experience to date and for improved implementation of soil fertility and pest control practices. Farmers nevertheless remain enthusiastic and committed. For them, it seems that the advantages of lower production costs, timely payments with premium, freedom from indebtedness and the high level of support outweigh the disadvantages.

Organic cotton production in Benin
SIMPLICE DAVO VODOUHE

Introduction

Benin, like Senegal, is a former French colony. It is surrounded by Nigeria, Togo, Niger, Burkina Faso and, on its southern side, the Atlantic Ocean. It has an area of 112 600km^2 and a population of about 5 million. Cotton is one of the main exports from Benin and averages 38 per cent of the total exports per year and is therefore of major economic importance to the country.

Cotton is also of great importance at household level. For most farmers and farming families, particularly in Central and Northern Benin, cotton is the main cash income. Other crops are used mostly for home consumption or for food processing. Official statistics indicate that an average of about 125 000 farming families grow cotton. Both the area under cotton cultivation and actual production are increasing at a considerable rate annually. Cotton production increased from 31 200 tonnes of seed cotton in 1982 to nearly 318 000 in 1996. The area under cultivation increased from 26 800ha to over 340 000ha over the same period of time. This boom in cotton production can be attributed to the use of new technologies such as improved seed varieties, fertilizers, pesticides, animal traction and the effective institutional framework.

The cotton sector in Benin is highly organized by the government. State intervention has provided farmers with a guaranteed outlet for their harvest and access to markets. Institutions involved in cotton production are: Fonds de Stabilisation et Soutien (FSS), Centre d'Action Régional pour le Développement Rural (CARDER), Societé Nationale pour la Promotion Agricole (SONAPRA), Recherche Coton et Fibres (RCF), Direction de la Promotion de la Qualité et du Conditionnement (DPQC). Private companies are also now gaining importance in ginning, in supplying inputs to farmers, and in marketing activities as the sector is gradually privatized. Farmers' organizations are becoming important in the cotton sector, taking over many activities previously carried out by government services. Many activities previously performed by, for example, CARDER are now left to farmers' organizations including input distribution, marketing of seed cotton, etc. However, the benefit from these organizations has so far tended to accrue to a few dominant individuals rather than to the organizations as a whole.

In 1995, the Beninese Government began privatizing ginning activities as capacity was falling behind production. Private investors have been invited to invest in eight new factories with a total ginning capacity of 225 000 tonnes. Four factories are already functioning, while four others are under construction.

Agriculture in the main cotton regions of Benin is characterized by shifting cultivation. Rotation patterns include sorghum and maize in the North, and yam, maize and cassava in Central Benin. Chemical fertilizers and pesticides are used mainly in cotton production, and to a lesser extent for other crops such as maize. Pesticides are sprayed on cotton on a calendar basis with about six applications per year. Efforts are being made to reduce the quantity of pesticides used by applying the IPM techniques. These techniques are known as 'lutte étagée ciblée' (LEC). The main pests are: *Helicoverpa armigera, Diparopsis watersi, Sylepta derogata, Dysdercus voelkeri, Polyphagotarsonemus latus, Pectinophora gossypiella, Tetranychus* spp., *Aphis gossypii* and *Cryptophlebia leucotrata*.

There is growing interest in alternative production methods as a result of rising input costs and awareness of the environmental impact of current cultural practices. The increase in the total area for cotton and the use of synthetic agrochemicals are creating environmental problems especially in North and Central Benin. Soil erosion and shortened fallow periods are affecting soil fertility. In addition, producers have become increasingly aware of the high costs of imported chemical products, which have risen dramatically since the devaluation in January 1994. The health of farmers and their families are endangered by the casual use of pesticides and by, for example, recycling empty pesticide cans for domestic use.

The decision to experiment with organic cotton arose from a feasibility study on developing new forms of trade links between Benin and the Netherlands, and a European Study Tour in late 1994 organized by the Pesticides Trust. The tour visited buyers of organic cotton and investigated the potential market. A new NGO was formed, the Organization Beninoise pour la Promotion de l'Agriculture Biologique (OBEPAB) with the objective of promoting organic cotton pilot projects, information dissemination and policy advocacy. There are currently two experimental organic projects under way in Benin: Aklampa and Dan in the South, and Kandi in the North.

The Aklampa and Dan Project

The OBEPAB pilot project in the South is supported and financed by the Pesticides Trust. It employs two extensionists and a supervisor. The first step taken was a meeting with farmers in the village of Aklampa (Glazou District) and Dan (Djidja District) in 1995 to discuss cotton and the environment. In a brainstorming session, farmers exchanged experiences and observations on cotton production. Cotton was produced because it provided financial security, as purchasing prices were known in advance. Extension services, through the system of contract farming, and provision of technical inputs were good. Farmers were aware nevertheless that:

○ cotton was more time and labour consuming than their other crops;
○ increasing areas for cotton growing was forcing farmers to move far from the village for cultivation, and land for cotton growing was increasing at the expense of land for food cultivation;
○ cotton growing prevented them from harvesting their main food crops of maize and yam, and from carrying out cultural operations related to yams (the main staple crop) and as a result they were becoming food importers, instead of food exporters; and
○ the fertility of the land was becoming poorer and alternatives which would restore soil fertility and increase income were sought.

Farmers did not believe, however, that organic cotton would be a workable alternative to conventional cotton growing, and were anxious about the market for the crop.

The strategy produced in response to the farmers' discussions involved a mutual control arrangement whereby the farmers themselves chose who would participate in the first experiment in organic cotton growing. About 50 farmers were proposed and a contract established between them and OBEPAB. Farmers are the main actors in the project. They meet regularly to discuss the development of their cotton crop and the OBEPAB agent offers them advice and gives information on pest control and fertilization during field visits.

Cultivation
The programme is aimed at progressively restoring the balance between different insects in the cotton farms with the goal being biological control

of pests. During the pilot project natural products were used for pest control, mainly oil- and water-based neem products. Treatment began 45 days after sowing, depending on the level of infestation in the field, at intervals of 10 days. OBEPAB's agent visited the farms shortly after treatment to test its effectiveness, and treatment was repeated if necessary. Participatory evaluation by the farmers and the OBEPAB agent concluded that treatment had begun too late and that for good-quality organic cotton, treatment should begin sooner as a preventive and be applied more frequently.

The 1996/7 harvest produced 4.8 tonnes of seed cotton which were judged by the farmers to be of organic standard. The yields vary from farmer to farmer and are between 118kg/ha for farmers who did not follow the instructions to 850kg for farmers who followed all instructions.

In the 1997/8 season, 34 farmers planting 21ha will be involved in the village of Aklampa and 13 farmers with 15ha in the village of Dan. Local gins and spinning mills have expressed interest in carrying out the processing.

Relations between cotton producers

OBEPAB has met with members from similar organic cotton projects—PADEC Kandi and the Koussanar project from Senegal—to compare experiences and identify opportunities for using natural pest control. It would also be useful if farmers came together to exchange views on organic cotton providing initially a village-level network, and in time regional networks. A seminar was held in Abomey in March 1997 which brought together interested people from neighbouring countries and Europe to examine issues involved in organic cotton production and to learn from each other about crop protection, marketing and certification.

The Kandi Project

The project in Kandi was initiated in 1996 as a part of the integrated rural development project, PADEC-Kandi which is supported by SNV, the Dutch development organization. Interest in organic cotton experimentation was generated by two seminars on Cotton and the Environment (1995) and Organic Cotton Growing: Feasibility and Perspectives (1996) which were organized by a group seeking co-ordination and greater relevance in the development activities in the Kandi area. Farmers, extensionists and policymakers were initially very sceptical about the possibilities of success. In the 1996/7 season, some 32 individual farmers in 8 groups of men and women grew organic cotton on plots of 0.36ha on average. They became convinced that cotton can be produced organically even though yields are low. Farmers were particularly interested in the experiment from the economic standpoint. Credit provided for the purchase of synthetic chemical inputs in the conventional sector is about 25–30 per cent of cotton revenues on average and farmers run the risk of becoming indebted. Organic production can therefore sustain a yield loss of up to 25–30 per cent without the farmer's income being threatened. Total yield loss was estimated to be 40–50 per cent and a premium of 20 per cent was paid by the project to make up the balance. In the first season, farmers have concentrated on soil fertilization with organic material and bat 'guano' and on pest control using neem powder. Women farmers have problems with fertilization because they do not own cattle. In 1997/8 the numbers of farmers increased to 59 women and 49 men with an average plot size of 0.25ha. Average yields have increased to 400kg/ha which is still low, but some farmers obtained 900–1000kg/ha.

Activities in the 1998/1999 season will focus on two questions: whether it is possible to produce organic cotton as a viable economic alternative for the farmer to conventional production, and how to promote setting up an organic cotton industry in Benin, in collaboration with local farmers' organizations and local cotton institutes, in order to maximize local added value before export. Efforts will focus on extension work and improving yields at the field level whilst networking and information dissemination will be important activities in persuading the conventional sector of the importance of the organic approach.

Conclusion

The state in Benin dominates the cotton sector and is well organized, but the actual practices contribute to environmental degradation. The introduction of organic cotton is appreciated by farmers and the numbers engaged in the programme are increasing. The success of such programmes depends mainly on the effectiveness of farmers' organizations and the exchange of knowledge between farmers on fertilization and pest control methods.

15
Future challenges

DOROTHY MYERS and SUE STOLTON

Introduction

The book has aimed to describe work in progresss on organic cotton production, processing and marketing. It is the first book on the subject and it is hoped that it will generate more research, analysis and publication on the topic. The objective was to be as comprehensive and up-to-date as possible at this point at the end of the 1990s. This is a recent area of endeavour, however, and information is inadequate, difficult to obtain and unsystematic. It is a new and dynamic area, and things are changing rapidly. A great variety of people are involved from farmers to agronomists to business people to researchers and scientists to designers to consumers. There is no established structure as there is in the conventional cotton world and ways of working have had to be developed from scratch, which has led to much innovation. Projects and experiments are taking place in a wide range of settings in more than 17 countries in North America, Latin America, Asia, Australasia, Africa and Europe.

Despite all the uncertainties and limitations, a number of issues emerge from the discussion which need to be addressed or which require further attention if organic cotton production and processing is to expand and make its contribution to changing the conventional agricultural paradigm. Although some of the points set out below are drawn from specific country experience, they are seen as having more general relevance. In considering cotton specifically, it must be remembered that it is only one part of the organic system and, although it is dealt with as a separate entity in this book, it is always part of an organic system. Many of the points below are relevant to organic systems overall insofar as the system may require additional resources, research, capacity-building, and market resources.

There are several important issues which need to be addressed generally throughout the cotton chain which include:

○ Awareness of the problems associated with conventional cotton production and the possibilities offered by organic cotton is crucial.
○ Gender issues in general need to be addressed at the production level especially. Decision-making in agriculture tends to reflect a gender bias, with extension services being provided by men for men in spite of the fact that, especially in Africa, the farmers are often women. In the interests of the further development of organic agriculture, structures should

aim for equity in decision making. Women play a crucial role in manufacturing, design, retail and purchasing as well as at the production level.

○ There is a need for greater transparency at all points in the chain in order to make experience and information widely available. It is necessary to build a body of expertise related to the whole organic cotton chain which can be drawn upon to develop the sector further.

○ In addition to information and expertise along the cotton chain, there is a need for conversion support, including appropriate and accessible information for farmers at field level, training, extension, temporary financial support and contacts related to all aspects of organic conversion.

○ Research and analysis of the economics of organic cotton is crucial. In particular, there is a need to conduct more research on the internalization of environmental costs in conventional agricultural prices in order that proper comparisons can be made with conventional production.

Research needs at the farm level

Improvements are needed in production technology through research and development at farm level including:

○ biologically based pest management;
○ non-chemical weed control;
○ soil-fertility management;
○ and, for mechanically harvested cotton, management techniques to replace chemical defoliants.

Some research priorities identified at the technical level include:

○ identifying suitable seed varieties for organic systems sowing;
○ alternative seed treatments;
○ the costs and benefits of green manures;
○ the composting of crop residues and its effect on pests;
○ ways to monitor and enhance the presence of natural enemies.

A co-ordinated research programme could be developed involving industry, government, research institutes, extensionists and farmers. Farmers should be closely involved through participatory extension techniques. Research and extension must not be considered separately from farmers' themselves and their organizations.

Farmer training and extension

Research in farmers' fields and farmer field school approaches to training are effective ways of training farmers and increasing their awareness of the principles of organic agriculture.

Extension should be organized through farmers' organizations, using participatory methods. Training should start in farmers' fields, with the principals of agro-ecology and organic production, and should also include certification, marketing, business management, accounting and fundraising. A firmly based understanding of the principals of organic production is vital, as is an understanding of organic agriculture as a system which brings benefits over the medium to long-term, rather than in the short-term. Farmers' need for food security must be understood by all actors in the system. Farmer-to-farmer exchanges should be emphasized as a way of extending uptake and generating new projects.

Farmer support
The structures that are required to start and maintain an organic project were discussed in Chapter 4. As well as providing suitable information systems, the need to ensure adequate financing (particularly during conversion) and material support (such as livestock and pest control equipment) is essential to project success.

Inspection and certification

Problems faced by producers in the South having to certify according to the requirements and systems developed in the North have been discussed in Chapter 6 and in the case studies. Several areas could be investigated:

○ National regulatory systems for organic agriculture and processing, especially in the South, could be developed in more countries through broad consultation processes. Such local systems could reduce the costs of certification and contribute to the further development of the organic sector. It is important that laws address the current needs of the organic sector within the country as they currently exist.
○ Internal control systems need to be an integral part of certification schemes in countries where small-scale farmers predominate. Such systems empower small farmers, support organic farming development, ensure compliance with certification requirements, and reduce the costs of certification.
○ Existing national certification bodies in the South need to be strengthened, leading to IFOAM accreditation, thus facilitating access to the European and North American markets.

Processing

Chapter 6 describes current processing standards and highlights the inconsistencies amongst the systems. At present, organic standards are more developed for agricultural production systems. The adoption of the IFOAM processing standards will be an important step forwards, but further work is needed to develop organic fibre processing standards.

There is a continuing need for research and development into the whole life-cycle of an organic cotton product and for education of those working in the organic cotton business to the environmental and social effects of the whole life-cycle. Improvements in technology, such as those developed in response to environmental legislation in Europe need to be disseminated throughout the organic cotton industry worldwide. Likewise, techniques from the South such as knowledge about natural dyes and traditional processing are relevant for processing organic cotton.

Manufacturing and design

It is important that designers gain a greater understanding of the issues because their impact at the processing stage is crucial. The role of the environmental designer is to integrate environmentally responsible approaches into normal design requirements and business considerations. Lack of information in textile colleges is striking, although more colleges are incorporating environmental considerations into their curricula. If students have access to relevant and accurate information within the industry there will be greater prospects for change.

Labelling

Labelling confusion in the market place must be overcome if consumers are to have confidence in labelling systems. Most eco-labelling schemes have low budgets for marketing their products. They need to make alliances with other organizations to present a common approach to conventional and alternative textile production methods. The Clean Clothes Campaign in the Netherlands is an example of a coalition of trade unions, environment and fair trade organizations which promotes fair trade and environmentally responsible approaches to clothing manufacture.

Raising consumer awareness

Raising consumer awareness about the environmental and social aspects of textile and clothing production is a key element in building a market for organic cotton textiles. Consumer education and public outreach could include:

○ Support for consumer education and advocacy projects that focus on organic cotton.
○ The publishing and dissemination of resource materials related to organic cotton, including technical reference material for producers, handling and market-related materials for the clothing industry, general reference materials for consumers and NGOs. Existing material in Swedish, Dutch and German should be translated and more widely distributed.

213

Marketing

International markets can be further extended into countries where they do not exist. Local markets, which are beginning to appear in India, Peru and Egypt, can also be further expanded.

International marketing information continues to be sparse but is improving. Transparency in the cotton chain is seen as desirable and this type of information could be made available at all levels of the production chain, including the farmer level. Market and consumer surveys for organic cotton and eco-textiles should be carried out in Europe, especially in the countries where the market is still underdeveloped, such as UK, France and Italy. Information about possible markets in Japan and Australia, for example, is noticeably lacking.

Approaches to marketing should be diverse and can include:

○ developing the niche market;
○ blending organic cotton with conventional cotton in textile production (see Chapter 8);
○ approaches to environmentally sensitive companies; and
○ linking with local industries geared to making organic products (such as the hand-loom industry in India).

Project management

All actors in the organic cotton production chain should be involved at the beginning of projects up to importers' level at least. In this way, a guaranteed market for organic produce can be obtained before sowing starts and obstacles to production and marketing can be identified.

Advocacy and policy-level initiatives

Information can be provided to official bodies at local, national and international levels in order to draw attention to problems such as pesticide usage, irrigation and genetically engineered cotton; to report successful organic cotton projects; and to show where and how organic projects have made a difference. At the industry level, organizational efforts in the organic cotton industry should be strengthened in order to:

○ Actively incorporate organic cotton production research into the activities of the major cotton trade organizations.
○ Promote uniform international certification and processing standards for organic cotton and a standardized audit procedure for verification.
○ Strengthen membership of national organic cotton trade associations and support the implementation of organic cotton standards.

○ Support the creation of comprehensive directory of European suppliers, brokers, mills, companies, advocates, government agencies, consultants, support organizations and technical resources involved with organic cotton at a regional or international level, as has been done in the US (see Chapter 9).

Policy initiatives (particularly in Europe and the US) could be designed to favour the entry of organic and eco-textiles into the market. Governments could, for example, be encouraged to apply environmental criteria to their own buying policies for institutions such as police forces, schools, army, and so on.

Conclusion

Organic cotton has developed as a viable, albeit small-scale, alternative to conventional cotton in many countries under many different ecological and social conditions. This development has, in general, been without the support and assistance of established, conventional research and extension facilities. In some cases the establishment has even obstructed development, rather than stimulating support to this new direction in agriculture. Moreover the industry structures which exist at the processing, manufacturing and marketing levels are not appropriate or do not exist for environmentally responsible cotton clothing and textiles.

The development and successes of the projects described in this book therefore attest to the positive desire for change which is beginning to take place across the textile sector. That so much has been achieved in such a short time with relatively little assistance is in many ways remarkable. What the organic cotton sector now needs is a major input of resources to tackle the many areas described above which require further work. We hope this book will contribute to this effort by spreading the message both within and beyond the organic cotton sector of new developments and directions.

Acknowledgements

This chapter draws on ideas from, among others, Nathan Boone, Bo van Elzakker, César Morán, Susanne Hagenfors, Tadeu Caldas, Peter Ton and Lynda Grose.

References and Further Reading

The following section includes the principal references and further reading, by chapter. In a book of this size the references could have taken many pages, so the authors have listed only the most important references and provided the most useful information on the issues raised in the chapters. At the end of this section is an overview of key publications relating to organic cotton and further sources of information, such as the internet, journals and magazines.

Chapter 1

de Vries, H. and H. Kox (1995); *An international commodity-related environmental agreement (ICREA) for cotton: An appraisal*, Economics Department, Free University, Amsterdam.

Katz, D. and N. Boone (1996); *Organic cotton: world supply and strategies to strengthen the market*, Second International IFOAM Conference on Organic Textiles, Bingen, Germany, IFOAM, Germany.

Pretty, J. (1995); *Regenerating agriculture: policies and practices for sustainability and self-reliance*, Earthscan, London.

Robins, N. and S. Roberts (1997); *Unlocking trade opportunities: changing consumption and production patterns*, IIED and the UN Department of Policy Co-ordination and Sustainable Development, London and New York.

Ton, P (1996); *The European market for organic cotton and textiles: a market survey*, Foundation Ecooperation, Amsterdam.

Chapter 2

Allan Woodburn Assoc. (1995); '*Cotton—The crop and its agrochemicals market*', Edinburgh, UK.

Boone, N. and M. Reeves (1998); *Organic cotton directory 1998–1999*, The Organic Fibre Council and the Pesticide Action Network, USA.

British Agrochemical Association (BAA) Annual Reports, London.

de Vries, H. and H. Kox (1995); *An international commodity-related environmental agreement (ICREA) for Cotton: An appraisal*, Economics Department, Free University, Amsterdam.

Dinham, B. (1993); *The pesticides hazard: A global health and environmental audit*, the Pesticides Trust, UK.

Goldenberg, S. (1998); 'King Cotton reaps tragic harvest in Indian fields', *The Guardian*, Wednesday 21 January 1998.

Hamdy, M. E., S. Barghouti, F. Gilham and T. Al-Saffy, (1994); *Cotton production prospects for the decade to 2005: A global overview*, World Bank Technical Paper No 231, 1994.

Murray, D. (1994); *Cultivating crisis: The human cost of pesticides in Latin America*, University of Texas Press, Austin, Texas.

Pease, W. et al (1993); *Preventing pesticides-related illness in California agriculture: Strategies and priorities*, California Policy Seminar, Berkeley, California.

Pesticides Trust (1995); *A cotton reader*, Pesticides Trust, UK.

Rissler, J. (1997); '*Bt* cotton—another magic bullet?' *Global Pesticides Campaigner*, March 1997, PAN North America, San Francisco.

Rissler, J. and M. Mellon (1996); *The ecological crisis of engineered crops*, MIT Press, Cambridge, MA, USA.

Verma, J. (1998); 'Cotton, pesticides and suicides', *Global Pesticide Campaigner*, Vol 8: No. 2, PAN North America, San Francisco.

Wild cotton

Bell, A. A. (1984); 'Cotton protection practices in the USA and the World. Section B: Diseases', in: R.G. Khohel and C.F. Lewis (ed.) *Cotton*. Agronomy monograph No. 24, ASA-CSSA, Madison, W.I.

Hutchinson, J. B. (1962); 'The history and relationships of the world's cottons', *Endeavor*, Vol. 21, pp. 5–15.

Purseglove, J. W. (1984); *Tropical crops*. Vol: Dicotyledons. London; Longman 282pp.

Ruwitah, A. (1997); 'The mystery of cotton', *The Zimbabwean Review*, Vol. 3, No. 4, pp. 3–5.

Sloan, A. (1923); 'The black woman', *NADA* Vol. 1, No. 1, pp. 60–69.

Chapter 3

Bertoldi, M. et al (1987); *Compost: production, quality and use*, Elsevier.

Caldus, T. (1997); 'Organic cotton: not just a matter of fibre', *Ecology & Farming*, Vol. 14, IFOAM, Germany.

Coste, R. (1988); *Cotton*, The tropical agriculturist series, CTA/Macmillan.

CTA, (1994); *Preparation and use of compost*, Agrodok 8, Agromisa.

Gray, K. et al (1987); *Soil management: Compost production and use in tropical and sub-tropical environments*, FAO Soils Bulletin 56, FAO, Rome.

Jansen, H. G. (1995); '*Integrated cotton production in Nicaragua*', GATE, D-65726 Eschborn.

Munro, J. M. (1987); *Cotton*, Longman.

Matthews, G. A. and J.P. Tunstall (1994); *Insect pests in cotton*, CABI, Wallingford, UK.

Chapter 5

AFMA (American Fiber Manufacturers Association) (1993); *Resource and environmental profile analysis of a manufactured apparel product: Woman's knit polyester blouse*, American Fiber Manufacturers Association, Washington D.C.

Cooper, P. (ed.) (1995); *Colour in dyehouse effluent*, Society of Dyers and Colourists, London.

UNEP (United Nations Environment Programme) (1993); *The textile industry and the environment*, Industry and the Environment Technical Report No. 16, United Nations Publications, Paris.

Watson, J. (1991); *Textiles and the environment*, Special Report No. 2150, Economist Intelligence Unit, London.

SKAL (1994); *Standards for sustainable textile production*, September 1994, SKAL, The Netherlands.

Naturally pigmented cotton

Dabney, C. W. (1896); *The cotton plant, its history, botany, chemistry, culture, enemies and uses*, USDA Bulletin No. 33, Office of the Experiment Stations, Washington DC.

Fryxell, P. (1979); *The natural history of the cotton tribe (malvaceae, tribe gossypiae)*, College Station and London, Texas A & M Press.

Vreeland, J. M. (1981); *Coloured cotton, return of the native*. IDRC reports Vol. 10, No. 2, pp. 4–5.

Vreeland, J. M. (1993); 'Naturally coloured and organically grown cottons: anthropological and historical perspectives', *Beltwide Cotton Conferences*, pp. 1533–36, National Cotton Council, Memphis.

Ware, J. O. and L. I. Bennedict (1962); 'Coloured cottons and their economic value', *Journal of Heredity* Vol. 53 No.2: 57–65.

Chapter 6

Geier, B. (1997); 'Reflections on standards for organic agriculture', *Ecology and Farming*, IFOAM, May 1997 pp 10–11.

IFOAM (1997); *IFOAM basic standards of organic agriculture and food processing*, 1997 edition, IFOAM, Germany.

IFOAM (1997); *Guide to the regulatory requirements for importing organic foods and agricultural products into international markets*, IFOAM, Germany.

Neuendorff, J. (1997); *Certification of organic foodstuffs in developing countries*, GTZ, Germany.

Rundgren, G. (1997); *Building trust in organics: A guide to setting up organic certification programmes*, IFOAM, Germany.

Standards are constantly evolving; for the most up-to-date version of the Standards referred to in the chapter, contact the following Standard Setting Organizations, details of which are included in the Contacts List: SKAL (EKO Label), Texas Department of Agriculture (TDA), KRAV, Arbeitskreis Naturtextil (AKN), EU Ecolabel, SIS Eco-labelling AB (the Nordic Swan), Swedish Society for Nature Conservation (Bra Miljöval), Stichting Milieukeur.

Chapter 7

de Vries, H. and H. Kox (1995); *An international commodity-related environmental agreement (ICREA) for Cotton: An appraisal*, Economics Department, Free University, Amsterdam.

Caldus, T. (1997); Organic cotton: not just a matter of fibre, *Ecology and Farming*, Vol. 14, IFOAM, Germany.

Klonsky, K., L. Tourte, S. Swezey and D. Chaney (1995); 'Production practices and sample costs for organic cotton—northern San Joaquin Valley, 1995', Department of Agricultural Economics, University of California, Davis.

Paxton, A. (1994); *The food miles report: The dangers of long-distance food transport*, The Safe Alliance, London.

UNCTAD (1996); *Organic production in developing countries: Potential for trade, environmental improvement and social development*; UNCTAD secretariat, Switzerland.

UNCTAD and IFOAM (in press); *Comparison of cost building of organic and conventional cotton cultivation and processing*, IFOAM, Tholey-Theley, Germany.

University of California and the United States Department of Agriculture (1996); *Production practices and sample costs for organic cotton*, USDA, USA.

Walsh, J. and M. Brown (1995); 'Pricing environmental impacts: a tale of two T-shirts', in *Illahee*, Vol. 11, No. 3 and 4, pp. 175–82.

Chapter 8

Chouinard, Y. and M. Brown, (1997); 'Going organic: Converting Patagonia's cotton product line', *Journal of Industrial Ecology*, Vol 1, No. 1, The Massachusetts Institute of Technology and Yale University, USA.

CBI (1994); *Health foods: A survey of the Netherlands and other major markets in the European Union*, CBI, Rotterdam, The Netherlands, 6pp.

International Herald Tribune (1995); ' "Green" clothes take root', June 8, p. 3.

Ton, P. (1996); *The European market for organic cotton and eco-textiles*, Foundation Eccoperation, Amsterdam.

Ton, P. (1997); *Le marche europeen du coton biologique et des textiles ecologiques*. Foundation Ecooperation/SNV-Benin, 40 pp.

Chapter 9

Organic Cotton Production in the USA

Economic Research Service (1997); *Cotton and wool outlook*, Issue number CWS-1197, U.S. Department of Agriculture, Washington, D.C.

National Agricultural Statistics Service (USDA) (1996); *Upland cotton: Agricultural chemical usage. Field Crops Summary*, US Department of Agriculture, Washington, D.C.

National Agricultural Statistics Service (1997); *Crop values 1997, Summary*, US Department of Agriculture, Washington, D.C.

Woodburn Assoc. (1995); *Cotton: the crop and its agrochemicals market*, Edinburgh, UK.

Organic cotton in California: Technical aspects of production
This section of the chapter was based on the paper '*Technical aspects of organic cotton production in the northern San Joaquin Valley of California, USA*' by Swezey, S.L., K. Klonsky, L. Tourte and P. Goldman. Some of the key sources included:

California Institute for Rural Studies (CIRS) (1993); *Second annual organic cotton conference, An edited collection of farm profiles, scholarly papers, statistics, and clippings on sustainable cotton production*, University of California, Davis, California.

Klonsky, K. and L. Tourte (1995); 'Statistical review for California's organic agriculture 1992–1993' Department of Agricultural Economics, University of California, Davis, California.

Klonsky, K., L. Tourte, S. Swezey, and D. Chaney (1995); *Production practices and sample costs for organic cotton, northern San Joaquin Valley, 1995*, Department of Agricultural Economics, University of California, Davis.

Swezey, S. L. (1995); 'Conversion of cotton production to certified organic management in the Northern San Joaquin Valley: Transition phase plant growth and yield (1992–94)', in the proceedings of the *Beltwide Cotton Conferences* 1:125–6. San Antonio, Texas.

Swezey, S. L., P. Goldman, R. Jergens, and R. Vargas (in prep.); 'Three-year farm-level comparison of organic and conventional cotton production systems', for submission to *California Agriculture*.

Swezey, S. L. and P. Goldman (1996); 'Conversion of cotton production to certified organic management in the northern San Joaquin Valley: Plant development, yield, quality, and production costs', in proceedings of the *Beltwide Cotton Conferences* 1: 167–1. Nashville, Tennessee.

The Texas Organic Cotton Marketing Cooperative
Richards, K. and D. Wechsler (1996); *Making it down on the farm—increasing sustainability through value-added processing and marketing*, Southern Sustainable Agriculture Working Group.

Chapter 10

Bergman, S. (1995); *The white treasure*, Verner Frang AB, Sweden.

UNCTAD and IFOAM (in press); *Comparison of cost-building of organic and conventional cotton cultivation and processing*, IFOAM, Tholey-Theley, Germany.

Chapter 11

UNCTAD and IFOAM (in press); *Comparison of cost-building of organic and conventional cotton cultivation and processing*, IFOAM, Tholey-Theley, Germany.

Chapter 12

UNCTAD and IFOAM (in press); *Comparison of cost-building of organic and conventional cotton cultivation and processing*, IFOAM, Tholey-Theley, Germany.

Chapter 13

UNCTAD and IFOAM (in press); *Comparison of cost-building of organic and conventional cotton cultivation and processing*, IFOAM, Tholey-Theley, Germany.

Chapter 14

Cauquil, Jean (1988); *Cotton pests and diseases in Africa—South of the Sahara*, IRCT-CIRAD-CFDT, Paris.

Hamdy, M. E., S. Barghouti, F. Gilham and T. Al-Saffy, (1994); *Cotton production prospects for the decade to 2005: A global overview*, World Bank Technical Paper No 231, 1994.

PAN Afrique (1997); *Coton biologique en Afrique*, (1997); the Pesticides Trust, London, ENDA/PRONAT, Senegal.

Ton, P. and Vodouhe, D. S. (1994); *Des opportunités d'établir des liens commerciaux entre le Benin et les Pays Bas*, Report to the Foundation of Ecooperation, the Netherlands.

Vodouhe, Simplice Davo (ed.) (1997); *Le Coton Biologique—Une chance à saisir par l'Afrique pour un développement plus harmonieux*, PAN Germany, Hamburg, OBEPAB, Benin and Pesticides Trust, London.

Chapter 15

Geier, B. (1997); 'Reflections on standards for organic agriculture', *Ecology and Farming*, IFOAM, May 1997, pp. 10–11.

IFOAM (1997); *IFOAM basic standards of organic agriculture and food processing*, 1997 edition, IFOAM, Germany.

Sources: General

de Vries, H. and H. Kox (1995); *An international commodity-related environmental agreement (ICREA) for cotton: An appraisal*, Economics Department, Free University, Amsterdam.

Boone, N. and M. Reeves (1998); *Organic Cotton Directory 1998–1999*, The Organic Fibre Council and the Pesticide Action Network, USA.

Buley, M., P. Grosch and S. Vaupel (1997); *Exporting organic products*, Protrade, Germany.

Carson, R. (1965) *Silent spring*, Penguin Books, UK.

Hamdy, M. E., S. Barghouti, F. Gilham and T. Al-Saffy, (1994); *Cotton production prospects for the decade to 2005: A global overview*, World Bank Technical Paper No 231, 1994.

Hummel, J. (1996); *Öko-Textilien:Vonder Nische zum Massenmarkt*, IWÖ-Diskussionsbeitrag Nr. 30, Institut für Wirtschaft und Ökologie an der Hochschule St. Gallen, Switzerland.

IFOAM (1996); *Proceedings of the second international IFOAM conference on organic textiles*, Bingen 1996, IFOAM, Germany.

IFOAM (1997); *IFOAM basic standards of organic agriculture and food processing*, 1997 edition, IFOAM, Germany.

Pesticide Action Network (1996); *Cotton connection: Towards sustainable cotton production*, proceedings of the international conference 'Cotton connection: for ecologically, socially and economically sustainable cotton production', November 1994, Hamburg, Germany, PAN Germany, Hamburg.

Pesticide Action Network (1997); *Organic cotton in praxi*, proceedings of the seminar 'Organic cotton in praxi—problems and strategies in organic cotton production in selected countries', December 1995, Erfurt, Germany, PAN Germany, Hamburg.

Pesticide Action Network North America (1998), *The organic cotton briefing kit*, PAN North America, San Francisco.

Pesticides Trust (1995); *A cotton reader*, the Pesticides Trust, UK.

Pesticides Trust (1995), 'The cotton chain' in *Pesticides News* No. 28, the Pesticides Trust, UK.

Ried, M. (undated); *About the art of growing cotton without chemicals*, Pesticide Action Network (PAN Germany), Hamburg, Germany.

Robins, N. and S. Roberts (1997); *Unlocking trade opportunities: Changing consumption and production patterns*, IIED and the UN Department of Policy Coordination and Sustainable Development, London and New York.

Rundgren, G. (1997); *Building trust in organics: A guide to setting up organic certification programmes*, IFOAM, Germany.

Sustainable Cotton Project (1998), *Cleaner cotton campaign tool kit*, Sustainable Cotton Project, Oraville, California, USA.

Ton, P. (1996); *The European market for organic cotton and textiles: a market survey*, Foundation Ecooperation, Amsterdam.

van den Berg, H. and Cock, M. (1993); *African bollworm and its natural enemies in Kenya*, International Institute of Biological Control, Kenya Station, Nairobi.

Information on the Internet

Green Trade Net: Protrade's international database for organic products is at
http://www.green-tradenet.de
GTZ/ISAT: http://gate.gtz.de/isat
GTZ/TOEB: http://gtz.de-toeb
ICAC: http://www.icac.org
IFOAM: http://www/ifoam.org
PANNA: http://www.panna.org/panna
The Pesticides Trust: //www.gn.apc.org/pesticidestrust

Journals

Enlace: the Journal of RAAA Peru (Spanish).
Ecology and Farming: the journal of IFOAM (English).
Pesticide News: the journal of the Pesticides Trust (English).
Global Pesticides Campaigner: the journal of PAN North America, San Francisco.
Various journals of the International Cotton Advisory Committee, (ICAC), Washington DC.

Appendix 1
Sources of support

The section below provides some background information on some of the important organizations which support organic agriculture in general, and organic cotton in particular, and some of the more important funding bodies of organic cotton projects to date.

IFOAM: The International Federation of Organic Agriculture Movements
BERNWARD GEIER

Principles and objectives of organic agriculture

Organic agriculture encompasses agricultural systems that promote environmentally, socially and economically sound food and fibre production. These systems take local soil fertility as a key to successful production. By respecting the natural capacity of plants, animals and the landscape, organic agriculture aims to optimize quality in all aspects of agriculture and the environment. It dramatically reduces external inputs by refraining from the use of synthetic chemical fertilizers, pesticides and pharmaceuticals.

Organic agriculture complies with globally accepted principles, which are implemented within local social-economic, geoclimatic and cultural settings. As a logical consequence, the organic movement stresses and supports the development of self-supporting systems at local and regional levels.

The principle aims of organic agriculture are summarized in the *IFOAM Basic Standards for Organic Agriculture and Food Processing*. They are:

○ to produce food of high nutritional quality in sufficient quantity;
○ to interact in a constructive and life-enhancing way with all natural systems and cycles;
○ to encourage and enhance biological cycles within the farming system, involving micro-organisms, soil flora and fauna, plants and animals;
○ to maintain and increase the long-term fertility of soils;
○ to use, as far as possible, renewable resources in locally organized agricultural systems;
○ to work, as far as possible, within a closed system with regard to organic matter and nutrient elements;

- to work, as far as possible, with materials and substances which can be reused or recycled, either on the farm or elsewhere;
- to give all livestock conditions which allow them to perform the basic aspects of their innate behaviour;
- to minimize all forms of pollution that may result from agricultural practice;
- to maintain the genetic diversity of the agricultural system and its surroundings, including the protection of plant and wildlife habitats;
- to allow agricultural producers a life in accordance with the principles of UN human rights, to cover their basic needs and obtain an adequate return and satisfaction from their work, including a safe working environment; and
- to consider the wider social and ecological impact of the farming system.

The IFOAM Basic Standards have provided a framework for many national regulations on organic agriculture, and at the international level the draft proposal of the WHO/FAO *Codex alimentarius*, and are used by organic farmer organizations all over the world as a common platform. The Standards have been translated into many languages. Organic agriculture is, however, a developing production system and the standards are constantly being revised by the IFOAM Standards Committee.

To facilitate international recognition of certification programmes, IFOAM has established the IFOAM International Organic Accreditation Services Inc. (IOAS). IFOAM membership requirements alone do not provide any mechanism for establishing compliance with IFOAM Basic standards or criteria for accreditation. The IOAS aims to ensure that certification programmes meet accreditation criteria in addition to IFOAM Basic Standards, thus ensuring consistency and compatibility world-wide. The IOAS is a voluntary system open to all private or state certification bodies, whether or not they are IFOAM members. The accreditation criteria are drawn from international norms (ISO Guide 65 and EN 45011 which are both norms for certification programmes) as well as from the experience of the global organic community. By 1997, 20 programmes had been, or were becoming, accredited.

Organic Fiber Council: USA

NATHAN BOONE

In 1994, the National Organic Cotton Association (NOCA) was formed in the US by organic cotton growers, manufacturers, and retailers to respond to the diverse needs of the expanding organic cotton industry. In 1996, NOCA formally merged with the Organic Trade Association to create the

Organic Fiber Council (OFC). The objective of the OFC is to provide a forum to address topics of interest to all sectors within the US organic cotton movement. As a working council of the Organic Trade Association, the OFC includes organic farmers, brokers, mills, manufacturers, wholesalers and retailers. OFC goals are:

○ to promote awareness and understanding of organic cotton and agricultural fibre by educating consumers and the textile industry;
○ to provide leadership to unify the diverse sectors of the organic cotton and agricultural fibre industries to exchange ideas and information in order to address industry-wide problems;
○ to increase the sales and sustainability of the organic fibre industry;
○ to leverage public and private funds to invest in the organic fibre industry;
○ to provide a strong and unified voice on legislative, regulatory and policy issues.

OFC's marketing programme disseminates educational information through media, publications, trade shows, and wholesale and retail outlets. OFC acts as a clearing house for source and supply referrals to improve the availability of organic cotton and develop new markets. OFC is developing the first Organic Cotton Spot Market on the internet, which will improve market access for organic cotton growers. Using the internet, companies and mills will be able to find and buy organic cotton directly from growers. A key output is the *Organic Cotton Directory* which aims to link producers with manufacturers. The directory includes details of US and Canadian producers, researchers, ginners, mills and others.

The OFC is working with the USDA's National Organic Program, as well as certifiers, mills, manufacturers and clothing companies to develop uniform standards for organic cotton production, handling, processing and labelling, and also collaborated with IFOAM in developing the first international standards for organic textile processing.

Pesticide Action Network (PAN)

DOROTHY MYERS

The Pesticide Action Network (PAN) is an international coalition of citizens' groups and individuals who advocate the adoption of ecologically responsible practices in place of pesticide use. Established in 1982, PAN now encompasses more than 400 non-governmental organizations (NGOs) working in more than 60 countries. PAN participants believe that citizens' action is essential to challenge global pesticide proliferation, to defend basic rights to health and environmental quality, and to ensure the transition to more just and sustainable societies. Network activities are co-ordinated through five independent regional centres based in Asia, Africa, Latin America, Europe and North America.

Since 1992, PAN has conducted campaigns to highlight the health and environmental problems of pesticides and accelerate the adoption of alternatives. PAN's regional co-ordinating groups work together to focus on stimulating organic cotton production and environmentally responsible processing. Projects include assistance to organic cotton experiments in Africa and Latin America, and public education for more responsible cotton processing, manufacturing and retailing in Europe and the US.

PAN groups around the world promote organic cotton production and processing in an effort to generate environmental and health benefits while providing a model for sustainable agricultural production, research and marketing. PAN participants have made a variety of contributions towards expanding the production and consumption of organic cotton.

PAN Africa

PAN Africa was founded as an independent organization in 1997 and later that year organized a workshop on organic cotton bringing together farmers, NGOs, researchers and policymakers from projects within the region to provide an example of how to develop actions with practical and political orientation. PAN Africa co-ordinates the Organic Cotton Network for Africa and provides training in agro-ecology as well as producing a quarterly journal.

PAN North America (PANNA)

PANNA promotes organic cotton production and consumption by generating public awareness of cotton issues and by helping connect consumers, companies and organic cotton producers in the US and internationally. The focus is on public outreach and education, utilizing its extensive clearing house and on-line information services. PANNA supports the Organic Fiber Council, has collaborated in the production of the *Organic Cotton Directory*, and has produced a briefing pack for consumers, non-profit organizations and industry.

PAN Latin America (RAPAL) and Red de Acción en Alternativas al uso de Agroquímicos (RAAA)

RAAA promotes organic cotton production among a group of small-scale farmers in the Cañete Valley (see Peru case study). Through public workshops, and farmer training programmes for adults and schoolchildren, RAAA teaches techniques of ecological soil and pest management as well as the importance of cotton to the culture and economy of the valley. This has involved collaborating with commercial interests on research, training and building awareness. RAPAL will organize a regional meeting in 1999 to bring together all actors interested in organic cotton.

PAN Germany

The PAN Germany cotton project began in 1994. The project is organized through a working group, Cotton Connection, which co-ordinates a network of people and organizations throughout Germany interested in organic textiles. Conferences in Germany and West Africa and consumer awareness projects have been supported.

The Pesticides Trust, UK

After many years of work on the 'safe use' of pesticides and challenging their negative impact, the Pesticides Trust made the decision to support work promoting positive alternatives and to focus initially on organic cotton. In consultation with PAN partners, farmers, a technical expert and donors, a programme of work was defined which includes drawing attention to the problems of pesticides use in cotton, advocating alternative production methods, supporting pilot field projects with farmers, the dissemination of information and raising consumer awareness of cotton issues.

Activities in the first five years of the project have included:

○ research and information gathering, publications and consultations;
○ a study tour in Europe for people interested in initiating organic cotton projects in Senegal and Benin;
○ support for a pilot organic conversion project in Koussanar, Senegal in partnership with ENDA-Pronat, and in Benin in partnership with OBEPAB;
○ funding and non-funding support for research into natural pest control for cotton in Zimbabwe, in collaboration with Zimbabwe Institute for Permaculture (ZIP) Research; and
○ support for information exchange within Africa.

The Trust's involvement in this publication is an integral part of the project.

Germany: GTZ

PETER FÖRSTER

The structure of GTZ allows for a diverse role in the promotion of organic cotton. In 1994, a working group on organic cotton within GTZ was established in order to work collaboratively amongst the different programmes, to identify possible projects and to co-ordinate the services and expertise of different GTZ projects and divisions involved in organic cotton production.

Protrade, the trade promotion department of GTZ, has been supporting and advising organic cotton initiatives in Tanzania, Senegal and Kenya in the last three years. They work with expert consultants who visit the project for 1–2 weeks twice a year. The goal of Protrade is to maintain and increase the competitiveness of small and medium-sized businesses in developing countries. Protrade offers advice on trade promotion, market analysis, fact-finding, selection of companies, and products, marketing consultancy, preparation and participation in trade fairs, and promotion within EU. Projects are chosen where there is local potential to build cultivation, ginning, purchasing, packaging and distribution structures. A local consultant is assigned along with the outside expert as a local contact for the farmers and the companies. The main aim of the projects is to advise on the best ways to manufacture and sell a product in the international market.

Other services are offered by GTZ in relation to the promotion of organic cotton, including the following.

ISAT/KPF-GATE
Information and Advisory Services on Appropriate Technology (ISAT) provides services for NGOs and development workers of all organizations and institutions working in development co-operation. Activities include the promotion of NGOs and NGO networks, south–south exchanges and support for small-scale NGO projects.

Crop Production, Plant Protection and Agricultural Research Division
The division has conducted studies on the economics of organic cotton production at small-holder level and provides consultancy services for projects.

Pesticide Service Project (PSP)
The project carries out studies on alternatives to synthetic pesticides. The formulation of alternative pesticides are promoted and supervised and advice for research projects on alternative plant protection is provided. The project pursues the aim of enhancing the expertise and know-how of individuals and NGOs, governments and consultancy agencies responsible for pesticides.

Sweden: Sida

In 1994, Sida recognized the potential for the export of organic products from Africa. A first, successful organic cotton project in Uganda confirmed the potential, and a specific programme, Export Promotion of Organic

Products from Africa (EPOPA) was created. It is administered by the Business and Enterprise Development Division, a unit of Sida's Department of Infrastructure and Economic Cooperation (INEC). The actual management of the programme is sub-contracted to Agro Eco consultants based in the Netherlands.

The objective of the programme is to develop the export of organic products, thus providing an opportunity to increase and diversify exports, while exposing the agricultural and agro-industrial sector to innovative and environmentally responsible practices. It also aims to demonstrate the 'development through business' concept.

Projects can be initiated in all countries of Africa where Sweden is engaged in private sector development. At present, work is underway in Uganda and preparations for future work are in progress in Tanzania and South Africa with possibilities for extending to other countries.

Organic agriculture is seen as the most advanced form of sustainable agriculture and is well regulated both by industry self-regulation (IFOAM standards) and by national regulations. The inspection and certification of products generated are sub-contracted to a third party, GroLink, a subsidiary of the Swedish national organic certification organization, KRAV.

EPOPA encourages processing in the country of origin, giving preference to high-volume or high-value products. It is export-oriented but care is taken that farmers do not forego the production of food crops for domestic consumption, and some assistance is provided for improved marketing of cash crops for domestic markets.

In each country where EPOPA works, a local co-ordinator or country manager is employed to identify potential products, exporters and production areas, provide information on organic requirements, ensure communication between the business partners, facilitate visits by buyers, consultants and inspectors and, above all, provide management assistance. When a product is promising, a feasibility study is carried out which will cover market potential and the difficulties to be anticipated in shifting to organic production. The study determines future project structure and management, the quality control system, and the training and initial management support needed. When the product and project set-up look promising, memoranda of understanding are prepared outlining the roles and commitments of the various actors.

EPOPA provides assistance in project organization, research and extension, and marketing contacts. It can fund the costs of the feasibility study, consultancy and initial certification. Costs for third-party certification are part of the price of the product and should be taken over by the exporter as soon as possible.

Appendix 2
Glossary

Acaricide: Synthetic chemical which kill spiders and mites.

Accreditation: A procedure by which an authoritative body gives a formal recognition that a body or person is competent to carry out certification or product inspection.

Boll: The seed-vessel of the cotton plant.

Boll weevil: *Anthonomus grandis*, a weevil found in North and South America that develops in the cotton boll, feeding on the developing seed.

Bollworm: Several species of Lepidoptera that feed on cotton bolls.

Botanicals: Botanical pesticide, such as extracts of the neem tree, that have insecticidal properties.

Biodegradable: Capable of being decomposed naturally.

Biodiversity: The total variability within all living organisms and their habitats.

Cash crops: Production of income-earning crops for export or local consumption.

Certification: Procedure by which a third party gives written assurance that a product, process or service conforms to specific requirements.

Certification agency: The organization performing certification.

Certified organic: Certification of a predefined organic production system or method.

Codex Alimentarius Commission: Codex is a standard-setting organization jointly administered by WHO and FAO which produces evaluations on pesticide residues in food and on the toxicology of particular active ingredients. The primary objective of Codex is to establish Maximum Residue Limits (MRLs) for pesticides in food that will facilitate internal trade and protect the health of consumers. Organic agriculture is under discussion within Codex.

Companion planting: A technique in which different species are planted close together for the benefit of one or both in order to, for example, keep away pests or diseases.

Compost: Decomposed vegetable matter and, in most cases, animal waste; one of the best forms of organic matter for feeding the soil.

Conventional agriculture: The current intensive agricultural production system which is dependent on synthetic chemical fertilizers and pesticides.

Cotton bale: A package of compressed cotton lint after ginning, tied with wire or metal bands and wrapped in cotton, jute or polypropylene. Bales vary in weight in different countries, but the universal density bale weighs 220 to 225kg and has a density of 448kg/m^3.

Cotton fibre: An extension of cells in the walls of developing cotton seed; the product that results from the separation of cotton fibre from the cotton seed in the ginning process.

Cotton gin: A machine used for separating the cotton fibre from the seed.

Cotton lint: Fibre that develops as an extension of cells in the walls of developing cotton seed; product that results from the separation of cotton fibre from the cotton seed in the ginning process (see cotton fibre).

Cotton seed: The seed of the cotton plant.

Defoliant: Synthetic chemical which kills leaves.

Desi cotton: Old World cotton of the species *Gossypium arboreum* and *G. Herbaceum*, grown mainly in South Asian countries.

Dioxin: A group of chemical contaminants formed during the manufacture of certain compounds and the combustion of many others.

Eco-label: Independent, third-party monitored, criteria for products produced with lower environmental impacts than the conventional norm.

Eco-textiles: Products made with processes described as environmentally responsible.

Eco-trend: A period in the early 1990s when environmental considerations had an influence over a wide range of consumer choices from food to clothing.

Environmentally responsible: Description of steps taken towards reducing the environmental impact of certain procedures and practices.

Extension: The provision of information to farmers to enable them to improve their practices.

Extensive agriculture: Forms of agriculture characterized by larger land surfaces per farmer who are then not pressed to intensify production, for example through the use of external inputs, to make a living.

Fungicide: Pesticide which kills fungi.

Fibre: See cotton fibre.

Finishing: The final stages in fabric processing which includes preparation of the fabric for dyeing and printing and the application of any specialized fabric finishes, such as that for water resistance.

Genetic diversity: The genetic variability within a species.

Genetic engineering: The transfer of genetic characters between species to enhance the performance of the recipient species in some specific characteristics.

Green manure: Crops cultivated to improve the nutrient content of the soil and soil structure.

Grey goods: A term applied to 'raw', unbleached fabrics before they are bleached, dyed or printed.

Ginning: The process of separating the cotton fibre from the seed.

Herbicide: Synthetic chemical which kills plants.

In conversion: A period of conversion to organic agriculture required by the organic standards before products can be certified as fully organic.

IFOAM: International Federation of Organic Agriculture Movement (IFOAM) is a co-ordinating network for the organic movement worldwide.

IFOAM Basic Standards: Standards produced by the International Federation of Organic Agriculture Movement (IFOAM) which provide a platform for international agreement on standards for organic agriculture and provide an important reference for NGOs and regulators when creating national standards.

Insectary plants: Plants which promote the presence of natural enemies.

Insecticide: Synthetic chemical which kills insects.

Inspection: Conformity assessment by observation, analysis and judgement, accompanied, as appropriate, by measurement, testing or gauging.

Intercropping: Secondary crops planted between the rows of primary crop.

IPM: Integrated Pest Management (IPM) is a system of pest control which involves the integrated use of a variety of pest control methods including pest resistant varieties, planting time, use of natural enemies and other forms of biological control. IPM includes the use of synthetic chemical pesticides only on an as-needed basis and as a last resort.

Land races: Early, cultivated forms of crop species, developed over a long period of time by local farmers. They are still grown today and are often well adapted to the local conditions.

Life cycle: The product life cycle encompasses all activities from raw material cultivation, processing, transportation, distribution and use, to final disposal.

Micronaire: A measure of the cross-sectional size of the individual cotton fibre.

Monoculture: Growing one crop continuously without using rotation.

Naturally pigmented cotton: Coloured cotton fibre which has a botanically formed pigmentation lodged in the centre, or lumen, of the fibre.

Nitrogen-fixing crops: The relationship between species of Leguminosae and the nitrogen-fixing soil bacterium Rhizobium, which lives in nodules on the legume roots, which allows the fixation of atmospheric nitrogen.

Organic agriculture: According to IFOAM, organic agriculture describes various systems for producing food and fibres according to specific standards which promote environmental, social and economic health without the use of chemical and genetically synthesized fertilizers, pesticides and pharmaceuticals. Organic agriculture adheres to globally accepted principles, which are implemented within local social-economic, agro-ecological and cultural settings.

Organic matter: Any material of living origin including manure, leaves and plant debris.

Organic premium: An extra element in the price paid to farmers for growing certified organic cotton to offset risk and uncertainty and a possible drop in yields.

Organic standards: A written document which defines acceptable practices for organic agriculture.

Organophosphates: Organic chemical containing phosphorus; organophosphate insecticides are nerve poisons which kill the target pest (usually insects).

Pesticide: Synthetic chemical which kills pests.

Pesticide resistance: Resistance developed by some pests and diseases species to specific pesticides, rendering them worthless or less effective.

Pheromone: Complex chemical substances produced by insects for communication; laboratory-synthesized pheromones have been developed for the biological control of pests.

Predator species: Insect or vertebrates eating plants or pest species.

Pyrethroid: Botanical chemical extracted from a Kenya chrysanthemum species (see Synthetic pyrethroids).

Rotation: The changing of crop species grown on the same field over the years. Rotation of crops helps maintain soil fertility and breaks the life cycle of many pests and diseases. Rotations depend on a farmer's needs and locality.

Seed cotton: The contents of the cotton boll, consisting of the seeds with the fibre attached as harvested from the plant and before ginning.

Sizes: A substance added to cotton yarn during weaving which gives it extra strength and minimizes yarn breakages.

Staple length: The average length of cotton fibres.

Synthetic pyrethroids: Synthesized copy of the active ingredient in pyrethrum which kills insects (see also Pyrethroids).

Treated seeds: Seeds which have been treated with fungicide and/or insecticide to ward off disease and pest damage during storage, planting and germination.

Transitional: Term for organic systems in-conversion, used primarily in North America.

Trap crop: An alternative host plant to particular pest species planted to siphon the pest off the main crop.

WHO Recommended Classification of Pesticides by Hazard: An internationally recognized system for classifying pesticides according to their acute toxicity ranging from WHO 1a (Extremely Hazardous) and WHO 1b (Highly Hazardous) to WHO II (Moderately Hazardous) and WHO III (Slightly Hazardous).

Appendix 3
List of contacts

AFTA
PO Box 1521
Oud-Beyerland
3260 BA
Netherlands
Tel: +31 186 619122
Fax: +31 186 619886
Email: Peter.Bolt@inter.nl.net
Group: Company
Contact: Peter Bolt

Agreco
Mündener Straβe 19
Witzenhausen-Gertenbach
D-37218
Germany
Tel: +49 5542 4044
Fax: +49 5542 6540
Email: agreco@font-online.de
Group: Certifier
Contact: Richard F Göderz

Agro Eco Consultancy
PO Box 23058
Kampala
Uganda
Tel: +256 342919
Fax: +256 342919
Email: aptulip@imul.com
Group: Consultant
Contact: Alan Peter Tulip

Agro Eco Consultancy
Postbus 63
Bennekom
6720 AB
Netherlands
Tel: +31 318 420405
Fax: +31 318 414820
Email: b.vanelzakker@agroeco.nl
Website: www.agroeco.nl/agroeco/
Group: Consultant
Contact: Bo van Elzakker

Agro Eco Consultancy
PO Box 4135
Harare
Zimbabwe
Tel: +263 4 781500/1
Fax: +263 4 781502
Email: agroeco@fontline.co.zw
Group: Consultant
Contact: Tom Deiters

Algodonera Pyma SA
Santa Fe 47 Oeste
San Juan
CP 5400
Argentina
Tel: +54 6421 4468
Fax: +54 6421 4468/8797
Group: Company
Contact: Sergio D. Kalierof

Arbeitskreis Naturtextil e.V.
Hauβmannstraβe 1
Stuttgart
D-70188
Germany
Tel: +49 711 232752
Fax: +49 711 232755
Group: Standard setting organisation
Contact: Frank-Michael Mähle

Australian Cotton Research Institute
NSW Agriculture
PMB Myall Vale
Narrabri
New South Wales 2390
Australia
Tel: +61 2 67 991500
Fax: +61 2 67 931186
Email: robertm@mv.pi.csiro.au
Website: cotton.pi.csiro.au
Group: Consultant, Researcher
Contact: Dr Robert Mensah

Bioherb
PO Box 1216
Witzenhausen
D-37202
Germany
Tel: +49 5542 6466
Fax: + 49 5542 72891
Email: bioherb@t-online.de
Website: www.agrar.de/bioherb
Group: Consultant
Contact: Birgitt Boor/Ulrich Helberg

Bo Weevil BV
Postbus 236
Ermelo
3850 AE
Netherlands
Tel: +31 341 562 767
Fax: +31 341 562 767
Group: Broker
Contact: Marck van Esch

Boller, Winkler AG
Organic Cotton Spinning
Turbenthal
CH 8488
Switzerland
Tel: +41 52 396 2222
Fax: +41 52 396 2200
Email: info@textil.ch
Website: www.textil.ch
Group: Producer
Contact: Ernst Ehrismann

C & M Organic Enterprises
23199 Road 7, Unit B
Chowchilla
California 93610
USA
Tel: +1 209 665 3925
Fax: +1 209 665 3916
Group: Broker, grower
Contact: Claude Sheppard

California Certified Organic Farmers
(CCOF)
1115 Mission Street
Santa Cruz
California 95060
USA
Tel: +1 831 423 2263
Fax: +1 831 423 4528
Email: dianeb@ccof.org
Website: www.ccof.org
Group: Certifier
Contact: Diane Bowen

Center for Agroecology and
Sustainable Food Systems
University of California
1156 High Street
Santa Cruz
California 95064
USA
Tel: +1 831 459 4367
Fax: +1 831 459 2799
Email: findit@cats.ucsc.edu and
phgo
Website: http://zzyx.ucsc.edu/casfs/
Group: Resource, training
Contact: Dr. Sean L. Swezey/Polly
Goldman

Charity, Richard B
Sertão Verde Avenida Oliveira
Paiva, 1840
Bairro Jacareí
Fortaleza
Ceará CEP 60.822-131
Brazil
Tel: +55 85 271-3479
Email: sertaoverde@sec.secrel.com.br
Group: Consultant
Contact: Richard B. Charity

Chelsea College of Art and Design
Lime Grove
London
W12 8EA
UK
Tel: +44 171 514 7848
Fax: +44 171 514 7848
Email:
katetfletcher@compuserve.com
Group: Consultant
Contact: Kate T Fletcher

Classico, Textiles & Fibres
Postfach 1271
Böblingen
D-71002
Germany
Tel: +49 7031 95630
Fax: +49 7031 956386
Group: Company
Contact: Ulrich Depken

Coop Schweiz
Postfach 2250
Basel
CH-4002
Switzerland
Tel: +41 61 336 6666
Fax: +41 61 336 6040
Group: Company
Contact: Mr H Traris-Stark

Demeter-Verband
Brandschneise 2
Darmstadt
D-64295
Germany
Tel: +49 6155 8469
Fax: +49 6155 8469 - 11
Email: demeterbd@aol.com
Group: Certifier

ECO Textiles
Hessenplatz 3
Frankfurt a.M.
D-60487
Germany
Tel: +49 697 71387
Fax: +49 697 06479
Group: Company
Contact: Mrs Ulrike Schönherr

Ecocert International
Suite 20A
Am Schlagbaum 5
Osterode-Förste
D-37520
Germany
Tel: +49 55 2295 1161
Fax: +49 55 2295 1164
Email: ecocert@compuserve.com
Group: Certifier
Contact: Andreas Kratz

Eco-Logic
8 Politechniou Street
Athens
10433
Greece
Tel: +30 1 522 1230/093 2868834 (mobile)
Fax: +30 1 522 1230/1022
Group: Consultant
Contact: Dmitris Dmitriadis

Ecotropic
Parracombe
Chapel Lane
Forest Row
East Sussex RH18 5BU
UK
Tel: +44 1342 824622
Fax: +44 1342 824949
Email: 106110.2305@compuserve.com
Group: Consultant
Contact: Tadeu Caldas

Egypt Centre of Organic Agriculture (ECOA)
PO Box 68
Hadaik Shoubra
Cairo
ET 11241
Egypt
Tel: +20 2221 0459/452 5885
Fax: +20 2221 6958/5885
Group: Certifier
Contact: Dr Ahmed El-Araby

Egyptian Biodynamic Association (EBA)
PO Box 1535 Alf Maskan
Cairo
ET 11757
Egypt
Tel: +20 2 281 8886
Fax: +20 2 281 8886
Email: sekem@sekem.com
Website: www.sekem.com
Group: Company
Contact: Klaus Merckens

ENDA-PRONAT
BP 3379
Dakar
Senegal
Tel: +221 225565
Fax: +221 235157
Email: pronat@enda.sn
Group: NGO
Contact: Mariam Sow

Equilibrium Consultants
23 Bath Buildings
Bristol
BS6 5PT
UK
Tel: +44 117 942 8674
Fax: +44 117 942 8674
Equilibrium@compuserve.com
Group: Consultant
Contact: Sue Stolton

ESPLAR
Centro de Pesguisa e Assessoria
Rua Princesa Isabel 1968
Fortaleza
CE 60015-061
Brazil
Tel: +55 85 221 1324
Fax: +55 85 252 2410
Group: NGO
Contact: Pedro Jorge BF Lima

EU Ecolabel
European Commission, DGXI.E.4
Rue de la Loi
Brussels
B-1049
Belgium
Tel: +32 2 295 7755
Fax: +32 3 295 5684
Email: ecolabel@dell.cec.be
Website: europa.eu.int/en/comm/
dg11/ecolabel
Group: Standard setting organization

Finkhof e.G
St Ulrich Straße 1
Arnach
D 88410
Germany
Tel: +49 7564 931718
Fax: +49 7564 931712
Group: Consultant
Contact: Wilfried Leupolz

GroLink AB
Torfolk
Hoje
S-684 95
Sweden
Tel: +46 563 72345
Fax: +46 563 72066
Email: gunnar@grolink.se
Website: www.grolink.se
Group: Consultant, Certifier,
Standard setting organisation
(KRAV)
Contact: Gunnar Rundgren

GTZ, German Appropriate
Technology Exchange
Postfach 5180
Eschborn
65726
Germany
Tel: +49 6196 793186
Fax: +49 6196 797352
Email: Carsten.hellpap@GTZ.de
Website: http://gate.gtz.de/isat
Group: Aid Agency
Contact: Carsten Hellpap

GTZ, Pesticide Service Project
Post fach 5180
Eschborn
65726
Germany
Tel: +49 6196 791081
Fax: +49 6196 797180
Email: peter-foester@gtz.de
Group: Aid Agency
Contact: Peter Förster

GTZ, Tropical Ecology Support
Programme
Postfach 5180
Eschborn
65726
Germany
Tel: +49 6196 793284
Fax: +49 6196 797413
Email: TOEB@gtz.de
Website http://gtz.de-toeb
Group: Aid agency
Contact: Kirsten Hegener

Hermann Buhler
Winterthur-Sennhof
CH-8482
Switzerland
Tel: +41 52 233 5550
Fax: +41 52 233 5585
Group: Company
Contact: Martin Kagi

Hess Futur Trade GmbH
Hessenring 82
Bad Homburg
D-61348
Germany
Tel: +49 6172 1214 78
Fax: +49 6172 1214 88
Group: Company
Contact: Martin Jedersberger

Hess Naturtextilien GmbH
Marie-Curie-Straße 7
Butzbach
D-35510
Germany
Tel: +49 6033 9910
Fax: +49 6033 991120
Email: k.paulitsch@hess-natur.com
Website: http://www.hess-natur.com
Group: Company
Contact: Ute auf der Brücken/
Katharina Paulitsch

Imhoff, Dan
268 Prospect Street
San Francisco
California 94110
USA
Tel: +1 415 282 8138
Fax: +1 415 282 6934
Email: dcimhoff@igc.apc.org
Group: Journalist, consultant
Contact: Dan Imhoff

INKA CERT
Miembro de Biolotina
Av. Avenales 645
Lima 1
Peru
Tel: +51 1 423 0645
Fax: +51 1 433 1073
Group: Certifier
Contact:

Institut für Marktökologie-IMO-
Scheiz
Poststrasse 8
Sulgen
CH-8583
Switzerland
Tel: +41 71 642 3616
Fax: +41 71 642 3663
Email: IMOCH@compuserve.com
Website: http://www.imo.ch
Group: Standard setting organisation,
Certifier
Contact: Dr Rainer Bachi

Institute for Environmental Studies
Vrije Universiteit
De Boelelaan 115
Amsterdam
1081 HV
Netherlands
Tel: +31 20 4449 555
Fax: +31 20 4449 553
Email: onno.kuik@ivm.vu.nl
Website: www.vu.nl/english/o—o/
instituten/IVM/
Group: Researcher
Contact: Onno Kuik

Instituto do Algodoa de
Mocambique
Caixa Postal 806
Av. Eduard Mondlane
Maputo
Mozambique
Tel: +258 1 431 015/16
Fax: +258 143 0679
Email: iam@algodao.uem.mz
Group: Government
Contact: Norberto Mahalambe

International Cotton Advisory
Committee
1629 K Street NW, Suite 702
Washington
DC 20006
USA
Tel: +1 202 463 6660
Fax: +1 202 463 6950
Email: rafiq@icac.org
Website: http://www.icac.org/
Group: Research, Trade organization
Contact: Dr. Terry Townsend/Dr M.
Rafiq Chaudhry

International Federation of Organic
Agriculture Movements
(IFOAM)
Head Office
Oekozentrum Imsbach
Tholey-Theley
D-66636
Germany
Tel: +49 6853 5190
Fax: +49 6853 30110
Email: IFOAM@t-online.de
Website: http://www.ifoam.org
Group: Standard setting organisation,
NGO
Contact: Bernward Geier (General
Secretary)

IFOAM-Asia, IIRD
PO Box 562
Kanchan Nagar, Nakshatrawadi
Aurangabad
Maharashtra 431 002
India
Tel: +91 240 332336
Fax: +91 240 331036/335304
Email: iird-daniel/
aurangabad@dartmail.dartnet.com
Group: NGO, Consultant
Contact: Dr Alexander Daniel

IOAS
118½ First Avenue South
Suite 15
Jamestown
ND 58401
USA
Tel: +1 701 252 4070
Fax: +1 701 252 4124
Email: ioas@daktel.com
Website: http://www.ecoweb.dk/
ifoam/accredit/index.html
Group: Accreditation
Contact: Ken Commins

Israel Bio-Organic Agriculture
Association (I.B.O.A.A.)
121 Hachashmonaim St.
Tel-Aviv
67011
Israel
Tel: +972 3 561 0538/562 1082
Fax: +972 3 561 8633
Email: iboaa—m@netvision.net.il
Group: NGO
Contact: Micha Tiser

Japan Organic Agriculture
Association
Nishidaira 2384
Tokigawa-Mura
Hiki-gun
Saitama 355-03
Japan
Tel: +81 493 67 1743
Fax: +81 493 67 1743
Group: NGO
Contact: Mayumi Morizane-Saito

KRAV
Box 1940
Uppsala
S-751 49
Sweden
Tel: +46 18 100290
Fax: +46 18 100366
Email: info@krav.se
Website: www.krav.se
Group: Certifier, Standard setting
organization
Contact: Åke Natt och Dag/Martin
Holmberg/Eva Mattsson

Lango Cooperative Union
Lira 59
Uganda
Email: aptulip@imul.com
Website:
Group: Farmers' Cooperative
Contact: Patrick Oryang

Lichtschatz Projekte GmbH
Gockelmannweg 13
Isny-im-Allgau
D-88316
Germany
Tel: +49 7562 56 002
Fax: +49 7562 55 200
Group: Company
Contact: Jurgen Erlenburg

Lower Guruve Development
Association
PO Box 165
Guruve
Zimbabwe
Tel: +263 1 583 46
Fax: +263 1 583 54
Group: Farmers' Group, NGO
Contact: Ephraim Murendo (Co-
ordinator)

Lynda Grose, Inc.
30 Homestead Street
San Francisco
California 94114
USA
Tel: +1 415 641 9135
Fax: +1 415 647 6715
Email: lyndagr@aol.com
Group: Consultant
Contact: Lynda Grose

Maikaal Fibres Limited
Flat # 2C + 2D
25 Ballygunge Circular Road
Calcutta
700019
India
Tel: +91 334 757811
Fax: +91 334 756759
Email: maikaal@giasc101.vsnl.net.in
Group: Company
Contact: Morgan Jalan

Naturland e. V.
Kleinhaderner Weg 1
Gräfelfing
D-82166
Germany
Tel: +49 89 853842
Fax: +49 89 855974
Email: Udo.Cen@naturland.de
Website: www.Naturland.de
Group: Certifier
Contact: Udo Censkowsky

Naturtextilberatung
Postfach 3305
Konigswinter
D-53628
Germany
Tel: +49 22 448 2339
Group: Company
Contact: Claus Muller

OBEPAB
BP 8033
Cotonou
Republic of Benin
Tel: +229 301 975
Fax: +229 301 975/300 276
Email: obepab@bow.intnet.bj
Group: NGO
Contact: Simplice Davo Vodouhe

Okotex Fachmesse für Naturtextilien
Stresemannallee 35-37
Frankfurt am Main
D-60596
Germany
Tel: +49 69 631 5031/2
Fax: +49 69 631 3009
Group: Company
Contact: Heike Scheuer

Organic Crop Improvement
Association (OCIA)
1405 South Detroit Street
Bellefontaine
Ohio 43311
USA
Tel: +1 513 592 4983
Fax: +1 513 593 3831
Email: ociantl@bright.net
Group: Certifier

Organic Fibre Council
1927 Tulare Avenue
Richmond
California 94805
USA
Fax: +1 510 215 7253
Email: ofc@igc.org
Group: NGO
Contact: Sandra Marquardt

Organic Growers & Buyers
Association
8525 Edinbrook Crossing, Suite 3
Brooklyn Park
MN 55443
USA
Tel: +1 612 424 2450
Fax: +1 612 315 2733
Email: ogba@mwt.net
Group: Certifier
Contact: Sue Cristan/Cathy Walters

Pakucho Pax - Native Cotton Project
of Peru
San Isidro F-3
Vallecito
Peru
Tel: +5154 24 7221
Fax: +5154 22 7128
pakucho@mail.interplace.com.pe
Website: http://www.interplace.
com.pe/pakucho.htm
Group: Company
Contact: James M. Vreeland Jr

PAN Africa Regional Centre
PO Box 15938
Dakar-Fann
Senegal
Tel: +221 254 914
Fax: +221 254 914
Email: panafric@sonatel.senet.net
Group: NGO
Contact: Abou Thiam

PAN Asia and the Pacific
PO Box 1170
Penang
10850
Malaysia
Tel: +60 4 657 0271
Fax: +60 4 657 7445
Email: panap@panap.po.my/
panap@GEO2.poptel.org.uk
Group: NGO
Contact: Sarojini Rengam

PAN Germany
Nernstweg 32-34
Hamburg
D-22765
Germany
Tel: +49 40 39 9191 0-0
Fax: +49 40 390 7520
Email:
pan-germany@umwelt.ecolink.org
Group: NGO
Contact: Susan Haffmans

PAN Latin America/'RAPAL'/
RAAA
Apartado Postal 11-0581
Av Mariscal Miller
2622 Lince, Lima
PE-11
Peru
Tel: +51 1 421 0826
Fax: +51 1 440 4359
Email: rapalpe@mail.cosapidata.com.pe
Group: NGO
Contact: Luis Gomero

PAN North America Regional
Center (PANNA)
Coordinator of Cotton and Latin
America Programs
49 Powell St., Suite 500
San Francisco, California 94102
USA
Tel: +1 415 981 6205 ext 326
Fax: +1 415 981 1991
Email: mreeves@panna.org
Website: www.panna.org/panna/
Group: NGO
Contact: Margaret Reeves

Patagonia
259 West Santa Clara Street, 93001
PO Box 150
Ventura, California 93002
USA
Tel: +1 805 643 1643
Fax: +1 805 648 8002
Email: mike-brown@patagonia.com
Group: Company
Contact: Jill Vlahos/Mike Brown/
Kevin Sweeney

Peru Consult AB
Höganäsgatan 3
Helsingborg
254 33
Sweden
Tel: +46 42 15 16 80
Fax: +46 42 15 16 80
Email: Per.jiborn@swipnet.se
Group: Consultant
Contact: Per Jiborn

Pesticides Trust
Eurolink Centre
49 Effra Road
London
SW2 1BZ
UK
Tel: +44 171 274 8895
Fax: +44 171 274 9084
Email: pesttrust@gn.apc.org
Website: http://www.gn.apc.org/
pesticidestrust
Group: NGO
Contact: Dorothy Myers

Prakruti
620 Jame Jamshed Road, 4th Floor
Dadar East
Bombay
400014
India
Tel: +91 22 414 9688
Fax: +91 22 415 5536
Email: manishk@glasbm01.vsnl.net.in
Group: NGO
Contact: Kisan Mehta

Protrade: GTZ
PO Box 5180
D-65726 Eschborn
Germany
Tel: +49 61 96 79 0
Fax: +49 61 96 79 74 14
Email: protrade@gtz.de
Website: http//www.green-tracknet.
de
Contact: Marion Buley

Quality Assurance International
(QAI)
12526 High Bluff Drive, Suite 300
San Diego
California 92130
USA
Tel: +1 619 792 3531
Fax: +1 619 792 8665
Group: Certifier
Contact: Griffith McClellan/Howie
Ross

Rapunzel
Refik Tulga Caddesi 11
Cambidi
Izmir
Turkey
Tel: +90 462 6175
Fax: +90 462 6176
Email: raporg@superonline.com.tr
Contact: Atila Ertem

Rapunzel Anbau Projekte
Haldergasse 9
Legau
87764
Germany
Tel: +49 8330 910143
Fax: +49 8330 910109
Group: Company
Contact: Lisa Walcher

Ratter, Gerd
Edward Schröder Strasse 12
Witzenhausen
37213
Germany
Tel: +49 5542 910756
Fax: +49 5542 910757
Email: gerdratter@t-online.de
Group: Consultant
Contact: Gerd Ratter

Remei AG
Lettenstrasse 9
Rotkreuz
CH-6343
Switzerland
Tel: +41 41 790 3304
Fax: +41 41 790 1624
Email: remei@csi.com
Group: Company, broker
Contact: Patrick Hohmann

Schmidt & Bleicher Ltd
Lintzingsweg 3
Marburg
D-35043
Germany
Tel: +49 6421 958100
Fax: +49 6421 958161
Email: IDEEN@l-online.de
Website: http://www.ideen.com/
exit2.htm
Group: Company
Contact: Ralph Bleicher

Sekem
PO Box 2834, El Horrya
Heliopolis
Cairo
Egypt
Tel: +20 2 280 7994/7438
Fax: +20 2 280 6959
Group: Company
Contact: Helmy Abouleish

Servicio Agropecuario
Box 494
Loma Plata
Chaco c.de c.883
Paraguay
Tel: +595 918 301
Fax: +595 918 306
Group: Farmers' co-operative
Contact: Wilhelm Giesbrecht Wiebe

SIS Eco-Labelling AB
Box 6455
Stockholm
113 82
Sweden
Tel: +46 8 610 3042
Fax: +46 8 34 2010
Email: svanen@sis.se
Website: www.sis.se/Miljo/Nordic/
Swanindex.htm
Group: Standard setting organization
Contact: Monica Backlund

SKAL
Stationsplein 5
PO Box 384
Zwolle
8000 AJ
Netherlands
Tel: +31 38 426 8181
Fax: +31 38 421 3063
Email: skal@euronet.nl
Website: www.skal.com
Group: Standard setting
organization, Certifier
Contact: Programme Manager

Soil Association
Bristol House
40–56 Victoria Street
Bristol
BS1 6BY
UK
Tel: +44 117 929 0661
Fax: +44 117 925 2504
Email: soilassoc@gn.apc.org
Group: Standard setting
organization, Certifier, NGO
Contact: Francis Blake

Stichting Milieukeur
Eisenhowerlaan 150
Den Haag
2517 KP
Netherlands
Tel: +31 70 3586300
Fax: +31 70 3502517
Website: www.milieukeur.nl
Group: Standard setting organization

Stilo Print
PO Box 5045
Tilburg
5004 EA
Netherlands
Tel: +31 13 463 4285
Fax: +31 13 463 4528
Group: Company
Contact: Mr Loek Bloemist

Sustainable Cotton Project
PO Box 2965
Santa Cruz
CA 95063
USA
Tel: +1 408 476 6432
Fax: +1 831 470 9915/6
Email: jobaumgart@aol.com
Group: NGO
Contact: Jo Ann Baumgartner

Sustainable Cotton Project
6176 Old Olive Highway
Oroville
California 95966
USA
Tel: +1 530 589 2686
Fax: +1 530 589 2688
Email: will@sustainablecotton.org
Group: Resource, Training, NGO
Contact: Will Allen

Sustainable Solutions/Design
Association
Skt. Peders Straede 41
Copenhagen K
DK-1453
Denmark
Tel: +45 33 33 97 38
Fax: +45 33 33 97 38
Email: psd@psd-dk.com
Website: http://www.psd-dk.com
Group: Consultant, NGO
Contact: Kristian Dammand Nielsen

Swedish Society for Nature
Conservation
Good Environmental Choice (Bra
Miljöval)
PO Box 7005
Göteborg
S-40 231
Sweden
Tel: +46 31 711 64 50
Fax: +46 31 711 64 30
Email: gbg@snf.se
Website: www.snf.se
Group: NGO, Ecolabelling
organization
Contact: Susanne Hagenfors

Texas Certified Organic Program
Texas Department of Agriculture
PO Box 12847
Austin
Texas 78711
USA
Tel: +1 512 475 1641
Fax: +1 512 463 8225
Email: lmckinno@agr.state.tx.us
Website: www.agr.state.tx.us
Group: Certifier, Standard setting
organization
Contact: Leslie McKinnon

Texas Organic Cotton Marketing
Cooperative
Route 1, Box 120
O'Donnell
Texas 79351
USA
Tel: +1 806 439 6640/6646
Fax: +1 806 439 6647
Email: lvpepper@juno.com
Group: Broker, Farmer's co-
operative, company
Contact: Mary Furlow/LaRhea
Pepper

Textile Environment Network
Manchester Metropolitan University
Dept. of Textiles/Fashion
Cavendish Building, Cavendish St
Manchester
M15 6BG
UK
Tel: +44 161 247 3533
Fax: +44 161 236 0820/247 6341
Group: NGO, Researcher
Contact: Jo Heeley

Ton, Peter
Ceramplein 58–2
Amsterdam
1095 BX
Netherlands
Tel: +31 20 668 1032
Fax: +31 20 668 1032
Email: peterton@xs4all.nl
Group: Consultant
Contact: Peter Ton

Triconor AB
PO Box 390
Ostersund
S-83125
Sweden
Tel: +46 63 14 8500
Fax: +46 63 103479
Group: Company
Contact: Bo Ottosson

Union of Concerned Scientists
1616 P Street NW
Suite 310
Washington
DC 20036–1495
USA
Tel: +1 202 332 0900
Fax: +1 202 332 0905
Email: jrissler@ucsusa.org
Website: www.uscusa.org
Group: NGO
Contact: Jane Rissler

Universidad Nacional Agraria
Departamento de Horticultura
La Molina, Apartado 456
Lima 1
Peru
Tel: +511 3495877
Fax: +51 1 3480747
Email: rugas@lamolina.edu.pe
Group: Consultant, resource, training
Contact: Roberto Ugás

Verner Frang AB
PO Box 313
Borås
S-503 11
Sweden
Tel: +46 33 127800
Fax: +46 33 106499
Email: stephan@vernerfrang.se
Website: www.ecocotton.com
Group: Company
Contact: Stephan Bergman

Vidharba Organic Farmers
Association (VOFA)
Vasundhara Chambers
New Union Bank, Main Road
Yavatmal
Maharashtra 44 5 001
India
Tel: +91 7232 4250
Group: Farmers' Co-operative
Contact: Mr Subhedar

WWF Switzerland
Project Management Textile Ecology
Postfach, Hohlstr. 110
Zurich
CH-8010
Switzerland
Tel: +41 1 297 21 21
Fax: +41 1 297 21 00
Email: christine.baerlocher@wwf-
ch.wwf-switzerland.inet.ch
Website: http://www.wwf.ch
Group: NGO
Contact: Christine Bärlocher

ZIP Research, Zimbabwe Institute of
Permaculture
Box 301
Causeway
Harare
Zimbabwe
Tel: +263 4 336130
Fax: +263 4 726911
Email: samp@fontline.co.zw
Group: Resource, training
Contact: Shepherd Musiyandaka/
Fortunate Nyakanda/Dr Sam L J
Page

For further contact details in the US
see the *Organic Cotton Directory*.

Appendix 4
IFOAM Basic Standards for the Processing of Textiles

The *IFOAM Basic Standards* describe the ideals and principles of organic farming, and processing of the products of organic agriculture. They include additional sections on specific crops such as coffee, cocoa and tea, as well as general principles on social justice, and labelling and consumer information.

The standards are reviewed regularly; a new set is published every two years after having been approved by the General Assembly of IFOAM members.

The standards are not used for certification purposes as they stand, rather they provide a basis upon which certification programmes worldwide develop their own national or regional standards.

In the last two years the IFOAM Standards Committee have been overseeing the expansion of the standards in a number of new areas including textile processing. The textile processing standards were approved by the General Assembly in November 1998, after amendments, for inclusion within the *IFOAM Basic Standards*, where they appear in Chapter 8. They are published here for the first time. It should be noted that there may therefore be minor differences between the version published here and the final version, which will be published by IFOAM.

The *IFOAM Basic Standards* are the basis upon which the IFOAM Accreditation Programme (IOAS) operates. Until the next revision in 2000, the textile processing standards will be referred to as *draft* standards for technical reasons related to the IFOAM Accreditation Programme (IOAS).

For further information about the organic textile processing standards, contact IFOAM direct (see details in the Contacts list).

Scope

The standards are applicable to all kinds of natural fibre products including, but not limited to: yarn; fabrics; ready-made clothes, clothing, rugs and furnishing textiles; and non-woven products. These standards cover the processing of certified organic fibres and certified wild fibres.

Raw materials

General principles
○ The textile raw materials in a textile product should be 100 per cent organically produced.
○ The processing of raw materials into fibres should be done with consideration to the environment.
○ The non-textile raw materials in a textile product should be harmless to the environment and humans, both in production, consumption and disposal.
○ The raw materials should contain the characteristics of the desired end-product (e.g. natural coloured fibres, natural flame retardant).

Recommendations
○ Natural fibres should be used.
○ The certification programme should regulate the contents and/or the emission of nickel, and chrome and other undesirable substances in non-textile accessories.

Standards
Cotton defoliation
○ The use of cotton defoliants is prohibited.
○ Certification programmes may allow exceptions for calcium chloride, magnesium chloride and sodium chloride until 2002.

Retting
Field retting of flax and other fibres is permitted. If wet retting and steam retting is used, the certification programme shall require appropriate waste water treatment or use, to avoid water pollution.

Silk Production
○ Mulberry trees for silk production shall be organically cultivated.
○ If silk is certified, the certification programme shall develop standards for egg cultivation, silkworm cultivation and reeling. Such standards shall require that all agents including disinfectants in silkworm cultivation, egg cultivation and reeling shall fulfil the requirements for processing as laid down in these standards.
○ Hormones and veterinary treatments are regulated in line with IFOAM animal standards.
○ Tensides used in silk degumming (cocoon boiling) shall be readily bio-degradable (OECD 301), and there shall be an appropriate waste-water treatment.

248

Wool Scouring
○ Tensides used for wool scouring shall be readily biodegradable (OECD 301) and there shall be an appropriate waste-water treatment.

When needed to produce a long-life quality, a certain function or fashion, the certification programme may allow the use of non-certified materials according to the following:

Non-certified natural fibres   When a certified organic natural fibre is not available in the required quantity and quality, the certification programme may allow non-certified natural fibres to be mixed with the certified fibres or used in certain details. The same fibre shall not be of certified organic and non-certified origin.

Synthetic fibres   When synthetic, regenerated cellulose or recycled fibres are used, the following are excluded:

○ Halogen-containing fibres (chlorofibre, teflon, etc.)
○ Fibres which are, or whose production is, hazardous to humans, workers or the environment.

The certification programme shall develop lists of approved synthetics. The mixing in of non-organic fibres must be in accordance with IFOAM labelling standards.

The certification programme shall not certify products where non-textile accessories constitute the major part of the product, unless they have developed criteria for such details. Accessories may not contain more Cadmium than 0.1mg/kg.

Processing in general

General principles
All processing units should follow an integrated environmental management system.

Recommendations
Processing should take place using appropriate and least damaging environmental techniques.

Standards
IFOAM standards for storage, separation, identification, hygiene and pest management apply. IFOAM standards for food additives and processing aids do not apply.

The certification programme may grant individual exceptions for the requirements of separation in instances where such separation could lead to substantial environmental or economic disadvantages, and where there is no risk of the mixing of raw materials (e.g. the possible contact of an organic product with recycled fluids that have been previously used for conventional production (mercerizing, sizing, rinsing, etc.). When granting such exceptions, the certification programme shall establish that there is no contamination by the actual process.

Environmental criteria for wet processing

General principles
The wet processing of organic fibres into textiles should prevent any negative environmental impact.

Recommendations
The certification programme should develop standards for the sewage treatment and the effluents regarding BOD and COD (or TOC or TOD), heavy metals and phosphorus, as well as the disposal of sewage sludge and solids.

The quality of the waste treatment must be considered with respect to the inputs being used.

Standards
The certification programme shall require that any production unit:

○ at least complies with national regulations regarding environment.
○ documents the use of chemicals, energy, water consumption and waste-water treatment, including the disposal of sewage sludge and analysis of effluents
○ no later than one year after the initial certification, has developed an environmental plan for how to improve the environmental performance of the production.

The certification programme shall certify production units only where there is at least a functioning internal or external sewage water treatment (sedimentation, temperature, pH regulation).

The certification programme may apply these environmental criteria only to the processing of the certified textiles and not to the whole factory.

Input products – general

The use of chemical products (dyes, auxiliaries, etc.) in textile processing is regulated. These inputs are referred to as 'products' in the text. The standards do not apply to lubricating oils for machinery, paints for machines and facilities, unless they are likely to contaminate the fabrics.

General principles

The processing of organic fibres should utilize organic or natural substances. Where this is not possible, the processing should avoid the use of synthetic chemical and substances that may pollute the environment or pose a hazard for workers or consumers.

When assessing products, the total environmental impact should be considered.

Recommendations

The processing of organic textiles should avoid the use of synthetic chemicals, substances which are environmental pollutants and substances which pose a health or safety hazard for workers or consumers.

The use of bio-accumulating products and heavy metals should be avoided.

Standards

All products shall be declared by the operator, including relevant data to assess (safety data sheets). Preservatives shall always be declared.

The certification programme shall have all recipes used on file.

The certification programme shall develop criteria for the evaluation of products. Such criteria shall consider both the biodegradability and the toxicity e.g.:

	Biodegradability 28 days (OECD 302 A)	Toxicity for aquatic organisms (LC_{50} or EC_{50} or IC_{50} for algae, water-fleas and fish)
Can be approved	< 70%	> 100 mg/l
Can be approved	> 70%	10–100 mg/l
Prohibited	< 70%	< 100 mg/l
Prohibited		< 1 mg/l

The same rules should apply for metabolites.

Considering the need for gaining more experience in the evaluation of products, the certification programme may develop alternative models or use other existing models if these ensure satisfactory environmental performance. Such alternative models shall be published and the certification programmes shall document the results of such a model compared to the model given in the Table.

251

In any case, products may not be used if they are either:

o Carcinogenic (R45)[1]
o Mutagenic (R46)
o Teratogenic (R60–63)
o Toxic to mammals – LD_{50} <2000 mg/kg shall not be allowed
o Known to be bio-accumulative and are not biodegradable (<70 per cent 28d OECD 302A)
o Listed on the negative list (see below)

[1] 'R' refers to the European system as described in Reg. 92/32/EEC.

In addition, the certification programme shall not approve the use of a certain product if there are appropriate alternatives available that are natural, and have less environmental impact.

The certification programme shall maintain a positive list of substances allowed or a negative list where substances not allowed shall be identified.

Biocides, including PCP, TCP and PCB, may not be included in any input.

The following chemicals may not be present in any product at more than 1 per cent:

o α-MES.
o Antinomy.
o AOX – Absorbable halogenated hydrocarbons, and substances that can cause their formation.
o APEO.
o DEHP.
o DTPA.
o EDTA.
o Halogenated flame-proof agents.
o Heavy metals.
o LAS.
o Organo-chloride carriers.
o Quarternary Ammonium compounds (DTDMAC, etc.).

Special regulations for different steps in processing

Standards
Apart from the general criteria these special regulations for different steps apply:

Spinning oils (avivage) and knitting oils (needle oil) shall be readily biodegradable or made from vegetable or animal origin.

Sizes shall be ultimately degradable, or be recycled to a minimum of 75 per cent.

Sodium hydroxide or other alkali is permitted for mercerizing, but shall be recycled to the highest possible extent.

Chlorine and perborate bleaching agents shall not be permitted for bleaching, colour removal or stain removal.

Mordents may not contain heavy metals above the limits indicated under 'dyestuffs'.

The following dyes may be used:

○ Dyes derived from plants (CI 75 000–75 999).
○ Mineral dyes not containing heavy metals.

The following are excluded:

○ Heavy-metal dyes.
○ Complex-bonded metals in excess of 1g metal/kg textile.
  The certification programme may grant limited exceptions for pigments containing copper if other alternatives are not available.
○ Dyes capable of releasing aromatic amines that are known or suspected carcinogens.
○ Dyes that are, or are suspected of being, allergenic or carcinogenic.

For other dyestuffs the general criteria should be applied for evaluation of their use (ETAD Agreement).

Dyestuffs must not contain more than:

Antimony 50ppm	Arsenic 50ppm	Barium 100ppm
Lead 100ppm	Cadmium 20ppm	Chromium 100ppm
Iron 2500ppm	Copper 250ppm	Manganese 1000ppm
Nickel 200ppm	Mercury 4ppm	Selenium 20 ppm
Silver 100ppm	Zinc 1500ppm	Tin 250ppm

Note: While heavy metals as dyestuffs are prohibited, they can appear as contaminants in other dyes. The limits above relate to such contamination.

Only printing methods based on water or natural oils are allowed. Aromatic solvents are prohibited. Colour residues shall be recycled or disposed of in a safe way.

No restrictions apply to mechanical and physical treatments.

Certification programmes must develop standards to regulate other methods and treatments, which must at least satisfy the general criteria for chemicals.

Labelling

General principles
The labelling should be correct and contain information useful to the consumer.

253

Recommendations
The certification programme should require that any substances known to cause allergies and which have been used during textile processing should be mentioned on the label.

Standards
The labelling of textiles follows IFOAM standards on labelling with the following special regulations:

o The calculation by weight shall exclude weight of non-textile accessories (buttons, zippers, etc.).
o The materials in non-textile accessories shall be declared.
o Inputs used during processing do not have to be declared.
o Information on fastness, shrinking and washing shall be included in the labelling, whenever appropriate and applicable.

Where the certified textile constitutes only part of the final product (i.e. furniture), the textiles can be declared according to this standard, but it must be clear from the labelling that this relates only to the textile part of the product.

Abbreviations in the textile standards

CI	Colour Index
COD	Chemical Oxygen Demand
EC_{50}	Effect Concentration (50 per cent effect)
ETAD	Ecological and Toxicological Association of the Dyestuff Manufacturing industries
IC_{50}	Inhibition Concentration (10 per cent inhibition)
LC_{50}	Lethal concentration (50 per cent mortality)
OECD	Organisation of Economic Co-operation and Development
TOC	Total Organic Carbon
TOD	Total Oxygen Demand
α-MES	α-methyl ester sulphonate (C16/18)
AOX	Absorbable halogenated hydrocarbons, and substances that can cause their formation
APEO	Alkylphenoloxylate
DEHP	Di-2ethylhexylphthalate
DTPA	Diethylenetriamine penta-acetate
EDTA	Ethylenediamine tetra-acetate
LAS	Linear alkyl benzene sulphonate
PCB	Polychlorinated Biphenyls
PCP	Pentachlorphenol
TCP	Tetrachlorphenol

Index

256

European market 109, 112
eutrophication 16, 156
experimentation 41
export 4, 5, 8, 109, 144, 160, 164–6, 174, 188, 194
Export Promotion of Organic Products from Africa (EPOPA) 40, 189, 195, 199, 228, 229
extension 41, 177, 179, 180, 195, 197, 211

fabric finishes, specialist 57, 63, 79
   see also easy-care
fabric finishing 53, 57–63, 79
fabrics 45, 53, 56–7, 105, 106, 113, 134, 135
fair trade 5
fallow 23–4, 178, 179, 189
false codling moth (*Crytophlebia leucotreta*) 33, 206
farm systems 21–4, 87
farmers & agricultural workers 2–3, 14–15, 18–19, 22, 40–1, 126, 134–5, 144, 174, 191, 206–7
farmers organizations/groups 39, 134–5, 194
farming *see* agriculture
fashion 6, 49–50, 71–2, 73, 101, 102, 122
fennel 24
fertilizers 15, 16, 26–8, 88, 122, 126–7, 145, 156
   see also compost; guano; manure; organic fertilizers; soil fertility
fibre 6–9, 81, 85, 92, 124, 173
field boundaries 30
field sanitation 31, 32
Fieldcrest-Cannon 49
FIJESA 142, 144
finance 142, 168, 193
   see also costs; debt; economics; incomes; pre-payment; premiums; prices; subsidies; taxation
finishing 10
Finland 76
fishing nets 47
fixing agents 61, 62
flame/fire retardant finishes 77, 79
flat knitting 57
fluorocarbons 63
fodder 138, 167, 181, 182
Fofana, Bakary 204
Fonds de Stabilisation et Soutien (FSS) 206

food 2, 14, 23, 184, 189, 192, 207
   contamination of 15, 31
   organic/health foods 5, 74, 112, 122, 150, 162
   food security 177, 212
   see also individual crops & plants
forage 23
forest cotton 137
formaldehyde 63, 76, 79, 80, 162
France 112, 214
FUNDA 31
fungi & fungal diseases 25, 28, 29, 170, 171
   see also individual fungi
fungicides 25
   see also individual fungicides
furnishing textiles 46
Fusarium spp. 25, 29, 170
FVO 143

Gap, The 6, 109, 110, 111
garments 81, 92–100, 102, 105, 114, 118, 137, 151, 168, 174
   see also clothing; fashion
gender 4, 177, 203–4, 210
   see also women
genetically-engineered cotton 16, 17–18, 19
Geocoris spp. (bigeyed bugs) 129
Germany 74, 76, 77, 102, 103, 114–15, 227
GFF (Good Food Foundation) 5–6
ginning 35, 54, 92, 130–1, 138–9, 141–3, 173, 206
globalization 50
glucose 62
glyphosate 17, 19
glyphosate-tolerant cotton 19
Good Food Foundation (GFF) 5–6
Gossypium (cotton) 11
Gossypium arboreum 47, 147
Gossypium barbadense 47, 48, 136
Gossypium herbaceum 11, 47, 147
Gossypium hirsutum (linted cotton) 11, 31, 47, 48
government/state involvement/ regulations 4, 18–20, 24–5, 40, 164, 176, 192–3, 205
Greece 38
'green cotton' 72
Green Cotton (Novotex) 72
green lacewing (*Chrysoperla* spp.) 30, 128, 129, 151, 153, 196

salt 34, 61, 133
San Joaquin Valley (SJV), California
   California 125, 127, 128, 130, 131
savings 88, 132
Savita cotton 147
Sclerotium rolfsii 170
scouring 56, 57, 58–9
SCP (Sustainable Cotton Project) 52,
   125, 246
screening 57
Scymnus 172
seed hairs 25
seed, cotton 16, 25, 127, 139, 152, 160,
   167, 170, 177–8
   cotton seed oil 15, 26, 54, 142
   treatment 25, 127, 139, 167, 170, 190
Sekem farms 165, 169, 172, 174, 245
selling direct 134
SENASA 139
Senegal 25, 34, 199–205
Senegalese Agricultural Research
   Insitute (ISRA) 201
separation of organic cotton 54, 141,
   144, 154, 168
sequestrants/sequestering agents 59, 78
seringa (*Melia azadirach*) 196, 197
sesame 23, 31, 152, 178, 182, 189, 192
Seventh Generation 108
sewing 63
Shalty 168
Sheppards, The 126
Sida 40, 176, 189, 190, 193, 199, 228–9
Sida Export Promotion of Organic
   Products from Africa (EPOPA) 40,
   189, 195, 199, 228
'Silica' preparation 172, 173, 174
sizes (coating) 57, 58, 78
SJV (San Joaquin Valley), California
   125, 127, 128, 130, 131
SKAL 74, 81, 115, 116, 143, 157, 245
skin contact products 77, 115, 116, 117
small-scale producers/small holders
   40–3, 69–71
social costs/impacts 9, 79–80, 143, 146,
   203
Societé Nationale pour la Promotion
   Agricole (SONAPRA) 206
Sodefitex (Senegal State cotton Board)
   200, 201, 202
sodium chlorite 59, 142
sodium hydrosulphite 62
sodium hydroxide (caustic soda) 50, 59,
   62, 142

sodium hypochlorite 59
sodium sulphide 62
soil 9, 13, 178
   fertility 15, 26, 42, 87, 89, 139, 141,
   150, 196, 207
   nutrients 15, 23, 26, 27–8, 127, 130,
   138
   structure 15, 28, 169, 171
   see also fertilizers
Soil Association 165, 166, 245
solvents 78–9
sorghum 23, 28, 150, 152, 178, 181, 184,
   189, 206
Soviet Union, the former 8, 10, 13, 48
sowing 28, 31, 127, 139, 140, 152, 170,
   181, 187
soya beans 24
spider mites (*Tetranychus* spp.) 128,
   156, 170, 206
spiders 128, 173, 187, 196
spinning 37, 54, 56, 78, 92, 142, 148
spiny bollworm (*Earias insulana*) 33,
   167, 173
Spodoptera littoralis (cotton leafworm),
   14, 33, 167, 172, 196
spraying of pesticides 13, 125, 180, 187
Srida, India 151–2, 245
SSNC (Swedish Society of Nature
   Conservation) 38, 76, 77, 79, 81, 85,
   114, 145
stainers (*Dysdercus* & *Oxycarenus*
   spp.) 33, 196, 206
standards & standard setting (organic)
   25, 43, 65–8, 123, 143, 161, 165, 191
   textile standards & labels 65, 73–7, 80
   two-tier standards/labels 74, 75, 85
starches 57, 58
steaming 62
Steilmann 73
step-by-step eco-labels 75–6, 77, 79, 80,
   84–5
sticky cotton 128, 134
storage of lint 54, 131, 135, 142, 144
strip cropping 152
subsidies 18, 19–20, 42, 86, 169, 194
Sudan 13
suicide 14, 185
sulphur 15, 128, 140
sulphur dyes 62
sun hemp (*Crotolaria juncea*) 27, 152
sunflower 31, 181, 182, 189
sunflower oil 181
supply chain 51, 52, 53, 135

breeding 11, 24, 29, 30
see also individual varieties
vat dyes 62
vegetables 30
Venezuela 31
Vermicompost 153
Verner Frang AB 141, 143, 144, 145,
    247
Verticillium spp. 25, 29
viability of cotton production,
    economic 14, 15 94, 100, 101, 209
Vidharba Organic Farmers'
    Association (VOFA) 149, 152–5, 248
village units 190, 192
VOFA (Vidharba Organic Farmers'
    Association) 149, 152-5, 248

war/unrest, civil 189, 192, 193, 194, 195
washing 60, 62, 78, 142, 162
    see also cleaning; laundering
wasps (*Trichogramma*) 32, 128, 140,
    151, 153, 154, 172, 187, 197
waste & waste water 10, 53, 54, 56, 58,
    59, 60, 63–4, 73, 76, 77
    see also effluents
water 13, 16, 57, 58, 63, 64, 79, 127, 128,
    156, 175, 197
    see also irrigation; waste water
water pollution 9, 15, 156, 185
water-repelling finishes 57, 63, 79
WCGA (Western Cotton Growing
    Area) 177, 178

weaving 56–7, 58, 78, 92
weeds & weeding 16, 28, 29, 30, 129,
    153, 172, 181
Week's Guatemala cotton 47
Western Cotton Growing Area
    (WCGA) 177, 178
wheat 23, 127, 150
White Cotton 143
whiteflies (*Bemisia tabacii*) 151, 153,
    156, 170
wild cotton 11, 17
Wingwiri, Emelda 186, 187–8
women 3, 4, 186, 203–4, 209,
    210–11
    see also gender
World Wide Fund for Nature (WWF)
    38, 248
woven fabrics 53, 58
Woven Wind Orgainic Project 161
WWF (World Wide Fund for Nature)
    38, 248

Xanthomonas malvacearum 25, 29

yarn 52, 54, 174, 206
yields 8–9, 88–91, 128, 131–3, 147–8,
    153, 158, 174, 198, 203, 208–9
Yuma cotton 48

Zimbabwe 4, 40, 184–8
zinc sulphate 34, 130
ZIP Research 187, 227, 248